HOW the WAR was REMEMBERED

DATE DUE			

HOW the WAR was REMEMBERED

HOLLYWOOD & VIETNAM

Albert **Auster** & Leonard **Quart**

New York
Westport, Connecticut
London

Library of Congress Cataloging-in-Publication Data

Auster, Albert.
  How the war was remembered : Hollywood and Vietnam / Albert Auster
and Leonard Quart.
    p. cm.
  Bibliography: p.
  Includes index.
  ISBN 0-275-92383-5 (alk. paper). ISBN 0-275-92479-3 (pbk. : alk.
paper)
  1. Vietnamese Conflict, 1961-1975—Motion pictures and the war.
2. Motion pictures—United States—History—20th century.
I. Quart, Leonard. II. Title.
DS557.73.A97   1988
959.704'3—dc19   87-36125

Library of Congress Catalog Card Number: 87-36125
ISBN: 0-275-92383-5
        0-275-92479-3 (pbk.)

First published in 1988

Praeger Publishers, One Madison Avenue, New York, NY 10010
A division of Greenwood Press, Inc.

Printed in the United States of America

The paper used in this book complies with the
Permanent Paper Standard issued by the National
Information Standards Organization (Z39.48-1984).

10 9 8 7 6 5 4 3 2

To my Mother, Molly Auster
and to Dr. Kurt C. Rawitt.

To my Wife, Barbara Quart
whose support and love gave
me enough confidence to begin
my writing career.

Contents

Illustrations ix

Acknowledgments xi

Introduction xiii

PART I
The War Film and Vietnam 1

PART II
The War That Dared Not Speak Its Name:
Wounded Heroes and Supermen 23

PART III
Hunter-Heroes and Survivors 75

PART IV
Confronting Vietnam 131

Notes 149

Bibliography 157

Index 163

Illustrations

China Gate   14

The Green Berets   32

Coming Home   53

The Deer Hunter   59

Apocalypse Now   69

Rambo: First Blood Part II   111

The Killing Fields   115

Platoon   133

Acknowledgments

Most books have a long gestation process and this book is no exception. This results in obligations to a great many people. Acknowledging everyone who helped would be impractical, but it is absolutely necessary to thank some.

Therefore, we would like to thank Lynda Sharp, who initiated this project, and Alison Bricken, who, with patience and understanding, saw it through to its completion. Also our gratitude to Barbara Schlapp-Gilgoff, whose scrupulous editing is a prime factor in the book's readability, and to Shelagh Krueger, Helen Johansen, and Jeanne Arnold, who typed various versions of the manuscript.

> "If I ever make a picture that's pro-war, I hope they take me out and shoot me."
>
> John Huston

Introduction

"Why write anything? . . . Who wants to be reminded?"[1] says a character in the very first sentence of Dr. Ronald J. Glasser's fine book on the Vietnam War, *365 Days*. Despite the Vietnam memorial in Washington, D.C., and a number of others in small towns and cities, it sometimes feels as if the significance of the war has been forgotten.

The Reagan administration has made its own rhetorical obeisance to the courage of the Vietnam dead, but it continues to often demonstrate an utter obliviousness to the war's murderous lessons. Its covert, overt, and illegal support of the contras in Nicaragua repeats many of the same strategies and arguments that led us into the Vietnam quagmire. Beyond Nicaragua, the administration offers inflated and ever-escalating military budgets, hardline posturing on arms control and the strategic Defense Initiative (SDI), and in general a penchant for cold-war oratory and confrontational politics that has softened under the spotlight of Gorbachev's *glasnost*.

Of course, there is no way to remove Vietnam from our collective memory. It remains an open wound that has never been healed or fully understood, either by successive political administrations or by the media that helps reflect and shape public opinion. While Vietnam has been the subject of a number of Hollywood films, few have gained even a partial handle on the surreal and real nature of the battlefield on which the soldiers fought and died, and almost all have left untouched the political logic (or illogic) behind the United States' commitment there.

Given the character of the war—a conflict where the GI felt adrift and alien and was viewed by many of the people he supposedly came to liberate as an invading aggressor—it's no wonder that the old World

War II-film genre conventions and heroics seem entirely inadequate to capture the reality of this struggle. That fact and Hollywood's fear that any profits would be mitigated by offending the mass audience in confronting such a divisive and controversial conflict resulted in only one film dealing directly with Vietnam while the war was still raging. *The Green Berets* (1968) essentially had John Wayne transform Vietnam into a pop-patriotic, right-wing version of cowboys and Indians. Other films that touched on the war in the 1960s did so via oblique suggestion and indirection. Audiences saw the unrest and rebellion of the young, resistance to draft, the Korean War, and screen biographies of jingoistic generals, all either circling the war, providing surrogates for it, or treating it as a peripheral theme.

As people's passions cooled, however, a number of films about Vietnam began to appear. In the 1970s, Hollywood discovered a suggestive symbol for the war in the returned veteran, a staple character of post-World War II films. Even back in those halcyon days when films usually provided vets with happy endings (e.g., *Pride of the Marines* [1944] and *The Best Years of Our Lives* [1946]), there was an undertone of anxiety and tension in the depiction of their supposedly harmonious homecomings.

However, happy endings were no longer imperative by the 1960s, and dark undercurrents became the dominant tone in Vietnam films. Vietnam vets were not returning from a popular and putatively just conflict, like WWII but from a war that could only be seen as a debacle for the United States. They were depicted as alienated, sometimes psychopathic figures (e.g., *Tracks* [1975] and *Black Sunday* [1976]) shattered by both their service in a meaningless war and their guilt for having survived a world where death was omnipresent. Hollywood didn't turn every returning vet into a psychopath, but these films are permeated by a bristling rage that creates a suggestive but somewhat distorted image of the veteran.

Despite Hollywood's penchant for reducing social reality to manageable social types and the continued absence of battlefield images, Vietnam finally came home on the screen. Beginning in the 1970s, a number of both small (*The Boys in Company C* [1977]) and epic (*The Deer Hunter* [1978] and *Apocalypse Now* [1979]) films appeared that attempted to convey directly some part of the Vietnam ethos. However, although these films aimed at (and sometimes succeeded in) capturing the chaos and extremity of the war, much of its complex texture was left untouched. Centered around metaphoric figures like the "superman" or the "hunter-hero," who supposedly encompassed the essence of the Vietnam experience, some of these films and their symbolic figures were clearly more socially and culturally resonant than others. Even those works dominated by false heroics and Hollywood stereotypes, however, still had political and cultural significance. What none of these films addressed, even the most intellectually and aesthetically sophisticated of the lot, were the political or historical bases for the war or the Vietnamese perspective of the conflict. None touched on North Vietnamese nationalism, Marxism-Leninism, or the character of that culture. In fact, the Vietnamese were depicted primarily as cannon fodder (although a few films evoked their military skill) and their country as nothing more than a landscape for American moral commitments and personal fantasies. Until *Platoon* in 1986, except for the small-budget, limited-release *Go Tell The Spartans* (1976) and two or three powerful scenes of battle action in *The Deer Hunter*, these films did not even aim at the realistic evocation of how it felt to be a GI on the war's front lines.

The purpose of this book is to trace Hollywood films about Vietnam from works like *China Gate* (1957)—made in the 1950s before the United States became directly involved—through the oblique works of the 1960s to the films of the 1970s and 1980s, which used a variety of symbols, metaphors, and images to encapsulate and interpret the war for the American public. Of course, the "wounded vets," "supermen," "hunter-heroes" and "survivors" that most of the Vietnam films centered on were not all of a piece. Their conceptualization and presentation varied formally and substantively from film to film, a fact that makes us wary of constructing airless and overly rigid typologies and keeps our analysis close to the concrete detail and particular images of each individual film.

Although the book is primarily about the social, political, and cultural meaning and value of these films, we have not treated them as mere social artifacts. Each film's editing, lighting, camera set-ups, and mise-en-scène are discussed, and we have made critical judgments about aesthetic qualities. We have also analyzed in detail the relationship of the film to the history of the Vietnam War and its postwar legacy.

Up to now, no one film has projected an image of the war that feels like a final or near-final word on the conflict. Of course, that may be impossible to realize. Still, given recent striking works like *Platoon* and Kubrick's *Full Metal Jacket* (1987), we begin to feel sanguine that the Vietnam film that combines both a feeling of verisimilitude and a profound political and psychological imagination may be in the offing. That film will be the indelible act of remembrance of the painful reality that the Vietnam War deserves.

PART I

The War Film and Vietnam

In his book *The Great War and Modern Memory*, Paul Fussell reminds us that in 1914 young men innocently went off to battle with words like *staunch*, *valorous*, *gallant*, and *brave* firmly implanted in their minds. This traditional moral rhetoric came from the novels of Scott and Kipling, the boys' romances of H. Rider Haggard, and the poems of Tennyson.[1] The world these young men lived in seemed stable, and history seemed purposive and progressive. Obviously, the boys who went to Vietnam 50 years later did not grow to manhood in a world as coherent and benign. But even though they no longer invoked honor or glory and literature played little role in their lives, many still carried heroic war images with them to Vietnam. Those images, a montage of heroic postures and actions culled from innumerable John Wayne and Audie Murphy World War II films, still had resonance in the 1960s.

Recognition of the influence of the war film on the American male in particular and the American psyche in general is by now commonplace. It has been more than just an impetus to patriotism and a model for bravery and courage, however. In the words of James Agee, these films are our "ritual dance,"[2] and, as those who have studied it know, ritual is often the key to a society's conflicts, ambivalence, and most-cherished values. Thus the remark of the GI in Tim O'Brien's National Book Award-winning novel about the Vietnam War *Going after Cacciato*, "Honest, it was such a swell war they should make it a movie,"[3] is more than just the narcissistic desire to see images of himself and his comrades on the screen. It reflects, rather, a feeling that only film can provide an adequate form for and sense of the war. Although the Vietnam war films never quite conveyed or defined the historical and political reality of the war or discovered a form that would evoke its full complexity, they consciously and unconsciously revealed a great deal about our society and culture. They constructed symbols and visual metaphors that, while often either too abstract or too predictable and conventional to encompass the war experience, still suggested a great deal about the American ethos. At moments these films also evoked with great immediacy the terrors of the war and produced a cathartic effect on its audience.

The war film as a genre was well established early in the history of American cinema. One can clearly trace its origins to that grandfather of all modern film epics, *Birth of a Nation* (1915).[4] This film is landmark, its brilliant cross-cutting, tracking, close-ups, irising, and lighting making it practically a grammar of film language. Such is the power of its editing that the film moves effortlessly from its more-personal dimensions, filmed in medium shot and close-up, to epic long shots. The film depicts with equal power a grieving mother and her children in close-up and the iris out to a long shot of Sherman's conquering Union army fanning out like ants to burn and pillage.

The long shots of armies marching, of masses of men facing each other in the trenches amid the smoke and thunder of battle, and of cities burning gave the Civil War a feeling of grandeur simultaneously with the horror of human waste and tragedy. Griffith constructed powerful images of dead bodies scattered all over the battlefield (with the ironic title *War's Peace*) while creating a hero—Colonel Cameron, the personification of Southern martial gallantry and chivalry—whose nobility and bravery gained cheers even from the enemy. Although there is no question about Griffith's pacifistic intent (the film's final image shows the God of War dissolving before the Prince of Peace), by stressing the South's martial prowess and chivalric traditions and by portraying the Ku Klux Klan (KKK) in a heroic mode, Griffith reflected and reinforced the warrior ethos that was so much a part of the era's popular culture.

Despite its pacifistic strain, *The Birth of a Nation* was responsible for the future development of the war film. Most of the central themes and images of later films originated in its battle scenes and in its depiction of the Reconstruction South. In the Reconstruction scenes, the heroes appear unambiguously virtuous and moral while carpetbaggers, scalawags, and blacks are corrupt, pitiless, barbaric, and even demonic (not far from the way the Japanese were portrayed in World War II films).

In its ambivalence about war's grandeur, the film prefigured one of the major contradictions of future war films. Its view of warfare, characterized by heroic action and gallant gestures, and the beautifully composed, painterly long shots of deadly battles are at odds with and even subvert the film's pacifistic message. Ironically, *The Birth of a Nation* became a metaphor for the romantic ideal of warfare, arousing and sustaining the martial spirit. Furthermore, its transformation of the KKK into a nine-teenth-century version of knights in armor (ridding the South of alien, destructive elements) was not lost on those who felt that the United States suffered from moral malaise and needed a national regeneration.[5]

It was the martial strain in *The Birth of a Nation*, not Griffith's pacifist leanings, that helped to mold the war films of World War I. Released soon after we entered the war, they set the proper polemical tone, encouraging patriotism and mob violence against German-Americans and radicals by depicting the enemy as coarse and brutal villains—a separate race characterized by a lust for power and an uncontrolled desire to rape, pillage, and murder. The films were totally entwined with the war effort, and consequently Germany was portrayed in utterly demonic and bestial terms while England and France were seen as godly nations. In many of the films, the Kaiser became the apotheosis of the German nation's savagery. The industry produced films crudely titled *The Kaiser, Beast of Berlin* (1918) and *The Prussian Cur* (1918), and even Chaplin's gentle, satiric contribution to the war effort, *Shoulder Arms* (1918), indulges in mild ridicule of the enemy. Although in *Shoulder Arms* heroic little Charlie wears a uniform and is committed to the war, the Germans are not viewed as unredeemably evil, and the war ends bloodlessly with Charlie capturing the Kaiser. On the other hand, World War I moved D. W. Griffith in *Hearts of the World* (1918) to drop the strong pacifistic strain in his work. The film was underwritten by the British War Office and depicts the Germans as absolute barbarians who attack women and murder innocent people. Griffith directed three other patriotic war films but later regretted his involvement with these propaganda works.[6]

Despite this outpouring of blatant polemic, the "beastly hun" stereotype only momentarily dominated the war film. With the end of World War I came a growing disenchantment with and even revulsion toward the war, and films dealing with it became relatively more complex. King Vidor's epic *The Big Parade* (1925) evokes some of the reality of army life and harrowing trench warfare without ever becoming an antiwar work.

Vidor's film was a great commercial success, mostly owing to its mixture of crude slapstick, romantic passion, and sentimentality. Its strengths were neither political nor psychological—it never questioned the political basis of World War I nor the nature of war itself. Instead, it portrays its protagonist, Jim Apperson (John Gilbert), as transformed by the war experience from a rich, idle parasite into a rough-and-tumble, ordinary doughboy, thereby sustaining the old cliché about the army's capacity to shape character and to create men.

Vidor was an intuitive director who created stunningly choreographed sequences of men apprehensively marching in silent formation through the woods while being shot at by an invisible machine gun—the images edited to march time played on a bass drum. To avoid any hint of war-film sentimentality, the men are seen as anonymous soldiers, part of war's merciless body count, rather than characters who elicit identification and sympathy from an audience.[7]

The Big Parade was followed by Raoul Walsh's *What Price Glory?* (1926) and William A. Wellman's *Wings* (1927). *What Price Glory?* is based on the Maxwell Anderson-Lawrence Stallings play that decried the waste of young lives in war. Even though paying lip service to some antiwar sentiments, the film focuses on the raucous, brawling antics of its marine protagonists, played by Victor McLaglen and Edmund Lowe. In fact, their behavior probably inspired nostalgia for military life rather than arousing pacifistic feelings in the audience.[8]

Wings director William Wellman, a member of the Lafayette Flying Corps during World War I, understood that war exhausts the body and spirit and that its landscape is suffused with pain and death. The film's emphasis, however, is on the heroism, romance, and glory of war. Its two banal, all-American heroes (played by Richard Arlen and Charles [Buddy] Rogers) impatiently confront the enemy and embrace danger. The uniqueness of the film lies in its spectacular aerial footage, the camera inside the aircraft vividly conveying what it feels like to engage in a dogfight, bomb a village, or fly through the clouds. In *Wings*, Wellman made such exhilarating use of a tracking camera that whatever antiwar sentiment the film contained is subordinate to the flamboyance of its military maneuvers and action.[9]

A wave of pacifism and isolationism in the early 1930s produced films like the antiwar *All Quiet on the Western Front* (1930) and *The Man I Killed* (1932), which convey the tragic and horrible nature of war. Directed by Lewis Milestone, *All Quiet on the Western Front* won Academy Awards for best picture and direction and was probably one of the strongest pacifist statements ever made by Hollywood. The film, based on a novel by Erich Maria Remarque, follows a group of German adolescent boys who innocently enlist in the war for the supposed good of the fatherland at the urging of their blindly bombastic, nationalist schoolmaster. Their naïveté is quickly disabused by the murderous intensity of trench warfare. The film powerfully and starkly evokes a war devoid of glory and heroism—just whistling rockets and bursts of gunfire, flares eerily lighting up the sky, barbed wire with bodies entangled in it, the endless cries of the wounded, and dugouts overrun with rats. The boys are help-less, frightened pawns, ground up like cannon fodder by a war whose roots and rationale they cannot understand. Milestone's camera travels endlessly along the muddy, crater-ridden terrain observing waves of soldiers being shot down. The troops spill over each other's trenches and are then repeatedly pushed back again to their own lines. To convey the immediacy and extent of this violence and destruction, Milestone uses a variety of camera angles, especially low-angle shots and long overheads.

The film is visceral rather than reflective, more interested in constructing searing closeup montages of the boys' exhaustion and fear of battle than in attempting to analyze the political nature of the war. Nor is the film much concerned with granting any individuality or dimension to its characters—most of the faces blur into an anonymous mass. In fact, the dialogue is generally stilted and declamatory and the humor is strained. The film's enduring strength lies in its images, which strikingly convey how fighting this war makes "every day a year" and how the German boys discover that their enemies are just ordinary men like themselves. Milestone's commitment is to the regular fighting man (very few officers appear on screen and their military strategies seem utterly self-destructive), absolutely endorsing the sentiment voiced by Paul (Lew Ayres), the one recruit given any personality, that "when it comes to dying for your country, it is better not to die at all."

All Quiet's final images, though heavy-handed in their irony, remain moving both in their sympathy for the tragic fate of the recruits and for the film's intense feelings about the futility of war. On Armistice Day, Paul sees a butterfly and reaches his hand out of the trenches to grasp it. The scene cuts with great fluidity from Paul's hand to an enemy sniper setting his gun sights on Paul, whose hand is finally stilled. Its poignance is also intensified by having a harmonica mournfully play on the sound track. The film concludes with a somber coda: the recruits march out to battle superimposed over a sea of graves and turn back to the camera with one last, haunted look on their faces.[10]

Milestone's film was without ambiguity or equivocation about its pacifism and it was followed by lesser films that echoed its vision. Lubitsch's *Broken Lullaby* (1932) and Hawks's *the Road to Glory* (1936) condemn the senselessness and irrationality of war and conclude a cycle of World War I films that ranged from unquestioning patriotism through a touch of realism to pacifism. Most of the pacifistic films focus on the German, French, and Italian roles in World War I, making it easier for Hollywood to condemn the war without ever confronting the United States' place in it. Nonetheless, these films had their effect. Indeed, novelist John Clennon Holmes would later write that he and his fellow soldiers went off to World War II with a great deal less enthusiasm and jingoist sentiment than the generation of 1914 just because of films like *All Quiet on the Western Front*.[11]

Between the opinion polls in the late 1930s showing that 90 percent of Americans wanted to keep out of the war and the moguls' fear of losing lucrative European markets and of arousing anti-Semitic feelings, Hollywood shied away from any commercially premature antifascist films. However, by the end of the "phony war" (the brief six-month period between the end of 1939 and spring of 1940 when war had been declared in Western Europe but no actual fighting had yet taken place) and the fall of France, Hollywood transformed the old beastly Hun stereotype into the swaggering, goose-stepping murderous Nazi. After Pearl Harbor, the public's rage and sense of betrayal placed the Japanese above the Nazis (race clearly playing a role) in the gallery of World War II villains.[12]

Pearl Harbor made the war effort palatable to the vast majority of the American public and, in fact, people bragged about their own or their family members' parts in the conflict. The war also aroused a great deal of community concern and involvement through civil defense activity, victory gardens, and soap and paper drives. Of course, it not only left the civilian population unscathed but expanded economic opportunity, making home support for the conflict easy to give.[13] The Hollywood films of the period were in accord with the public's view that the war was a just and necessary act, fought against an evil enemy who threatened civilization. They expressed little or no ambiguity about the reasons for fighting the war, the nature of the enemy, or life on the front itself.

In his memoir on World War II, *Not So Wild a Dream*, television commentator Eric Sevareid wrote that he "had a desperate desire to see the war, to be in the war, to know what the men of my generation were going through."[14] Sevareid went off as a journalist to the front, where he discovered an atmosphere that evoked intense feelings, heightened even at times beyond description. He created a portrait of a war where the "spirit of exaltation in mutual high endeavor" coincided with a sense of boredom, exhaustion, and moments of deliberate murder and wanton devastation.[15] Despite his feeling that the war was a tragic and complex event, the end of the conflict brought both a sense of relief and "a sneaking sensation of nostalgia and regret."[16]

World War II was clearly a conflict seen neither by civilians nor soldiers as unjustified, nightmarish, or absurd. Consequently, Hollywood had no difficulty playing an active part in promoting morale and projecting a positive image of the war. During the years 1942–44, nearly one-third of Hollywood's films concerned some aspect of the war. The films aggressively promoted and complacently defended U.S. democratic values, almost never pointing out the abuses and inherent contradictions of those values in American culture and society. They also affirmed a faith in the American Way of Life—in our warmth, our honor, and our egalitarianism. In fact, the war was made almost attractive, films presenting a world of camaraderie and courage where war's usual quota of horrors and tragedies were kept under control.

The vast majority of films portrayed military units filled with stock characters whose underlined and untroubled ethnic and regional diversity exemplified U.S. democracy in action. Hollywood platoons contained veritable melting pots of wisecracking, Dodger-loving, Brooklyn Italians and Jews; laconic, Midwestern farm boys; cool, crack-shooting Texans; feisty Irish non-coms; a lone Hispanic or Oriental; and a well-educated, articulate WASP officer all seamlessly meshing together. Films like *Gung Ho* (1943) portray a marine corps Raider platoon as men who, with little hesitation or anxiety, go into combat to kill Japs. Of course, they are seen as more than mere fearless fighting machines. Through its narration and fatherly commanding officer's pep talks, the film constantly promotes the fact that this unit is committed to togetherness, brotherhood, and team work (*gung ho* is Chinese for teamwork) and that they are ready to die for freedom and equality.

Lewis Milestone's *The Purple Heart* (1944) captures American fliers heroically standing up against their Japanese captors, demonstrating yet again that Americans are an indomitable people. More important, this film set out to reinforce the public's hatred of the Japanese by portraying them as a barbaric, treacherous, and cruel people who indulge in wild dances of fury and exotic samurai rituals. In Raoul Walsh's taut, action-filled, unpretentious *Objective Burma* (1944), an aging urbane newspaper-man-who-has-seen-it-all discovers the bodies of a group of American soldiers butchered by the Japanese. His world-weariness dissolves instantaneously, and he angrily cries, "Degenerate, immoral idiots! Wipe them off the face of the earth." This is of course the same cry echoed by most World War II films, whether they are set in Norway, North Africa, the Netherlands, or *Thirty Seconds over Tokyo:* the enemy was seen as arrogant, vile, and totalitarian and had to be destroyed.[17]

However, even before the end of the war, films like William Wellman's *The Story of GI Joe* (1945), lauded by James Agee as a "lean, subtle, eloquent work,"[18] began to convey some of the realities of the war. Based on Ernie Pyle's Pulitzer Prize-winning war dispatches, this dry, still, sober work avoids the inflated rhetoric, grandstand heroics, and stereotyping that characterized most other World War II films. Wellman's infantrymen are not clean shaven or well fed, and the war takes its toll—all are exhausted by the day-to-day slogging, one of the major characters has a breakdown, and many die in the course of action. The soldiers inhabit a somber, dark world, and the film's understated quality beautifully conveys the pathos and tragedy of war. In a similar fashion, though much more sentimental and self-consciously populist, Milestone's *A Walk in the Sun* (1946) communicates a genuine feeling for its melting-pot infantry unit's fear and anxiety about fighting and dying.[19]

Parallelng this film's naturalistic treatment of warfare is the treatment of the postwar readjustment of veterans in *The Best Years of Our Lives* (1946). This film still has its moments of doubt about the meaning of the war. These are most clearly seen in its portraits of complacent and even odious civilians who safely step into comfortable jobs while the GIs fight and die for them in Europe and the Far East. Thus, its ex-GI, banker hero Al Stephenson (Frederic March) wonders out loud at his bank's tight-fisted lending policy to ex-GIs and exclaims, "Last year it was kill Japs—this year it's make money."[20]

In Billy Wilder's cynical and nasty *A Foreign Affair* (1948), U.S. troops occupying Berlin become totally entwined in black market dealings and affairs with German women—including a ruthlessly pragmatic, sensual, ex-Nazi collaborator played by Marlene Dietrich. The film is given a conventional Hollywood ending, but the images of U.S. GIs quickly forgetting all about the nature of the war and pursuing their own needs and pleasures feels totally authentic and is clearly at odds with the official rhetoric of bringing democracy to the Germans.[21]

Based on the evidence from these films, it might be presumed that the post-World War II period would adhere to the pattern of its World War I predecessor by following up a series of patriotic films with a group of more realistic, subtle works dealing with the war and its aftermath. Of course, as Marx and others have taught us, history repeats itself, but not always in exactly the same way. Thus, instead of films that reevaluated the war, we see the war film caught between the demand for cartoonlike patriotic propaganda and the desire for content that truthfully depicts the complex nature of the period. As a result, war films oscillated back and forth between the two poles or were often schizoid blends of both.

The probable cause of this oscillation in our war films was the rise of our cold war with the Soviet Union. Despite our alliance with the Soviet Union during World War II, there had always existed among conservatives a wariness about Soviet intentions. With Stalin's breaking of the Yalta agreements, conservative resentments intensified, an unease that many liberals ultimately began to share. As cold war tensions worsened, relations between the United States and the Soviet Union became increasingly permeated with fear and distrust. The hostility was compounded by Soviet fears about their territorial security, coupled with their historic expansionism and and their ideological reflexes about the nature of U.S. capitalism. These notions collided with a U.S. vision of world domination based on economic and technological supremacy such as the world had previously not known.[22]

The prime battlegrounds of the cold war were not military but political and ideological. Nevertheless, the cold war did move U.S. foreign policy from its traditional isolationism into one that emphasized rearmament, military alliances, and covert as well as overt foreign interventionism. In addition, on a psychological level it gave many people, including liberal literary critics like Alfred Kazin, the sense of a "war that has never ended."[23] That feeling of continued weaponless conflict (until Korea) made it difficult for Hollywood to come up with a single, clear, unambiguous pattern in their war films.

On the home front, however, there seemed to be little ambiguity in the vitriolic and vindictive war carried out against the supposed domestic Communist fifth column—a group that purportedly took its marching orders from the Soviet Union. Even before Senator Joseph McCarthy made his name a synonym for witch hunting and Red baiting, the House Committee on Un-American Activities vigilantly pursued the homegrown Red menace. That Red hunt took eventually to Hollywood, where studio moguls (who otherwise bridled at the mere thought of government interference) willingly created a blacklist of former and suspected Communists and, as further proof of their loyalty, produced films devoted to exposing and combating the ominous Communist conspiracy.[24]

Consequently, what might have become a period of Hollywood revisionism in relation to World War II gave way to cold-war films like *Iron Curtain* (1948), *Red Danube* (1949), *I Was a Communist for the F.B.I.* (1951), *Walk East on Beacon* (1952), and *Big Jim McLain* (1952). These films closely conformed to genre conventons, were pseudodocumentary in style, and usually dealt with the evil conspiracies of foreigners and their native dupes to overthrow the country. They were overloaded with patriotic platitudes and built on simple-minded morality plays where Communist ideology was never defined or explored. The good guys were brave, fearless, and virtuous while Communists were either emotionally disturbed innocents or ruthless schemers and killers.[25]

The crude anticommunism of these films was reinforced by the pressures confronting U.S. power after World War II. The year 1949 had been a year of terrible shocks for Americans. We lost our atomic monopoly when the Soviets tested their A-bomb, and we had to face an even more profound political trauma with the victory of the Communists over the Nationalists on the Chinese mainland. Nowhere was this shock felt more keenly than at the State Department, where the loss of China meant attacks from the right (led by Senator McCarthy) and, in turn, the need to shape the policy of containment in Europe into an Asian pattern. While forging this Asian Maginot line, Secretary of State Dean Acheson forgot to mention South Korea. Nevertheless, Korea was definitely on President Truman's mind when he sent U.S. troops, as the main part of the U.N. force, to fight there in June 1950, after the North Korean invasion. The invasion, partially brought on by the adventurism of the corrupt South Korean government, quickly overran the country.[26]

The first U.S. troops had barely established their perimeter around Pusan, the last South Korean outpost, before U.S. film dealing with Korea was produced. *The Steel Helmet* (1951), directed by Samual Fuller, centered around a hard-bitten veteran, a South Korean orphan, and a black corpsman who link up with a wandering squad of deviants and fight off a host of North Koreans. However, despite the fact that it is something of an anticommunist cartoon, *The Steel Helmet* is nevertheless touched with a healthy dash of post-World War II film realism.

From its opening credits, *The Steel Helmet* seems determined to be second to none in its portrayal of Communists as the last word in bestiality and savagery. In fact, the opening scene has loud-mouthed, cigar-chomping Sergeant Zack (Gene Evans), Fuller's hero, crawling, hands bound behind his back, through a field littered with the victims of a Communist massacre. Nor is this the only sequence that provides examples of Communist atrocities: North Korean soldiers leave booby-trapped GI corpses, kill innocent children, and indulge in human-wave attacks that give clear evidence of their total disregard for the value of human life.

Nonetheless, Fuller gives ample hints that he is wary of all ideologies. Indeed, as evil as the Communists are, the Americans are hardly guiltless. (Although Fuller may have been skeptical about the expression of patriotic sentiments, he was still, however, totally committed to a U.S. victory in the cold war.) Here Fuller finds fault particularly with the cultural and racial blindness of GIs. For instance, within minutes after his young South Korean friend saves his life, Sergeant Zack refers to him as a "gook" and finally feels comfortable with him only when he converts him into a miniature American, complete with GI dogtags and an American name. By the same token, a hardcore North Korean Communist officer POW dies asking for the Buddhist last rites. Such is Fuller's unconscious primitivism that it allows him to stumble prophetically onto a bit of cold war revisionism about the true nature of so-called monolithic communism when he has a North Korean argue that he is not a Soviet, but a North Korean Communist.

However, *The Steel Helmet*'s most interesting element is its portrayal of the U.S. fighting man. In contrast to the grizzled but chivalric GI Joe heroes of the earlier war films, Fuller's alienated hero, Sergeant Zack, is interested only in survival and is untouched by the slightest hint of humanitarian or sentimental impulses. Thus, gorging himself on a watermelon, he warns a fellow GI not to touch a dead American's body to get his dogtags. When the soldier is blown up by the booby-trapped corpse, he sneers contemptuously, "Get his dogtags, big deal." In addition, Zack wantonly machine guns an unarmed prisoner (a North Korean officer) to death in a half-mad frenzy after the death of his South Korean ward.

This bit of candor about U.S. fighting men is duplicated in *The Steel Helmet*'s treatment of American racism. After joining up with a black corpsman (James Edwards), Zack and his little pal then link up with a wandering squad whose melting pot of the usual GIs is supplemented by a conscientious objector (Jim Hutton) and a Nisei (Richard Loo). When a captured North Korean officer tries to seduce the two minority-group members into helping him by reminding them of the discrimination they face back home, he is rebuffed by the rather bland assertion that it's not his but their problem. This facile dismissal doesn't totally obscure the fact that this is almost the first time the race issue appears in a film actually dealing with men at war.

Considering the desperate speed and limited budget with which it was made (the film is all studio sets and back lots), it is striking how much bite and reality *The Steel Helmet* contains. Indeed, despite its tabloid script and caricatured characters, it gives evidence that the war film could offer an opportunity for more than mere jingoistic rhetoric and imagery.[27] It could be that during a war like the Korean War, which unlike World Wars I and II did not threaten the United States' existence and make it imperative that the nation commit itself to a concerted collective effort to defeat the enemy; a situation that ensured that anything short of fullblown patriotism would be considered traitorous. In addition, despite conservative cries echoing General MacArthur's Why not Victory, the United States settled for a stalemate in Korea. Following the national path of bullets and butter, Hollywood had it both ways, churning out bellicose statements about wartime heroism in *Fix Bayonets* (1951) and *Retreat Hell!* (1952) along with films that presented a more jaundiced picture of the armed forces and war.

Of course, the latter films placed their action within the safe confines of World War II and even World War I rather than look at them directly in the context of the cold war. One of the first such films was the revisionist *From Here to Eternity* (1953). This film was a far cry from the pre-world War II films that dealt with the macho posturing and heroic hi-jinks of peacetime army life coupled with covert pleas for preparedness and glamorization of new weapons systems (e.g., *Test Pilot*, [1938]). The film version of James Jones's powerful, naturalistic work, though shorn of the novel's intimations of homosexuality and stockade radicalism, still conveys the petty and large-scale brutalities of the pre-Pearl Harbor army as it tries to force men to conform. Moreover, its portrait of a fawning, sadistic, and opportunistic officer corps hardly endeared it to the Pentagon (although they did assist the production, albeit reluctantly and only after numerous script revisions). Similarly, a film like Robert Aldrich's bleak World War II film *Attack!* (1956) suggests that the lives of GIs are wantonly sacrificed because the officer hierarchy is incompetent, corrupt, and cowardly. This film, with whose production the Defense Department declined to cooperate, portrays war as generally dehumanizing and absurd while still maintaining a place for men who can affirm and sustain traditional military virtues like loyalty and honesty in the midst of the madness.[28]

As often as Hollywood poured out post-Korean War films that gloried in guts and gore (*The Steel Bayonet* [1958] and *To Hell and Back* [1955]), it also produced *The Caine Mutiny* (1954), *Paths of Glory* (1957), and *The Bridge over the River Kwai* (1957), all of which projected a darker, more-complex vision about the nature of war. In fact, such is the impact of tragedy and waste depicted in these films that the doctor in *River Kwai* might speak for all of them when he is moved to shout, "Madness, madness!"

Historically, this blending of war and antiwar films paralled a deepening U.S. commitment in Asia. Despite the absence of a declared war, signs of coming involvement were apparent even before the guns erupted in Korea. A month before the war began *Time* magazine carried the following message:

The United States now has a new frontier and a new ally in the cold war. . . . The place is Indo-China, a southwest Asian jungle, mountain and delta land that includes the Republic of Vietnam, and the smaller neighboring kingdoms of Laos and Cambodia, all parts of the French Union.[29]

Within weeks of the invasion of South Korea, the United States began pouring money and munitions into French hands in order to help them hang onto their colonies in Indochina.

This policy was a clear reversal of our World War II anticolonialism, which saw the U.S. Office of Strategic Services (OSS) boost the Indochinese guerrilla forces of the Communist (but thoroughly antifascist) Ho Chi Minh. However, with growing fears of losing Southeast Asia to Communism, the United States gave France over $3 billion in military aid, over half of which went into the first Indochinese war during the years between 1950 and 1954.

That war ended for the French in 1954 with the disaster at Dien-Bien-Phu, but not before the United States skirted extremely close to plunging into the war. Only President Eisenhower's military restraint prevented the hawks in his administration (who ran the gamut from Vice-President Richard M. Nixon to Armed Services Chief of Staff Admiral Radford) from taking that step. Nevertheless, the United States quickly took up the role of receiver for the bankrupt French enterprise and did everything to stalemate the Geneva Accords that ended the war.

These efforts ranged from the dirty-tricks silliness of pouring sugar into the engines of Hanoi omnibuses in order to destabilize the incoming Communist regime in the North to serious attempts at nation building in the South. The main thrust of U.S. policy was to find a non-Communist nationalist leader as an alternative to Ho Chi Minh. Even President Eisenhower predicted Ho would win 80 percent of the votes if the free elections promised under the Geneva Accords were held.

A serious contender to Ho was found in Ngo Dinh Diem, a French-educated Catholic whose non-Communist nationalist credentials received their bona fides from Francis Cardinal Spellman, Senator Mike Mansfield, and a young Senator from the state of Massachusetts, John F.

Kennedy. Although considered a long shot at first, Diem (with U.S. military advice and aid) succeeded in subduing the independent sects and bandits who had long dominated South Vietnam. In short order, he was hailed by the Western press as the Asian counterpart of Joan of Arc and Winston Churchill. More substantially, he was the beneficiary of over $3 billion in U.S. aid (half of it military) by 1960.[30]

While U.S. military and economic commitment grew in Southeast Asia, Hollywood refought World War II in films like *Battle Cry* (1955) and *From Hell to Eternity* (1960) or tried to come to grips with the Korean conflict in *The Bridges at Toko Ri* (1955) and *Battle Circus* (1953). If anything, at that point Southeast Asia was seen as a patch of exotica where Alan Ladd chased down smugglers in *Saigon* (1948) or where Dick Powell hunted a Martin Bormann-like Nazi war criminal in *Rogue's Regiment* (1948). If Hollywood was any barometer, the French effort in Indochina (despite the proclamation of the domino theory) seemed hardly to touch vital U.S. interests or generate much of a sense of immediacy and urgency for Americans.

Nonetheless, with increasing U.S. involvement in Southeast Asia, a few film makers decided this war was a subject worth exploring. First on the scene (as he was with the Korean War) was Sam Fuller. Indeed, Fuller had almost prefigured his commitment to the cold-war struggle at the end of *The Steel Helmet* with a coda that explained, "There is no end to this story," as Sergeant Zack, the black corpsman, and the ex-conscientious objector—the sole survivors of the Communist assault—go off to continue the battle. The message implicit in the words and the image was of the United States accepting its reponsibilities in the cold war. Thus, finding American mercenaries like Johnny Brock (Gene Barry) and Goldie (Nat King Cole) fighting in Indochina with the French in *China Gate* (1957) should come as no surprise, for they were merely fulfilling that pledge.

Stripped of anything even connected with Vietnamese social or physical reality except for its opening documentary footage setting time and place (ironically probably the first shots to introduce a picture of Ho Chi Minh to the American public), Fuller's film hovers perilously close to the sophistication of a Steve Canyon comic-strip adventure. Nevertheless, the gross cartoonlike plot of a dangerous mission undertaken by foreign legionnaires and their "dragon lady" guide to destroy a secret Communist munitions dump contains some suggestive elements.

In *China Gate*, Fuller urges a greater U.S. commitment to the anti-Communist struggle in Southeast Asia. As is usual in his films, the American way is defended by pariahs and soldiers of fortune like his hero, Johnny Brock. Brock is a tough and cynical man without ideology who, in true *Casablanca* fashion, proclaims his political indifference with the remark that "soldiering is my business—Korea got cold and Indo-

China Gate

china got hot." In a similar manner, Lucky Legs (Angie Dickinson in a slit dress) is a charismatic, Eurasian saloon owner who has had her share of pain and trouble. She leads the legionnaires to the munitions dump not out of ideological commitment—she cares nothing for either side ("I'd prefer to let you and the hammer-and-sickle boys fight it out alone")—but only to get her son sent to the United States. However, Fuller's words and ideas are not particularly significant; it's action that counts, and Lucky and Johnny prove by their courage their commitment to the American ideal.

Through Johnny's relationship with Lucky (they were once married, but he left her when she gave birth to a son who looked Chinese), Fuller again sees racism not merely as a minor symbolic impediment to our democratic ideals but also as the major barrier to our claim to free-world leadership. In this aspect, Fuller's films are in accord with films of the period that have a similar message (e.g., *Sayonara* [1957]). However, Fuller does not trust the whole issue to revolve around the predictable romantic relationship between Brock and Lucky (they fall in love again, and at the film's end Brock's racism is expunged by his love for his Oriental-looking son). He also needs black crooner Nat King Cole to sing the title song and play Brock's anticommunist (he's in Indochina to kill "lying commies.") friend. Fuller's patronizing image of Cole is the embodiment of what a tolerant, nonracist society will produce: a sexless, smiling, black cold warrior, eternally singing and cleaning his gun.

In addition to the attack on racism, Fuller also conveys the notion that the Communists are ruthless destroyers who, in contrast to the supposedly civilized French, are ready to bomb civilians, both women and children. The personification of Communist commitment is Major Cham (Lee Von Cleef), a Eurasian lover of Lucky Legs who abhors the West for its softness and sentimentality. Cham is in fact the only Communist who gets to say more than a few words and is, like Lucky Legs, played by a white actor. (It's possible that antiracist Fuller had difficulty believing that an Oriental actor would be acceptable to the American public in an interracial romance.)

It is clear that Fuller wanted to fit *China Gate*'s Indochinese war into some kind of pattern Americans could understand. The film even goes so far as to invert the military reality of the war by making the foreign legionnaires into the guerrillas and the Communists into defenders of static positions. Nor is it any more enlightening about the Vietminh, since they are portrayed as hardly more than bandits who would as soon cut a French throat as sing the "Marseillaise."

This boys' adventure film might have been an attempt to make the war intelligible to Americans, yet its covert plea for racial tolerance is symbolic of the dialectic going on even within the most strident and bellicose cold-war film. It is evident from a film like *China Gate* that there was some feeling that American opinion should be mobilized in favor of maintaining U.S. cold-war responsibilities in the struggle against Communism. However, it was hard to arouse these passions when there wasn't any direct military threat to the United States. The lack of any imminent danger allowed Hollywood films to raise social and political issues that would hardly have been permitted if the situation were perceived as grave. Of course, they were always defined as minor problems that could be solved merely with the requisite good will. That kind of political fantasy was paralleled by the innocent assumption that we could do a better job than the French in dealing with Vietnam.

American naïveté was the bane of many foreign critics and is well reflected in Anglo-Catholic novelist Graham Greene's *The Quiet American* (1955), set against the background of the first Indochinese war. In fact, this innocence was perceived as so dangerous that one of Greene's characters goes so far as to call it a form of "insanity."[31]

In the book, Greene turns Vietnam into one of his characteristic tropical hells of heat and corruption, the domain where his inverted passion plays usually take place. This time the parts are played by solemn, ingenuous ("he never saw anything he hadn't heard in a lecture hall"), American CIA agent Pyle, who came to Vietnam to create a third force between the Communists and the French, and the cynical, weary, British foreign correspondent Fowler, who despises Pyle's ideas and finds his Vietnamese mistress the object of Pyle's affections. Although touched with religious symbolism, Greene's dialectic between innocence and guilt, ambiguity and certainty, is still politically pointed and incisive. Although his Judas-like betrayal of Pyle is bound up equally by personal and political considerations, Fowler acts out of his revulsion for Pyle's innocence and the mindless destruction it causes. Greene concludes the novel with a prophetic warning against involvement in Vietnam.

Despite this perspective, Joseph Mankiewicz's film version of *The Quiet American* (1958) seems firmly determined to ignore Greene's message and affirms American innocence without even Fuller's unsubtle qualifiers. As one of the major changes in the film, Pyle (Audie Murphy)—now devoid of any U.S. connection—is transformed into a selfless agent of an altruistic American organization called the Friends of Free Asia, whose intention is to help set up a plastics industry for the Vietnamese. Furthermore, the Communists (who were shadowy figures beneath the surface of Greene's Vietnam) become, in Mankiewicz's script, the active instigators of a devious plot to convince Fowler that Pyle is acting as the agent provocateur behind a scheme to supply plastique bombs to a terrorist, third-force Vietnamese general. Whatever political motivation Fowler has for betraying Pyle is made totally subsidiary to the mechanics of the bland, shallow love triangle played out by him, Pyle, and their passive Vietnamese girlfriend Phuong (played again by a white actress, Georgia Moll). However, if the Vietnamese conflict is subordinated to the romance and subsequent murder, there are still a number of scenes in which Fowler and Pyle get together and talk politics.

The film is shot primarily in static close-ups of two people talking. There is little that is visually arresting, and we have almost no sense of the social and physical life of Saigon or Vietnam. The dialogue is at times literate but often turns to lifeless sloganeering, with Pyle bearing the burden of smug and self-congratulatory lines about the United States being privileged by its own revolutionary history in understanding the minds of the Vietnamese. He inanely implies that the world waits for Americans to give answers that nobody else has been able to provide.

In the film, Pyle is supposedly the man with the political answers, and Mankiewicz weights the film against Fowler, who is depicted as a pathetic, emotionally retarded intellectual—pretentiously indulging in sardonic contempt for the American Way. Fowler inveighs against the United States as an antiseptic "consumer's paradise" and a "wide-screen world of romance." The attempt goes so far that even in death the courteous, virtuous, and courageous Pyle is victorious, as Phuong rejects Fowler (in the book she goes back to live with him) and the voice of another Englishman denounces him as "middle-aged, unwashed, unwanted."

However, it's possible that Mankiewicz felt he had to overstate his case, since the film is thrown out of balance by the performances of its two stars. Michael Redgrave makes Fowler a much more sympathetic and interesting figure than the boyish, affectless Murphy can make Pyle. The script may inform us that Fowler is a sad figure, but his wit and irony make Pyle in contrast seem like a dim fool. (Could it be that Mankiewicz unconsciously wanted to follow Greene's critique of American innocence?)

Nevertheless, Mankiewicz remains committed to the need for a U.S. presence in Vietnam. The sophisticated French police inspector speaks approvingly of Pyle as a "young man with an idea" who terrifies the Communists. Mankiewicz starts out by envisioning a vague third force, which can supposedly build a democratic Vietnam free of colonialism and Communism and committed to protecting individual freedom. However, as the film evolves, the idea of a third force dissolves and becomes personified in Ngo Dinh Diem. In fact, Pyle comes close to even naming Diem when he says that while a graduate student at Princeton, he met a man who "if all goes well, if Vietnam becomes an independent republic, this man will be its leader." Mankiewicz supplies the mystery man's name in his final dedication of the film to "the people of the Republic of Vietnam . . . and its president, Ngo Dinh Diem."[32]

If nothing else, Mankiewicz's dedication prefigures the commitment of the Kennedy administration in the early 1960s. It gives the impression that South Vietnam could be equated with the whole of Vietnam and implies that Ngo Dinh Diem was a popularly chosen leader rather than a creature of U.S. military aid. The film's essential message is that the United States was involved in Vietnam to help its people gain and maintain their independence and to protect the rest of Southeast Asia from falling to the Communists.

Both *China Gate* and *The Quiet American* are striking examples of American film makers' attempts to fit Vietnam into the mosaic of U.S. cold-war commitments. Nevertheless, despite a few low-budget films like *Jump into Hell* (1955) and *Five Gates to Hell* (1959), most film makers steered clear of Vietnam. With the exception of *China Gate*'s momentary rationale for commitment based on a rekindled love affair and its inter-racial progeny, there was precious little that Hollywood and the public could personally identify with beyond abstractions like *free world, self-determination*, and *freedom*. In essence, Americans felt they had little stake in Vietnam, a place, if public opinion polls of the period are to be trusted, most couildn't even locate on their maps.[33]

Unfortunately, this was hardly the case among the higher echelon of U.S. foreign-policy planners. From the very moment that President Eisenhower enunciated the domino theory, the struggle in Southeast Asia took on increasing significance for the United States. Subsequently this theory gained credibility when the revolutionary movement (the Vietcong) in South Vietnam, dormant since the signing of the Geneva Accords, revived as a result of the oppressiveness of the Diem regime and threatened to topple the Vietnam domino.

Elected by a slim margin of 118,000 votes as a consequence of U.S. economic difficulties (unemployment, frequent recessions, etc.) and foreign-policy malaise (Cuba, the U-2 incident) in the last years of the Eisenhower administration, John F. Kennedy adopted a foreign policy that intensified confrontations with the Soviet Union and its allies. He believed that the United States had the power to defeat guerrilla wars of national liberation, and, as a result, he increased the number of U.S. military personnel in South Vietnam from its peak of slightly over 1,000 under Eisenhower to over 15,000 by 1963.

Despite increasing U.S. commitment, the Diem regime continued to slide downhill. Diem suppressed all forms of dissent and imposed brutal taxation on the peasantry. Isolated from any kind of moderating influences, he came more and more under the spell of his power-hungry brother Ngo Dinh Nhu, and his wife. These factors precipitated the development of the National Liberation Front (NLF), which grew from a ragtag collection of armed guerrillas into a formidable revolutionary army of 15,000, capable of occupying cities.

The Buddhist crisis of 1962-63 created the catalyst for Diem's downfall. Ideally the third force that Graham Greene's Pyle so anxiously sought, the Buddhists were committed to a policy of neutrality, and they might have served as the basis for a coalition government had the United States been truly interested in a political solution to the war. However, bound to a military resolution of the conflict, the United States stood by as Diem ruthlessly attacked the Buddhists. Diem's suppression thoroughly eroded the last vestiges of his authority, and because this threatened to undermine the war effort against the Communist-dominated National Liberation Front, the United States gave covert support to the military coup that resulted in Diem's assassination.[34]

As the early years of the Kennedy administration were dominated by defense intellectuals (e.g., McGeorge Bundy and Robert McNamara) whose strategic thought was shaped by military premises, it is hardly surprising that the war film underwent something of a parallel renaissance. Most notable for their epic proportions were the star-filled, multi-million-dollar re-creation of D-Day *The Longest Day* (1962) and the equally illustrious (Gregory Peck, David Niven, Anthony Quinn) World War II action-adventure drama *The Guns of Navarrone* (1961). Ultimately, even the president himself was grist for the war-film mill with the making of the almost-campaign-biography tale of his wartime heroism *PT-109* (1963).

Nevertheless, films like the heavy-handed *The Victors* (1962) evidenced the persistence of pacifist themes. Even the Korean War film became infused with these ideas as a work by Dennis and Terry Sanders, the low-budget *War Hunt* (1962), conveyed a sense of the futility and madness of war.

Belligerence and self-doubt crept into George Englund's film *The Ugly American* (1963), based on the William J. Lederer and Eugene Burdick novel. A thinly veiled look at Vietnam set in a Southeast Asian country called Sarkhan, the book served as a primer on how to win the cold war in a Third World country. Little vignettes revolving around its characters carried the bulk of the novels dos (learn the language, study the culture) and don'ts (stay isolated, preach to them).[35] Instead of following this format, however, Englund pared the number of important characters down to two: the ex-OSS wartime officer and journalist-turned-ambassador MacWhite (Marlon Brando) and former guerrilla leader, national hero, neutralist, and MacWhite's friend Deong (Eiji Okada).

Perhaps the most judicious statement about this film came from Judith Crist, who wrote, "If the hero, played by Marlon Brando, is a good ambassador—God help us all!"[36] Her point is well taken, since Mac-White's consular manner seems to come from English drawing-room comedy and his sense of diplomacy from *The King and I*. Such is his tact that his first meeting with Deong winds up with each trying to outshout the other in epithets ranging from "Communist dupe" to "imperialist warmonger."

The upshot of this encounter is to bring to the surface the rigid cold warrior lurking beneath MacWhite's pipe-smoking, regular-guy liberalism. MacWhite responds to all Deong's protestations about the Sarkhanese people's need for self-determination and their wariness of the U.S. presence (they see it as auguring future military aggression) by feeling personally betrayed, and he authorizes the provocative act of building a "freedom road" right up to the border of North Sarkhan (North Vietnam). Of course, MacWhite's cold-war posturings are framed by liberal premises—the road is supposedly being built to save the people, not the ruling class. However, given MacWhite's arrogant, self-deceiving behavior, it's no surprise that Deong's uneasy, third-force commitment to neutralism and nonviolence begins to move to the left. The revolution breaks out and the Communists predictably (given the nature of the film) betray and murder Deong. A much-chastened Mac-White finally calls the Seventh Fleet to the rescue.

For the most part, *The Ugly American* indulges in a great many simplistic cold-war clichés about American virtue and Communist duplicity. There is even a folksy American engineer, Homer Atkins (Pat Hingle), and his wife Emma, who eschew ideology and MacWhite's rhetoric for good old American concern and compassion. Emma runs a children's hospital where she cares for starving children, and both are so loved by the people they work with that they are shielded from the Communists when the revolution begins. On the other hand, the film's Communists are without exception fanatical and insidious cardboard cutouts devoid of any shred of belief in human friendship or trust.

Although this film is filled with predictable stereotypes, it nonetheless contains moments that communicate something of the reality of the Third World. Despite its being essentially a static film, dominated by a great many shots of people talking and speechifying, it has one powerfully edited sequence—the airport demonstration riot that greets MacWhite's arrival. The images and action convey a chilling sense of the depth of Third World anti-Americanism, especially when the rioters seem about to break into MacWhite's sealed limousine. Also moving beyond the usual clichés is Englund's portrait of the aristocratic Sarkhanese prime minister Kwen Sai (Kukrit Pramai), who is neither caricatured as the shining hope of the free world or as a merely corrupt and decadent dictator. While it is true he engages in nepotism and has contempt for the people's capacity to govern themselves, his subtlety, sophistication, and dignity make MacWhite look even more muscle headed and dense than he is, especially when cunningly extracting a military commitment from MacWhite.

However, despite moments where one feels a more-complex political intelligence at work than is usual for Hollywood, *The Ugly American* predictably concludes with the prime minister committing himself to the American Way of democratic reform and coalition government and the reconciliaton of MacWhite and Deong (before he dies). The reconciliation is brought about by their individual decisions to submerge their sense of hurt and powerful egoism, admitting their errors and working together for political freedom (economic change is seen as a peripheral issue here). Just as in *The Quiet American* (but less overtly), political acts are influenced by personal conflicts, demonstrating the usual Hollywood uneasiness about abstract ideas and explicit political ideologies. Of course, ideas can be discussed and, in *The Ugly American*, even taken seriously, but granting them genuine complexity is another question altogether.

Moreover, *The Ugly American* tries to have it both ways in its depiction of the Third World's desire for self-determination in a world dominated by the two power blocs. Although the film raises the possibility that a country like Sarkhan might authentically desire to stay aloof from the big powers, it nonetheless portrays Deong's neutralism as naïvely playing into Communist hands. The basis for this purported belief is that the United States sincerely sees neutralism as a viable alternative for the Third World, while Communists use it as a ploy to cover their desire for domination. Therefore, even though MacWhite makes an impassioned plea (albeit a clichéd one) at his final press conference for the West to go beyond stereotypes and open itself to Third World revolutionary passions, the film is clearly pessimistic about the viability of the neutralist position.

The Ugly American was perfectly in tune with a Kennedy cold-war foreign policy that talked about Third World independence and neutrality and the moral struggle against ignorance, hunger, and disease while at the same time doing everything possible to undermine and corrupt such political movements. However, the film doesn't have the confidence in its rhetoric and posture that its less-complicated cold-war-film predecessors had. Indeed, it ends on a skeptical note. As MacWhite makes his television appeal for greater understanding of the Third World, the scene shifts to the living room of Mr. Average American. Dully chewing on a pork chop, he tunes MacWhite out, showing not the least shred of interest in his message. The scene is an implicit warning that if Americans do not listen to these wise words, the result will ultimately be a political nightmare.[37]

This moment of self-doubt reflects the kind of transformation the cold-war adventure-drama film had undergone from simple-minded stereotypes to a more-complicated vision. It also mirrors the war film's irregular development from propaganda and unquestioning patriotism through realism to a bifurcated genre that glorified and debunked war sometimes within the very same film. These changes were clearly the by-product of a political and military situation that was neither total war nor total peace, thus allowing the unequivocal and the skeptical to exist side by side. Enmeshed in this kind of ambiguity, it should come as no surprise that when the United States escalated its military involvement in Vietnam, the cinematic symbols, roles, and values that had served so well to justify and gain support for other wars lost their power to arouse a popular consensus in favor of the war. As a result, the problem facing the Hollywood producer, writer, and director wasn't solely the financial risk created by the increasing polarization of the audience as the war intensified. It was also the inadequacy of any known film metaphors to even fully encompass, much less illuminate the character of the Vietnam War.

Despite their inabilty to project totally unequivocal and unambiguous metaphors and characters, films like *China Gate, The Quiet American,* and *The Ugly American* did set a political tone. First and foremost, they were hardly reticent or subtle about portraying a ruthless, universal Communist conspiracy bent on world domination, in contrast to which they juxtaposed U.S. innocence and commitment to freedom. Most important of all, they conditioned the American public to accept the fact that the cold war was a global struggle and that we had a definite commitment to protect South Vietnam from Communist aggression.

PART II

The War That Dared
Not Speak Its Name:
Wounded Heroes and Supermen

In the late 1950s and early 1960s, the United States was primarily pre-occupied with areas in the cold war other than Southeast Asia, sometimes in direct confrontation with the Soviet Union. However, even where the ambiguities evoked by the tendency of indigenous Communist movements to overlap, fuse, or become indistinguishable with national liberation movements no longer existed, the complexities of the cold war persisted, for it was clear that any confrontation between the two super-powers held the potential for nuclear war and annihilation. The threat and fear of apocalypse rendered the simple idea of winning or losing absurd and profoundly affected the nature of the war film.

Such was the impact of the threat of nuclear warfare that Yale psychologist Kenneth Kenniston, studying a group of students organizing against the Vietnam War in his book *Young Radicals*, equated a fear of violence induced by a dread of nuclear disaster with the Victorians famed "dirty little secret" as a potent factor in motivating modern behavior.[1] Paul Cowan, a journalist and civil-rights activist, Peace Corps volunteer, and later radical protester against the Vietnam War, confirmed Kenniston's remarks, revealing that

ghoulish fantasies of imminent destruction had become fashionable within our small group of liberals. Sometimes we even seemed to be indulging ourselves in a subtle competition to see who was the most obsessed. Fisherman in the troubled sea of our psyches, we often exchanged yarns about our nightmares of buildings exploding, of charred victims of nuclear attacks gagging from the radiation poisoning they had suffered.[2]

These apocalyptic fears provided the impetus for a worldwide movement to Ban the Bomb. A network of writers and singers who wondered, "Where Have All the Flowers Gone?" or satirically proclaimed, "Goodbye Mom, I'm Off to Drop the Bomb" grew up around this cause. These anxieties almost came to horrifying fruition during the Cuban missile crisis.

For 13 perilous days the world seemed to be sliding inexorably toward nuclear war, as Soviet merchant vessels carrying rockets capable of delivering thermonuclear warheads steamed toward the U.S. blockade of Cuban waters. Although catastrophe was averted at perhaps the last moment, even the triumphant Americans were aware that such confrontations were a "collective death wish for the world."[3]

Although the scenario of the missile crisis might have served successfully as the plot for a Hollywood film (it was later made into a television movie), the grim reality of a thermonuclear war barely penetrated into films. In fact, Hollywood initially approached the bomb with the kind of reverence that ranked the destruction of Hiroshima alongside the raising of the flag on Iwo Jima as an act of World War II heroism. Indeed, in films like *Above and Beyond* (1952), *Strategic Air Command* (1955) and *Bomber's B-52* (1957), the bomb was actually pictured as a force for peace.

However, by 1959 the first glimmerings of détente and the agitations of the Sane Nuclear Policy movement breached Hollywood's battle-scarred worship of the bomb with the production of Stanley Kramer's antinuclear war drama, *On the Beach*, based on Nevil Shute's novel. Although a historically and politically important film event (it was simultaneously released in the United States and the Soviet Union), *On the Beach* was a kitsch-level assault on the bomb that probably had no more profound impact than making the film's obtrusive theme music "Waltzing Matilda" into a pop classic.[4]

The same could not be said of *Fail Safe* (1964) and *Dr. Strangelove: Or How I Stopped Worrying and Learned to Love the Bomb* (1964), both of which awakened audiences to the terrifying menace of nuclear war. *Fail Safe* and *Dr. Strangelove*, with their radically different cinematic styles, successfully conveyed what Susan Sontag called "the imagination of disaster,"[5] the sense of "living through one's own death and more, the death of cities, the destruction of humanity itself."[6]

In *Fail Safe*, based on the novel written by Eugene Burdick and Harvey Wheeler, the combination of the film's semidocumentary approach and a horrifying and powerful montage of the destruction of New York and Moscow gives the film its chilling measure of reality. Nevertheless, some of the most-compelling moments in the film arise from its image of the decent U.S. president (Henry Fonda), framed in almost total isolation, trying in dry, laconic tones to assure his Soviet counterpart that it was all a mistake. In these moments there is a feeling of unbearable and unspeakable tragedy hanging in the balance, as men representing very different political power structures and interests try to reason with one another. Viewing these scenes, an audience was hard pressed to avoid the visceral sensation of how close to the brink we actually were and what slender resources were available to cope with the impending disaster.

It is a bitter assault on the limits of reason that carries the often expressionistic *Dr. Strangelove* beyond a mere satire of liberal politicians, warmongering generals, compulsively spying Soviet ambassadors, and mad nuclear strategists to the primal instincts of sex and death. From its opening shots of a B-52 bomber in mid-air copulation with its refueling plan to the final detonation of the doomsday machine, there is hardly a moment in the film that doesn't connect nuclear war with eros and thanatos.

Dr. Strangelove launches some of its most caustic barbs at the liberal, humanistic tradition that holds that these destructive forces can be kept in check by reason and decency. We are reminded of the limits and inadequacy of reason as the bland president (Peter Sellers) tries to talk to a drunken Soviet premier about the mutual terror they are confronted with ("Now Dimitri, you know how we've always talked about the possibility of something going wrong with the bomb—the bomb, Dimitri, the hydrogen bomb!"). And paralleling the utter inadequacy of decent reasonable men in the face of such monstrous forces is the ex-Nazi scientist Dr. Strangelove, the personification of scientific reason gone amuck. With his self-propelled Nazi saluting arm, his belief in the divinity of computers, and his gleeful plans for a post-nuclear-holocaust society of subterranean polygamy, Strangelove emerges as a brilliant parody of the worst strains in U.S. politics and culture.[7]

Although neither *Fail Safe* nor *Dr. Strangelove* noticeably influenced any restraint in the arms race or even hinted at any sane strategy for dealing with nuclear weapons, they did force the audience to think about the unthinkable. By making both sides culpable in the drama, these nuclear war films additionally cut through the Gordian knot of cold-war mythology. As social philosopher Lewis Mumford noted in a letter to the *New York Times* about Dr. Strangelove, "The film is the first break in the Cold War trance that has for so long held this country in its rigid grip."[8]

No less significant than the demystifying elements in *Dr. Strangelove* is the black humor with which it treats nuclear war and U.S. politics. Its sense of the absurd provides a means of coping with a world that is perched so perilously on the brink of catastrophe. Indeed, laughter seems the only real alternative to either tears and hysteria or total paralysis.

In this approach, *Dr. Strangelove* reflected the influence of 1960s black-humor novelists like Bruce Jay Friedman, Thomas Pynchon, Kurt Vonnegut, Joseph Heller, and Terry Souther (coscenarist of *Dr. Strangelove*), all of whom used savage satire as a means of dealing with the insanity they saw around them. Unfortunately this perspective often came so perilously close to nihilism that, in real political terms, it undermined any possible activism except the assumption of probably an impossible degree of stoical detachment.

Nonetheless, if *Dr. Strangelove* did not bring about social change, it did encourage film makers to develop a sense of nightmarish comedy and irony in regard to war and politics. Its angle of vision became more and more useful to them as the society became more polarized in the late 1960s. In particular, it allowed the film industry to approach sensitive issues from a critical perspective without being stridently polemical, to use ideas that in another mode might have alienated the audience.

Needless to say, the 1960's film antecedents of this comic mode predated even *Dr. Strangelove*. John Frankenheimer's *The Manchurian Candidate* (1962) was built on the ironic 1950s liberal conceit that suggested that "if Joe McCarthy were working for the communists he couldn't be doing a better job." Taking this a few steps further, Frankenheimer made a film where not only were U.S. senators Communist agents, but so were war heroes and even the ne plus ultra of American virtue—Mom.

Using a conventional thriller format in which a Korean War POW returns home a brainwashed Communist assassin primed to kill a presidential candidate, Frankenheimer created a thoroughgoing world of illusion. It is a world in which dreams are more real than reality and irrationality is the norm: Congressional Medal of Honor winners turn into Red Chinese agents, and the ultimate patriotic act becomes killing your mother and stepfather.

In addition to this constant play between illusion and reality, Frankenheimer also resorted to a visual and verbal form of humor that became standard in the 1960s as the "put-on"—ironic and often bizarre effects and overstatements used to make a point or to get a laugh. For instance, in one scene a right-wing senator parades around a masquerade in an Abraham Lincoln costume, an overwrought liberal senator refers to a right-wing social event as a "fascist rally," and when he dies milk seems to spurt from his veins rather than blood.

Coupled with black humor and nightmare comedy, the practice of nothing really being what it is supposed to be (including most figures of authority) played an important role in the later films of the decade. In this visual and intellectual sleight-of-hand style, nothing can be taken for granted. Thus, as the films of the decade developed, one era might become a metaphor for another, one war a stand-in for another, and one of the world's most martial generals an argument for both pacifism and militarism.

Just as significantly, *The Manchurian Candidate* also contained (albeit unintentionally) harbingers of the future. Many of its scenes took place before the television cameras or under the baleful gleam of their screens, augering the media politics of the coming decades. Ultimately a more-chilling omen were the film's assassination scenes, particularly the Oedipal and vengeful Madison Square Garden shootings by the assassin of his own parents, linking private pathology with public and political action.[9]

The element of prophecy blended well with a new generation's attitudes toward film. Schooled in film classes to the nuances of composition, camera placement, and editing, this generation placed film even higher than the novel in the pantheon of artistic forms able to touch life's core. The idea that a film might be personal, visionary, or even prophetic, breaking out of the tradition of both Hollywood realistic and genre films, fitted well with a generation whose personal stamp not only touched film but the decade's politics as well.

In contrast, however, to some of the more radical ideas and feelings of the youth of the 1960s, the country (ever since the death of John F. Kennedy) continued to be controlled by men very much under the influence of older values and ideas. Representative of these was Kennedy's successor, Lyndon B. Johnson. Although a man of immense energy and consummate political skills (and some genuine populist concerns), Johnson was bound by an often outmoded commitment to the goals and programs of U.S. globalism. On the one hand, while he attempted to fashion a domestic Great Society, he undermined it as he resorted to provocations (Tonkin Gulf, Pleiku) intended to increase the U.S. military commitment to South Vietnam.

The inadequacies, inconsistencies, and contradictions of Johnson's policies were not lost on a growing number of liberal, white, middle-class American youth whose commitment to activism and social change had been inspired by the rhetoric and style of the Kennedy administration and the moral idealism of the civil-rights movement. Some of them formed Students for a Democratic Society (SDS) in the early 1960s and attempted to implement a program of social and political reform in the United States. This so-called New Left initially took the lead in recruiting and politicizing an effective and dynamic antiwar movement numbering thousands of Americans (most of whom were far from being New Leftists) repelled by U.S. conduct in the war, the growing number of U.S. casualties, and the rising draft calls.

The New Left was the most politically conscious of a larger movement of students and young and not-so-young men and women who felt also estranged by the spiritual emptiness and puritanical repressiveness they saw in American culture. A product of the post-World War II baby boom, the expansion of education, and the multiplying suburban affluence that characterized postwar America, the "hippies" and "flower

children'' gained intellectual legitimacy from the works of 1950s intellectual radicals like Norman Mailer and Paul Goodman and the poets and
novelists of the Beat Generation. Nonetheless, the basis of their
collective self-consciousness was not intellectual (indeed, many were
aggressively anti-intellectual) but the shared experience of drugs (mari-
juana, LSD), style (long hair, army cast-off clothes), music (Beatles, Bob
Dylan) and an increasingly aggressive underground press (*Los Angeles
Free Press, Berkeley Barb, East Village Other*).

Ultimately, a coalition of the New Left and the counterculture with
left-liberals helped drive Lyndon Johnson from power in 1968 and led to
the insurrections and riots that engulfed Columbia University and the
Chicago convention of the Democratic party in the spring and summer
of the same year. Although the event was much more shaped by the
ethos of the counterculture, this hybrid coalition realized a more utopian
moment in the communal experiences embodied in the Woodstock Music Festival in the summer of 1969.[10]

Writing in almost the same year as these events, Norman Mailer
responded to the coming of the young in his customary vein of
prophecy and ambiguity: ''Those mad middle class children with their
lobotomies   from   sin . . . their   innocence,   their   lust   for   the
apocalypse.''[11] Of course, Hollywood's response was less complex, but
Arthur Penn's *Bonnie and Clyde* (1967) did more than merely indulge in a
commercial paean to the young. *Bonnie and Clyde* helped transform the
nature of 1960s film making, not only bringing to fruition some of the
influences of works like *Dr. Strangelove* and *The Manchurian Candidate* but
also establishing a unique mood for 1960s films. Just how far it went
toward creating this new sensibilty can be seen from the vehement
attacks it received from the critical establishment—none showing more
venom and intransigent hostility than *New York Times* reviewer Bosley
Crowther, who called it (among other choice adjectives) ''pointless . . .
lacking in taste'' and ''sentimental claptrap.''[12]

In spite (or was it because?) of the extremes of these critical reviews,
Bonnie and Clyde's tale of two youthful outsiders who take to a life of
crime held a powerful fascination for its audience, who embraced its
celebration of the spontaneity and energy of the young. The sense of
freedom evoked by rhythmic banjo solos and kinetic jump cuts even
makes the duo's Keystone Kops-Robin Hood bank-robbing spree look
seductive.

In contrast, the film's older generation is portrayed as either exhausted
and defeated (old sharecroppers being driven off the land by the banks),
in conflict with Bonnie and Clyde (the forbidding, driven deputy Frank
Hammer who tracks them down), or malevolent (C. W. Moss's
duplicitous, Judas-like father). It isn't at all surprising that the film exalts
the ties among the outlaws (Clyde tells Bonnie that he is her family)

and sees relationships between parents and children (C. W. Moss and his father and Bonnie and her mother) as either brutal or remote.

References to the 1960s in *Bonnie and Clyde* are more than accidental. Part of its unique influence on other 1960s films (*M*A*S*H, The Wild Bunch*) is in the way it used a different era, the depression, to touch on and even illuminate contemporary issues. However, even though Penn wants Bonnie and Clyde's romantic rebellion to be in one way perceived as an act of rebellion against social injustice (the duo as premature Weatherpeople), their social consciences never seem more than a self-conscious contrivance of Penn's. What is most striking about their out-lawry is not its political content but how it evokes the sense of aliena-tion, restlessness, and style of the 1960s young.

In a similar fashion, the film's violence acts as a metaphor for the wars and assassinations of the decade. Moments like the violent firefights between the lawmen and the Barrow gang remind one not as much of the almost tame gangster-film shootouts of the past as the Vietnam War then being screened daily on the television news. Furthermore, the slow-motion, ballet like death scene of Bonnie and Clyde carries with it overtones of the obsessive slow-motion screenings of the Zapruder film of the Kennedy assassination.

Just as significant for film makers was *Bonnie and Clyde*'s use of French "new-wave" techniques. Arthur Penn, who directed (both Jean Luc-Godard and Francois Truffaut had been considered), and his editor, Dede Allen, made fine use of methods like freeze frames, jump cuts, and other special cinematic effects while adding bits of black humor and put-ons that carried overtones of *Dr. Strangelove* and *The Manchurian Candidate*. Indeed, it was the irony and joking in *Bonnie and Clyde*, such as their watching a Warner Brothers musical after their killing and the gang's "just folks" picnic with the kidnapped Velma (Evans Evans) and Eugene (Gene Wilder), that helped keep it from tipping too far in the direction of either conventional genre film or sentimental social melodrama.

For all its cinematic imagination and originality, *Bonnie and Clyde* had a pernicious influence as well. Its romanticization of criminality gave sanc-tion to some nihilistic tendencies prominent within the New Left and the counterculture, and fed their disdain for the adult world's belief in work and family. More important, by affirming criminality as a viable means of social and political protest, the film blurred the crucial distinc-tion between sociopathic violence and coherent political action and organization.[13]

Bonnie and Clyde also encouraged film makers to forgo dealing directly with contemporary issues (especially the war) and approach them in-stead by using genre forms or by indirect and oblique references. This evasive approach failed to meet the expectation of many antiwar Americans who, although aware that the media obfuscated and distorted the facts and realities of the war, still had enormous faith in its power to alter public opinion. As the war and protest against it escalated, so did demands that film makers produce an honest film about the war that, it was sanguinely and innocently assumed, would so startle Americans that they would immediately demand an end to U.S. involvement in Southeast Asia.

Of course the financial conglomerates that controlled the film industry did not confront the issue in a direct way. However, apropos of Lenin's comment that capitalists would sell the rope used to hang them, they still desired to cash in on the antiwar, pacifist spirit.[14] Consequently, even though they made no new films that might touch directly on too many nerves, film makers weren't reticent about making pacifist films about previous wars (the English *Oh! What a Lovely War* [1968]) or rereleasing older films that fit the temper of the times like *The Americanization of Emily* (1964), which meshed rather well.

Produced in 1964 on the same wave of antinuclear, antimilitarist sentiment that brought forth *Dr. Strangelove, Fail Safe,* and *Seven Days in May, The Americanization of Emily's* celebration of cowardice was somehow ahead of its time. Unfortunately, the only real stir it initially created was owing to the post-*Mary Poppins* dramatic debut of Julie Andrews. However, by 1967 the time was ripe for its pacifism. What's more, its ironic black-humor attacks on both war and heroism were by then on the way to becoming hallmarks of 1960s films.

The second coming of *The Americanization of Emily* found a ready-made audience for its cynical, wheeler-dealer antihero Lt. Commander Charles Madison (James Garner), whose credo is that cowardice ensures more for humanity than bravery. It's a belief that especially endears him to Julie Andrews, a British officer who has lost a husband, father, and brother in the war and whose passion is primarily stirred by the fact that he will "never get caught in the shooting. You can't imagine how attractive that makes you to me."

Not merely content with exalting cowardice, *The Americanization of Emily* also takes some shots at the madness of war, the prime target being Charles's superiors—specifically the psychotic Admiral Jessup (Melvyn Douglas)—who want the first dead man on Omaha Beach to be a navy man. Although hardly earth-shattering, the contemporary relevance of this kind of satire could hardly be mistaken. Moreover, although it wasn't the kind of film envisioned by the war's most militant opponents, it did maintain an irreverent attitude toward war, authority, and the military spirit.

No matter how deeply felt, however, these emotions were not the dominant ones in the country. Despite this, most producers, even the most patriotic, were loath to make prowar films about Vietnam, that is, with the exception of John Wayne, whose eagerness might be explained in part by the special niche he occupied in the pantheon of American heroes.

After the 1940s films like *They Were Expendable* (1945) and *The Sands of Iwo Jima* (1946), the name John Wayne became synonymous with the image of the tough, efficient U.S. fighting man as well as with the nation's most-cherished patriotic and social pieties. So indelibly imprinted on the imagination of American men was the Wayne image that more than one Vietnam War memoirist wrote that they joined the armed forces because they saw themselves "charging up the beach like John Wayne in *The Sands of Iwo Jima*." Nor was there anything ironic in Wayne's own devotion to that image (as evidenced by his Red-baiting leadership of the McCarthyite Motion Picture Alliance for the Preservation of American Ideals and his uninhibited support of bellicose conservatives like Ronald Reagan and Barry Goldwater). In his own mind (and possibly in others), only a John Wayne film about the Vietnam War could possibly win the hearts and minds of Americans.

As the subject of his apologia and polemic, Wayne chose the elite Green Berets' military unit. This decision at one stroke allowed him to connect the mythological worlds of his beloved mentor John Ford with a public devotion to the memory of John F. Kennedy's Camelot. Like Ford's frontier calvary units, Wayne's Green Berets became bastions of camaraderie, honor, decency, and Americanism fighting an often little-appreciated and even less-understood battle against Communist aggression. Their is a stronghold whose supposedly most-serious challenge is a domestic one—in the person of a liberal, skeptical newspaper columnist (David Janssen). For Wayne, soft liberals who undermined our patriotic will were far more dangerous than regiments of murderous Vietcong.

Combined with this is a depiction of the world of John F. Kennedy (Wayne's patriotism is not partisan; he recognized Kennedy's commitment to the politics of machismo) that might have made even the best and brightest blush. The choice of subjects itself—the Green Berets—was a reference to the Kennedy obsession with counterinsurgency, and the first scene in the film takes place conveniently enough at the John F. Kennedy Center for Special Warfare, Fort Bragg, North Carolina. And the film's mania for technology, complete with helicopters, gunships, napalm experts, and body bags that can lift a man hundreds of feet into the air, carries echoes of the missile-gap, space-race, and James Bond crazes—all of which were hallmarks of the New Frontier ethos. There is even a heroic black Green Beret medic (Raymond St. Jacques) to demonstrate the interracial nature of the prowar cause.

Nor is the film reticent about trotting out the by then all too familiar McNamara-Rusk-Rostow rationale for U.S. involvement in Vietnam.

The Green Berets

Speaking before a passive, applauding audience, the noncom, true-believer Sgt. Muldoon (Aldo Ray) informs them that the Soviets plan to dominate the world, compares South Vietnam to the American 13 colonies ("The 13 colonies took from 1777 to 1787, 11 years, before they came up with a paper all 13 could sign") and includes the almost ritualistic evidence of Soviet aggression in the form of Eastern European weapons captured from the Vietcong.

Muldoon's rhetoric is about as close as the film gets to providing a real picture of Vietnamese history or society or the war itself. If, in fact, Wayne's Green Berets are nothing more than muscular, war-loving cavalrymen, then the Vietcong are a modern version of renegade Indians, who scale a fortress aptly named Dodge City. Of course, the Vietcong are not allowed to have any redeeming human qualities. They are depicted in the main as a herd of faceless, endlessly dying barbarians who torture, rape, hatch conspiracies, rob the mountain districts of their rice, or insidiously infiltrate the Green Beret lines. They also, incongruously, include an aristocratic and decadent Communist general who is more interested in hedonistic pleasures and vices than in any revolutionary cause. Our South Vietnamese allies don't fare much better. Although they are viewed as a smart-looking, dedicated, efficient force, they are made to sound like Tonto ("We build many camps, clobber VC [Vietcong], affirmative?") and play a totally subordinate role to the Green Berets. There is also a Hollywood-style, Vietnamese Mata Hari (whose neutralist parents were killed by the Vietcong) thrown in, but she is merely there to provide the film with a bit of sexual interest and to demonstrate the impossibility of remaining neutral in Vietnam.

However, if the Vietnamese on both sides are no more than predictable stereotypes, there is a faint touch of something more complex in the portrait of the Green Berets. For all its win-the-war optimism, *The Green Berets* projects a curious note of fatalism. For instance, "Song of the Green Berets," which accompanies the film, has a lyric that refers to "fighting men who jump and die." In addition, there is the character of Sgt. Provo (Luke Askew), whose gung-ho attitude is undermined by his sepulchral looks and pathetic-comic posthumous wish to have a privy named after him. Of course, all the Green Berets face death with grace and courage; they may have a touch of fatalism, but they still remain recognizable Hollywood war heroes.

Underscoring this mood and making it even more striking is the film's intellectual and metaphoric exhaustion. Plot devices like the murder of a little Vietnamese girl, which turns the liberal newspaperman into a supporter of the war, and the comic relief and instant sympathy and tears provided by a cute, ubiquitous Vietnamese orphan named Hamchunk give the film the opportunity for indulging in every stock, patriotic film cliché used from *The Purple Heart* to *The Steel Helmet*. And through it all, impervious to bullets, age, despair, and criticism strides the war-hungry patriarch Wayne, here giving generous absolution to the columnist (who returns a cold warrior wearing army fatigues to write the true story), there granting fatherly comfort and care to the tearful Vietnamese orphan, and throughout the film casually justifying the necessity for a war built on scorched earth and mass killing.[15]

It was precisely this sense of weariness, this dependence on the banal and clichéd, that *New York Times* critic Renata Adler singled out for attack in her scathing review of the film. Hardly bothering to disguise her contempt, she wrote,

The Green Berets is a film so unspeakable, so stupid, so rotten and false that it passes through being funny, through being camp, through everything and becomes an invitation to grieve not so much for our soldiers or Vietnam (the film could not be more false or do greater disservice to them) but for what has happened to the fantasy-making apparatus of this country.[16]

Bitterness aside, Adler did touch on some crucial issues. Although *The Green Berets* was a financial success, that success seemed more likely to have been the result of audience response to the familiarity of another John Wayne film than agreement with his political vision. By breaking no new ground about the war either factually or metaphorically, *The Green Berets* seems nothing less than a cowboys-and-Indians movie caught in a time warp. The film's success provided cold comfort to producers or prowar politicians looking for profits or support for their policies.

This failure sheds some important new light on the dearth of Hollywood war films in the 1960s. As Adler shrewdly points out, Hollywood seemed unable to come up with new formulas that might make the war intelligible to Americans. Thus, to the oft-repeated explanations stressing the financial risk of Vietnam War films or television overkill must be added Adler's implicit suggestion of a failure of imagination. Hollywood could neither fit the Vietnam War into any of its old formulas nor create new ones for it.

A compelling reason for this (though hardly sufficient in itself) was the war's break from conventional patterns and certitudes. Just one small example, apropos of *The Green Berets,* might suffice to explain. By the time Wayne got around to glorifying the role of the Green Berets in Vietnam, there were hardly any of them left there (even as far back as 1963 there were only about 300 remaining in Vietnam),[17] a fact that was at odds with Wayne's and the American public's vision of the war. However, the United States would face much more serious shocks to its self-confidence and its notion of the Vietnam War as the result of the Tet offensive of late 1968.

The NLF and North Vietnamese stratagem (but falling far short of its tactical objectives) was a political and psychological victory of enormous proportions. Not only did it lay bare the emptiness of the U.S. military's avowals of "light at the end of the tunnel," it also underlined the fact that no amount of men and money could guarantee victory or produce anything better than a stalemate. The American public's post-Tet realization of this fact created such a popular stir that it forced the eventual withdrawal of Lyndon B. Johnson from the 1968 presidential race and brought about the offer of peace negotiations with the NLF and the North Vietnamese.

The repercussions of Tet were equally apparent in the war itself, with less sanguine results. Already notable for its brutality, the war seemed to go beyond any and all restraint and descended into a murderous irrationality bordering on barbarism. The American public was shocked by the post-Tet discovery of the mass grave of thousands of South Vietnamese slaughtered by the NLF and buried outside the city of Hue. Shortly thereafter (even though it didn't come to light for another year and a half), a U.S. patrol wantonly butchered 347 civilians in the village of My Lai.

This growing savagery soon began to take on an unreal quality, which is reflected in the comment of an army colonel after U.S. bombers leveled a town occupied by the Communists during Tet: "It became necessary to destroy the town in order to save it."[18] Less-dramatic but no less conclusive evidence of this state of mind were the GIs' references to the war as "Nam" and everywhere else as "the world," thereby conferring a special hellish distinction on the place.

Whether because of a paucity of inventiveness and financial cowardice or not, film makers evaded any and all direct opportunities to confront the escalating nightmare of Vietnam. The same, however, didn't extend to attempts to capitalize on the public's growing disenchantment with the war. This disposition inspired a number of late 1960s films with a decided antiauthoritarian, if not directly antiwar tenor; their tone was usually ironic and characterized by the black humor that had emerged as a special stamp of the decade. Although this irony was coupled with oliqueness (increasing in direct proportion to the divisiveness of the issue), these films could hardly be taken as referring to anything but Vietnam.

Almost synonymous with films about the War That Dared Not Speak Its Name was Robert Altman's formally imaginative and inventive (a seemingly anarchic but beautifully controlled collage of sounds and images in a quasi-*verité* style) *M*A*S*H* (1970). From its opening credits of combat helicopters landing wounded soldiers at a mobile army hospital unit to the ironically sweet pop music lyrics of a song called "Suicide Is Painless," the audience hardly needed critic Stanley Kauffmann's comments that "it really is Vietnam" to tell them that the film's Korean War setting was camouflage. Its principal heroes, the brilliant and madcap surgeons Trapper John (Elliot Gould) and Hawkeye (Donald Sutherland) carry out their own guerrilla war against army bureaucracy, football, organized religion, and a variety of other establishment devils—behavior more connected to the Vietnam era than the Korea of the 1950s. Finally, should anyone be confused, the film is permeated with references to dope and sex and contains so many obscenities that only the dimmest viewer could mistake what epoch and war it deals with.

*M*A*S*H* wasn't merely an attempt to milk counterculture antiwar, and 1960s references. Although at times the film is much too facile and superficial—too much a service comedy complete with conventional sexism (its women Lt. Dish and Hotlips Hoolihan are objects of use and abuse)—it does in its stylized, black-comic fashion evoke the madness of the war. The film strikingly captures the abbattoir like carnage (pieces of anatomy, buckets of spurting blood) of the operating room. As a result, the surgeons' macabre and adolescent practical jokes and slapstick routines and their silly, incongruous songs and off-color remarks are more than a straining for laughs. For Altman, their looseness, coolness, and sense of the absurd are the only ways of maintaining sanity in an insane world.

Altman's community of surgeons are able to both subvert the rhetoric and rituals of military life and successfully meet their military duties. They combine professional expertise with pot smoking and martini drinking, confidently and calmly sauntering about dropping wisecracks while cutting and stitching up the wounded and mutilated. And the conventional, conformist military officers in the film are no more than a collection of fools, incompetents, and hypocrites. The prime villain, Capt. Burns (Robert Duvall), is religious, patriotic, viciously sanctimonious, and easily deflated and defeated by the hip, cynical, and even at moments sensitive surgeons. They are, however, geniuses at no more than survival; they never really question, analyze, or rebel against the war. In fact, one feels that the pleasure they take in the war's male camaraderie and grotesque humor outweighs their contempt for its insanity.[19]

Despite the absence of a coherent political critique in *M*A*S*H*, it is clear that the old Hollywood war-film verities had little place in its orbit. If nothing else, *M*A*S*H* succeeded in revealing how anachronistic they truly were. This is a point made rather insistently by the cliché-spouting (Brechtian style) loudspeaker that continually trumpets the virtues of the latest showing of a morale-building war film (John Ford's *When Willie Comes Marching Home*) to the camp's obvious indifference.[20]

Nevertheless, even an anachronism had its proper use if it could be leavened with the appropriate ambiguity and irony. A carefully tailored product like Franklin Schaffner's *Patton* (1970) was made to appeal to both pro- and antiwar sentiments. It practically became a litmus test of one's feelings toward the war: hawks effortlessly saw it as the glorification of the martial spirit, and doves just as easily perceived it as a portrait of a monstrous war lover.

Perhaps nothing illustrates this better than the film's bravura opening. Set before an immense, wide-screen-filling American flag, a bemedaled, raspy-voiced, autocratic, pearl-handled-revolver-toting General George S. Patton (George C. Scott) delivers an oration to an unseen group of U.S. troops. The speech is at once bellicose, obscene, folksy, patriotic, and sentimental (a touch of Buck Turgidson and a little Vince Lombardi), beginning with the pugnacious aphorism that "no bastard ever won a war by dying for his country, he won it by making the other poor dumb bastard die for his country."

Although the harangue has a certain perverse charm (after all, here is a swaggering officer who makes no bones about what war is all about), it is also a parody of American patriotism. Patton takes this patriotism to its logical conclusion when he admonishes his invisible audience not merely to kill the enemy but to "tear his guts out."

Throughout the rest of the film (which traces Patton's World War II career from the Kasserine Pass to shortly after the Nazi surrender), there is no attempt to piously hide Patton's lust for battle; which prompts him to exclaim unabashedly over a corpse strewn battlefield, "God help me; how I love it." Nor is there much effort to gloss over his insensitive and almost barbaric callousness in the famous slapping of a frightened, shell-shocked soldier after the Sicilian campaign. But despite the film's willingness to portray Patton's ruthlessness, the ambiguity and parody inherent in the tight close-ups, the long shots, and the imagery of the prologue are never fully developed in the rest of the film.

Without even bothering to morally justify Patton's actions, explain them psychologically, or place them within a larger historical or political framework, the film begins to treat him as the apotheosis of the military hero. In fact, one gets the feeling that the film sees any attempt to explain Patton's behavior as a dilution of the grandeur of this modern, macho version of Don Quixote. Patton is conceived of as a man out of his time, a complex, bold, poetry-quoting and -writing, glory-hunting romantic who wants war to be a place for personal heroism. The film submerges all its other characters, making them bland and undefined, to Scott's dominant virtuoso performance as Patton. Even his friend and antithesis General Omar Bradley (Karl Malden) is low keyed, rule-book-bound, and compassionate, a vague, colorless figure totally dwarfed by the bigger-than-life Patton.

The film is subtitled "A Salute to a Rebel," and all Patton's manic war lust and right-wing opinions (he felt we should have fought the Communists, not the Nazis) are transcended by its evocation of his military brilliance (the massive mechanized sweep through France, his triumphant race against Montgomery to reach Palermo) his eccentricity (a belief in reincarnation) and his cultivation (he speaks fluent French, is a gourmet, and loves to live in luxurious villas). He's the sort of man who is characteristically seen in long shot, sitting ramrod straight upon a white horse (that mythical general on horseback who provides order and power to a nation). In the film's finale, he walks into the distance a solitary man amid an immense amount of wide-screen space, framed against a windmill. In short, the film informs us that Patton is either a powerful, brilliant military figure or a Quixote who tilts his lance against the world. If he's mad and self-destructive, it remains the madness of a romantic hero.[21]

Still, the fact that the film does not portray a Patton without warts is symptomatic of the cinematic treatment of war in the 1960s. Faced with the problem of an audience either disenchanted by or actively opposed to war and the inadequacy of traditional genres (*The Green Berets* is a perfect example), film makers drew on the 1960s trend toward black humor, irony, obliqueness, and ambiguity for a depiction of war—but not "the war" (Vietnam)—that would have some appeal to all shades of opinion.

Patton is unquestionably a powerful example of this sort of film. Proof, if necessary, comes from the reception the film got at the White House. President Richard M. Nixon saw it as an affirmation of our military policies and showed it repeatedly for inspiration shortly before the Cambodian invasion. On the other hand, a noted historian of the 1960s referred to this depiction of Patton as one that creates an image of "a dangerous war lover."[22] Even though the film never critically focuses on the warlike strain in his character, the fact that it is shown allowed some viewers to make the sort of judgments about Patton that the Wayne films never allow for.

Every evasion, every oblique reference, and every ambiguity of films like *Patton* whetted the demand for a genuine treatment of the war and its effects on Vietnam and the United States. Consequently, the Hollywood film about the Vietnamese war became for some Americans a vindication of our policies, for others our Nuremburg trials, and for all varieties of opinion a possible catharsis.

Although the films of the late 1960s (with the exception of *The Green Berets*) did not directly depict the Vietnam War, they were less reticent about reflecting its impact at home. Among the most significant of the war's effects were the swelling sense of disillusionment with American society in general and the resulting spread of social unrest and disruption.

The film that became practically synonymous with this feeling of alienation was *Easy Rider* (1969). In it, an oddly matched pair of aging hippie motorcyclists—the cool, detached, oracular Wyatt (Peter Fonda) and his tense, comic buddy Billy (Dennis Hopper)—sell a kilo of dope to a Los Angeles hip capitalist and then head east for the Mardi Gras in search of something they nebulously term "freedom." Their trip, enhanced by the film's eloquent use of landscape, space, light, movement, and sound, is for the first half of the film a paean to the American dream of the open road, this time pursued by hippies. In its inarticulate way, the film touches upon some of the counterculture's main themes and concerns: mysticism, drugs, the return to the land, communes, and especially freedom from convention.

Despite the banality of many of Wyatt's pronouncements (e.g., a homage to a toothless old rancher "doing his own thing, in his own time"), the film strikes a powerful emotional chord. In its second half, it evokes the conflict between "us" and "them": the free, spontaneous long-hairs versus the vicious redneck straights. Though the film may conceive of the conflict in cartoonlike terms, it succeeds in dramatizing the disillusionment with American culture and politics felt by many of the young (Vietnam being one of the prime causes of that disenchantment). While one might quarrel with both the intellectual fitness and presumptuousness of two dope-dealing hippies being used to symbolize social freedom and represent victims of U.S. repression, their violent end dovetails with the destiny of public figures like Martin Luther King and Robert Kennedy. In 1969, some feared that death was to be the lot of anyone who protested, dissented, criticized, or just did not conform.[23]

The sense of failure, frustration, and victimization that haunts *Easy Rider* was not solely confined to a film about the counterculture. In *Medium Cool* (1969), this feeling of disillusionment spills over into the political realm. Directed by the politically conscious, left-leaning director Haskell Wexler, the film provides a cinéma verité and neodocumentary rendering of the 1968 Chicago riots, National Guardsmen practicing riot control, and intrviews with subjects ranging from black militants to socialites. Nevertheless, like the tragic conclusion of the film's protagonist John (Robert Forster), a television cameraman, it results in nothing more than a dead end. He dies in a car crash, which is blandly recorded on television, a sardonic reminder of the power of the cameraman's own medium to shape and absorb our experiences and to ultimately undermine our capacity to react to them.[24]

No less a reminder (although more of campus rage and rebellion than of disenchantment) are films like *The Strawberry Statement* (1970) and *Getting Straight* (1970). Hardly documentary in style, they are instead chic, exploitative, and shallow portrayals of campus rebellion that suggest that the sources of discontent lay more in frustrated sexuality than any anger over political or social issues. Simon (Bruce Davison), the hero of *The Strawberry Statement* (James Simon Kunen's personal memoir

of the Columbia strike) joins the sit-in at his university (discreetly relo-
cated to a city somewhere in the Pacific northwest) because that's where
the girls are. This version of Holden Caulfield at the barricades is only
slightly less simplistic than the sophisticated, volatile, Selma-Vietnam
veteran Harry Bailey's (Elliot Gould) comment in *Getting Straight* that
rioting is sexy and that "getting laid was a radical act." It's an idea that
he has little difficulty putting into practice during the university riot at
the film's conclusion.

Even given these films facile and manipulative quality, they provide
glimpses of some of the decade's social commitments, angry confrontations, and political fantasies. For instance, although hyped and sensa-
tionalized, *Getting Straight*'s depiction of student rebellion and rioting
(the riot is all rapid cutting and reliance on zoom lens) captures something of the tension, rage, chaos, and gratuitous destruction that characterized many 1960s student-police confrontations. And in the same film,
the almost overnight conversion of an alumni president's extremely
conventional son into a flaming radical echoes the absurd ease and
swiftness with which some of the decade's young could without reflection turn America into "Amerika."

Just as significant and perhaps even more revealing about the impact
of the war at home (despite their often low-keyed approach) were films
that dealt with the draft, an institution that by the late 1960s had come to
personify all the home-front emotional trauma of the war as well as
some of the class and racial biases inherent in U.S. society. That these
emotions and insights coalesced around the draft was appropriate. On
the one hand the draft forced young men (some of whom were too im-
mature to realize the full impact of their decision) to make the terrible
choice between fighting in a war that might both repel them morally and
maim or kill them or resisting, thereby risking jail or what might turn
into permanent exile if they left the country. In addition, by allowing
middle-class youths to obtain educational deferments, the draft forced
the poor, the working class, and minorities to bear a disproportionate
share of the fighting and the dying.

However, films of the decade which dealt with the draft were not
filled with rage but with a kind of bittersweet humor and irony. In Brian
De Palma's independently made *Greetings* (1969), for example, the
theme that links together the escapades of the three heroes (played by
Gerritt Graham, Jonathan Warden, and Robert De Niro) is the effort of
two of them to figure out a way of helping their friend Jon (De Niro)
flunk his army physical or, to be more precise, his psychological. The
results are a wonderful romp through some of the hang-ups and mythol-
ogies of the 1960s, which ranged from assorted misadventures with
various women to a Warren Commission buff who doesn't hesitate to
use his girlfriend's body to draw diagrams showing where the panel

went wrong to the old counterculture chestnut of the draftee who uses homosexual mannerisms and fascist rhetoric in order to fail his army physical.[25]

In spite of this lighthearted, even whimsical approach, the film leaves its audience with the inescapable conclusion that the draft caused great turmoil among the young (for even the comparatively carefree tone of *Greetings* darkens toward the film's end as the Warren Commission expert is mysteriously shot, and Jon winds up in Vietnam.)

This tension is equally evident, but again dealt with in good-natured, folksy manner, in Arthur Penn's elegiac and episodic *Alice's Restaurant* (1969). This film is a critical but loving portrait of the counterculture that touches on how the young became alienated from their society (the draft being one of the prime reasons). *Alice's* hero, a solemn, honest, pure Arlo Guthrie (playing himself with consummate impassivity) is seen as a prototype of the alienated young and an heir to his legendary Old Left father, Woody. Arlo has long hair, plays a guitar, smokes dope, and constantly gets into trouble with college authorities and the police. It's this inability to conform that forces him to take refuge in a Stockbridge, Massachusetts, counterculture commune with his more-animated and complex surrogate parents, the sensual earth-mother Alice (Pat Quinn) and her insecure, hostile, dreamer husband Ray Brock (played with manic intensity by the late James Broderick).

However, even in the Stockbridge haven there is conflict between the "free" young and traditional American institutions. Symbolic of this conflict is the film's re-creation of the hit talking-blues number from which the film took its name, "Alice's Restaurant Massacre." Arlo and his pals are arrested by Officer Obie (played by benign, baffled, Stockbridge police chief William Obenhein himself) for illegally dumping their Thanksgiving dinner garbage and are then subjected to all the most advanced police technology (an oblique metaphor for the overkill used by the United States in Vietnam). The arrest has the ironic result of making Arlo ineligible for the draft, though he does go through a ferociously comic preinduction physical where he and the army confront each other in mutual confusion.

The satiric and bemused quality of both the arrest (complete with a blind Justice of the Peace) and the preinduction episodes (with its hall filled with obese, pretend mother rapers, homosexuals, and psychopaths all trying to escape the draft) wryly but pointedly captures the estrangement between the generations in the United States. Some of the young become figuratively if not literally outlaws, but if Penn's sympathies are clearly with youth's casualness, openness, and rebellion, he does not take Arlo's minor triumph over the draft board as a symbol for the ultimate victory of the counterculture. The film concludes, like *Easy Rider* and *Medium Cool*, with a sense of disillusion and defeat: both the commune and Ray and Alice's marriage seem to be heading for collapse.

Needless to say, the derisive barbs of *Alice's Restaurant* and *Greetings* only scratched the surface of the political and social impact of the war at home and hardly mentioned what was happening in Vietnam. Nevertheless, when this feeling of disillusion and oppression began to coalesce around the symbol of another of the war's victims, the returning Vietnam vet, a consciousness of the war itself did develop. The Hollywood film was not totally free from the conventions of the past, but regardless of its ambivalences and reticences, it still provided the first opportunity for some direct insight into the Vietnam War trauma itself.[26]

Symbolic of the war's horrific effects were the wounds that veterans bore in one form or another. Unlike their post-World War II predecessors Al Schmid (John Garfield) in *Pride of the Marines* (1945) and Ken Wiloceck (Marlon Brando) in *The Men* (1950), whose wounds were mainly symbols of anxiety and fear over the adjustment to postwar American society, the Vietnam-produced wounds were marks of equivocation, disillusion, and rage with war itself. In addition, the intact, coherent society to which Homer Parish (*The Best Years of Our Lives* [1946]) returned had been replaced by a violent and divided one.

Although these wounds might be treated as physical (*Coming Home* [1978]), the form they most often took was spiritual and psychological in nature, suggesting that the ambiguous and complex processes of the mind and heart could best exemplify the complicated and tangled issues and feelings aroused by the war. Although the psychological wound might be a commonplace survivor's guilt (*Heroes* [1977]), the implication was clear that something so terrible had happened in Vietnam—some act of war too horrendous to be shrugged off—that it shook veterans' moral perspectives and left them with terrible feelings of alienation and anomie.

The rather inauspicious debut of the Vietnam veteran occurred in the American International Pictures exploitational quickie *Born Losers* (1967). In what was an otherwise unremarkable script, a mysterious half-breed Indian karate expert name Billy Jack (Tom Laughlin) arrives to protect a town and its women from a pack of slavering Hell's Angels rapists. Billy Jack is a loner who is described as a "disillusioned war veteran," although the precise reason for his disillusion is never explained. However, in the ambience of the Vietnam decades it could be nothing less than some trauma associated with the Vietnam War,[27] the effects of which don't manifest themselves clearly until his appearance in the highly popular, top-grossing *Billy Jack* (1971).

Despite its cinematic, dramatic, and intellectual crudeness, the 1971 version of *Billy Jack* suggests in embryonic form all of the characteristics that were to become standard for the 1970s image of the returned Vietnam vet. True to his earlier appearance, Billy's mysterious background and strange behavior is explained by references to this half-breed Indian birth and his disillusion with the war. He again plays a savior who protects a racially mixed "free school" run by the saintly, pacifistic Jean (played without a touch of affect by Delores Taylor) from the vicious town boss, a bigoted cop, and a variety of squares. The latter often coming off as more reasonable than the self-righteous, shrill, and egregious overage hippies, runaways, and emotionally disturbed kids who constitute the school's faculty and student body.

Aside from its unrelieved exaltation of the counterculture, the film does give an interesting glimpse into the divided heart of Billy Jack and a suggestion of the complex character and feelings of the returned Vietnam vet. On the one hand, Billy Jack's disillusion has brought him back to his Indian roots. He participates in a mystical snake-biting ceremony (which presumably makes him invulnerable), and spouts Castenada-like aphorisms such as "being an Indian isn't a matter of blood, but a way of life." Not only does this link with the primitive and with unfettered nature, giving a sense of depth to his revulsion with American society, it also explains to some extent his affinity for the counterculture (which gloried in the primitive, the occult, and the liberated) and his susceptibility to the supposed charms and ideology of the emotionally empathetic, nonviolent Jean.

On the other hand, the most compelling things about Billy Jack are his self-confessed feelings of rage and the obvious relish he takes in demolishing or humiliating his enemies with a rifle or his skill in the martial arts. Indeed, his rage and fearlessness seem almost psychopathic, particularly the unnatural calm he shows in the brutal (but just) slaying of the son of the town's leading robber baron who, among other depredations, has savagely raped Jean. Moreover, Laughlin's lithe body and impassive features and his calm, cold eyes and monotone voice convey a menace that far surpasses any other character, including the whimpering, psychopathic, bad-seed villain Bernard Posner (David Roya).

The fact that the counterculture's nonviolence and Billy Jack's desire to follow Indian precepts and eliminate the ego do not seem to mesh with his murderous rage hardly seemed to bother Laughlin (also the film's director and coscreenwriter). He is clearly more intent on having it every which way he can than achieving any kind of intellectual coherence. Even though the film provides the audience with an unendurable number of murders, rapes, and beatings, it also exults in counterculture elements and activities ranging from street theater and psychodrama to a sweet, interracial romance and a climactic quasi-civil-rights demonstration (complete with clenched fist salutes) that greets a shackled Billy Jack.

Of course, contradictions of this sort were hardly new in Hollywood films, where holding two conflicting positions at the same time was practically a first principle. But in the case of the Vietnam vet, it may have meant something more than mere opportunism. In its undeveloped fashion, the film's depiction of Jack's rage and disillusion was the first real hint offered by Hollywood that all hadn't gone well in Vietnam and that instead of coming home a hero, more than likely the veteran was returning alienated, angry, unsettled, and unable to adjust to postwar society.

Billy Jack's solution is to convert the returned vet's anger into social commitment. The film concludes with the contrivance of Billy Jack surrendering to stand trial for murder only after the government agrees to investigate all broken Indian treaties.[28] This mixture of profound rage and social commitment was less a manifestation of opportunism than Hollywood's basic confusion about the war and its inability to deal with it successfully within the confines of conventional formulas. As a result of this muddle, the symbol of the Vietnam vet, rather than assuage public anxiety only reinforced the impression of the shattering nature of the Vietnam experience, especially its potential for creating traumatized, broken individuals.

This image grew daily more potent and credible as newspaper and television reports continuously revealed the devastating impact the war had on the moral and emotional heart of the U.S. fighting man. Foremost among these shocks was the disclosure of the My Lai massacre, an incident so savage (it was described by one of its participants as a ''Nazi type thing'') that it would lay to rest (possibly forever) the pious American belief that barbaric wartime behavior was foreign to U.S. troops.[29]

Just as damning was the testimony of a number of Vietnam veterans before a congressional investigating committee that provided first-hand verification that atrocities were almost a daily occurrence and that tactical stratagems like free-fire zones, defoliation, and forced draft urbanization were merely euphemisms for a type of genocide. Similarly, the sight of veterans in their wartime camouflage uniforms or in wheelchairs leading antiwar demonstrations, throwing away their medals, and pronouncing anathemas against their government was equally alarming as indication of the profound moral and emotional turmoil induced by the war.[30]

Nor was the sense of madness and spiritual disintegration solely confined to the battlefield. On the policy-making level, those events and activities that should properly have been perceived as a moral crisis generated by the war were treated rather as mere public-relations stumbling blocks to its conduct. Indeed, the entire Nixon administration war strategy was schizoid, consisting as it did of subterfuges like Vietnamization (the withdrawal of U.S. troops and the assumption of the battlefield burden by the South Vietnamese) and the simultaneous behind-the-scenes escalation of the war complete with an intensification of the bombing and an expansion into Laos and previously neutral Cambodia.

Perhaps in political recognition of this spreading sense of lunacy, President Nixon and Secretary of State Henry Kissinger called their international wartime strategy "the madman theory."[31] A bizarre concoction of the good policeman-bad policeman tactic introduced on the global level, it had the presumably reasonable Kissinger assuring the Soviets and the Chinese that if they didn't get the North Vietnamese to appease us, the vicious anticommunist nature lurking within Richard Nixon would likely throw off all restraint up to and including the use of nuclear weapons. With an avowed madman as a leader and madmen being created every day in the war, it should come as no surprise that the "madman" became the most easily recognizable and frequently used symbol of the war.

An early portrayal of this madness and its effects surfaced in John Frankenheimer's thriller *Black Sunday* (1976). Here, in a plot whose major action concerns the efforts of Israeli intelligence and the FBI to prevent the Palestine Liberation Organization (PLO) from bombing the Superbowl, the major character is a psychotic, ex-Vietnam POW and demolitions expert, Michael Lander (Bruce Dern), whose bitterness against his country (which he held responsible for his ordeal) is so intense that he is ready and willing to join the PLO in their murderous plot. Dressed in his naval officer's uniform, Lander talks about getting back at the United States and being remembered. It's an anger clearly viewed as pathological, not political (despite the PLO connection, which is mere plot contrivance), but it is seen as a genuine menace to the country. Although the film is more interested in technology—blimps and anti-personnel bombs are much more alive than people or politics— Dern effectively establishes himself in the role of the traumatized Vietnam veteran (as seen later in *Coming Home*).

Television superstar Henry (The Fonz) Winkler projects a more benign image of the emotionally disturbed vet in *Heroes* (1977). His self-consciously whimsical portrayal of Jack Dunne (a great many twinkly closeups) probably owes something to the producers' desire to appeal to the same prepubescent audience that watched Winkler go through his winsome paces on television. As a result, Dunne's mental illness (the cause of his confinement and constant attempts to run away from a veteran's hospital) is transformed into something like holy madness. In fact, Dunne is viewed as a man of sweet purity—an imaginative, free spirit who is more a counterculture eccentric than a pathological figure. Given that he is portrayed as a rebel against convention, the film uses him as a low-key, antiwar symbol in a scene where the escaped Dunne tries to convince a group of teenagers not to listen to a recruiter at a Times Square recruitment booth. It's these qualities that also allow him to win the love of Linda (Sally Field), a pert, cute, runaway bride-to-be, in their mutual flight across country.

Most of the effects of Dunne's emotional war wounds are benevolent, but there are moments when they emerge as something more ominous. Although never close to the explosive depths of Dern's rage, when provoked it does result in Dunne's fierce drubbing of a group of Neanderthal rural thugs who attempt to mug him. The war also has such a powerful hold over his imagination that just as easily as its horrors can blot out the memory of the death of a beloved army buddy, his memories can turn a placid small-town street into a vivid and terrifying recreation of the Vietnam firefight in which that traumatic event occurred. It's a flashback whose value as a powerful insight into the frenzied quality of the Vietnam experience contrasts sharply with the situation-comedy quality of much of the film.

The feverish effects of Vietnam that play such a low-key role in *Heroes* overwhelm Henry Jaglom's independently made and somewhat inchoate *Tracks* (1975). In this film, returned vet Jack Falen (Dennis Hopper) takes an almost surreal cross-country train ride accompanying the body of a GI to a home-town burial, and it illuminates some of the estrangement a returned vet might feel toward his society. The surreal and alienating quality of the trip is evoked by the sometimes bizarre, sometimes funny encounters Falen has on the train with a set of characters that include among others an autodidact sexologist, a nature-loving real estate developer, a disillusioned radical who is on the run, and a mysterious school girl with whom he has an affair.

Most telling of all is the film's depiction of the disruptive psychic impact of the war on Falen himself. Played in Hopper's usual intense, nervous manner, Falen seems merely a mass of idiosyncracies and emotional tics: he talks to himself and plays old World War II songs and Nixon speeches on a tape recorder. However, as the trip progresses his seemingly tenuous hold on reality slips. Haunted by guilty memories, Falen begins to hallucinate dangerously, until by the film's climax (at the GIs unattended funeral) he leaps fully armed from the grave screaming, "You want to know what it's like in Nam."[32] Caught in a final freeze frame, this armed vision of the returned Vietnam vet carries with it genuine menace.

In films that followed *Tracks*, the heart of the work was often the returned veteran's need to satisfy his rage. Besides the previously mentioned *Black Sunday*, *Rolling Thunder* (1977) and *Taxi Driver* (1976) dealt with veterans who go on bloody rampages. Both of them were written by Paul Schrader and share his penchant for gratuitous violence and a tendency to use characters as mediums for metaphysical abstractions. The homecoming of *Rolling Thunder*'s soft-spoken and withdrawn Major Charles Rane (William Devane) after seven years as a North Vietnamese POW represents more than a depiction of the estrangement of the returned vet. His estrangement is painfully evident in the silent, strained relations between the sleepless (he's haunted by memories of prison camp) Rane and his son and wife.

Schrader goes beyond depicting the psychological upheaval undergone by U.S. soldier's families as a consequence of the war. His major theme is the appetite for pain and violence that the war has helped arouse in both the returned veteran and in society. This is something he suggests in Rane's reply to the question of how he survived torture. "You learn to love the rope," Rane says, while displaying his obsession by reenacting the tortures he went through. This passion for "the rope" permeated American society during the Vietnam War years in a proliferation of nihilistic and vicious criminal violence (e.g., the Manson murders). Symptomatic of this in the film are the psychopathic hoods who, heedless of Rane's previous ordeal and hero's status, break into his home in search of silver dollars awarded him by the community for his heroism. They torture the stoical, unyielding Rane (his arm is gratuitously ripped apart in a garbage disposal unit) and murder his wife and child.

These heinous acts finally succeed in jolting the affectless, practically catatonic Rane out of his emotional inertness (even his wife's confession of an affair hardly ruffles him) and launch him into a gory rampage of vengeance. It's a task carried out with such zest (and filmed with similar passion) and relentlessness that any fears the audience may have about the explosive menace of the returned vet are supposed to be submerged in admiration of his strength of will and sense of purposiveness. Schrader obviously believes that society really needs an avenging angel capable of eliminating its criminal vermin. Of course, this avenger is not capable of ordinary human emotions. He tells his female traveling companion, "My eyes are open and I'm looking at you, but I'm dead." He has one passion left and, accompanied by another returning POW (who also can't adjust to ordinary civilian society), he releases his raging destructive impulses in the film's concluding murderous orgy.[33]

Schrader pursued this same theme within a larger intellectual context and with greater emotional force and directorial style and skill in his collaboration with Martin Scorcese, *Taxi Driver* (1976). Their feverish, claustrophobic efforts and those of the extraordinarily gifted actor Robert De Niro combined to create the character of cabdriver Travis Bickle, ex-Vietnam combat marine, insomniac, porno-movie habitué, and junk-food consumer, who works in New York at a job that sometimes includes ferrying about the pathological, the violent, and, for relief, the merely anxiety ridden.

Bickle himself is a mass of contradictions, combining simultaneously elements of Yeats' "rough beast" with an almost waiflike innocence and sensitivity. Lonely, frustrated, and angry, there is something terrible gnawing at his vitals, but he is essentially so inarticulate and out of touch with himself that he can't communicate what it is. It is, however, clear that the Vietnam experience has contributed to his alienation and paranoia. Travis' paranoia and his belief that the whole city (a red neon summer inferno with blistering pavements and smoke literally pouring out from its underground recesses) is out to destroy him leads to his focusing an almost Biblical fury on a brothel that houses a 12-year-old prostitute (Jodie Foster). The film views Travis' rage without making any moral judgments. He assaults and destroys the pimps, frees the girl, and finds himself an instant media hero.

Taxi Driver is much more a reworking of 1940s *film noir* conventions and an expression of Schrader and Scorcese's personal visions and fantasies about guilt and redemption than an evocation of the plight of the returned veteran or a critique of corrupt 1970s American culture. This corruption, often perceived by Hollywood in the 1970s as a product of the radicalism and permissiveness of the 1960s, placed Bickle and other Vietnam veterans in the company of civilian film crusaders against the 1960s ethos. Among these were the white working-class backlash of *Joe* (1970), the vigilanteeism of Charles Bronson in *Death Wish* (1971), and the redneck populism of Joe Don Baker in *Walking Tall* (1974). The archetype for this mood, of course, was San Francisco police inspector Dirty Harry Callahan (Clint Eastwood).

In the 1970s Dirty Harry films (*Dirty Harry* [1971], *Magnum Force* [1973], and *The Enforcer* [1976]), Eastwood portrays a solitary, indomitable figure whose relentless and ruthless pursuit of criminals is hampered by softhearted and often sanctimonious liberals who put the rights of the criminal ahead of those of the victim. Absolutely contemptuous of them, Harry is equally disdainful of the cultural decadence he sees around him (which, it is implied, are the fruits of their policy). Harry best summarized this attitude when he remarks, speaking about the bohemian North Beach area, that "I'd like to throw a net over the whole bunch."[34]

The apotheosis of such degradation is Scorpio (Andy Robinson), the psychopathic killer who holds a whole city at bay while he demands a ransom to stop his random killing, rape-murder of teenage girls, and kidnapping of an entire school bus filled with children. However, the long-haired, peace-symbol-wearing, racist, and homophobic Scorpio is hardly your routine movie maniac. In fact, he seems such a mass of contradictions that one might conclude he is a blend of Charles Manson and Lee Harvey Oswald with a bit of F. Lee Bailey thrown in for good measure (especially in the way he seems to know how to manipulate the Miranda and Escobedo decisions). In addition (and here director Don Siegel takes special pains to underscore the fact), he wears combat boots and has deadly sharpshooter kills with both a telescopic rifle and an M-16.

Of course, the film never tries to explain the source of these skills or the motives for Scorpio's criminal rampage, but the Vietnam implications are clear. The suggestions become explicit as the series continues, and in each succeeding film the villains are specifically defined as Vietnam vets. Thus, in *Magnum Force* (1973) a group of ex-Vietnam vets on the police force band together to from a fascist death squad in order to rid society of its criminal elements, and then in *The Enforcer* (1976) another group of vets become leftist revolutionaries who rob banks and murder in order to support their cause.

In the Dirty Harry series, the Vietnam vets are not only psychopathic individuals whose destructive fury has no possible redeeming value (e.g., Scorpio) but they are gradually given a more-frightening dimension, moving individual pathology to an ominous form of collective action. It's also clear in retrospect that Harry Callahan's lethal directness and contempt for bureaucratic authority and regulations and for the liberal establishment prefigures Rambo, the muscle-headed ''defender of the American Way'' of the 1980s.

These themes were not exclusive to the Dirty Harry series. In films like *Black Gunn* (1972) and *The Stonekiller* (1973), groups of black and white veterans are portrayed as eager recruits in a struggle against murderous dope pushers or as willing mercenaries in a fight between contending Mafioso families. This hardly constitutes political action and can just as easily be perceived as a function of Hollywood's action-genre tradition (possibly based on media reports of demonstrations by returned vets). Nonetheless, the films reflect a long-term historical and political truth (whether Hollywood filmmakers were aware of it or not): soldiers returning from a dirty, disruptive, and less than victorious war who find themselves without respect at home have in the past proven to be socially disruptive forces and powerful source for radical right and left movements.[35]

Despite the domestic turmoil caused by the war, the fact that there was no radical transformation or revolution testified to the stability and resilience of U.S. political and social institutions and to the power of the individualist ethic and ethos. Nevertheless, the image of the Vietnam vet still retained volatile potential. Although film magic could transform that alienation and rage into prosocial acts, a menacing edge still persisted. However, that edge faded some when confronted by one of Hollywood's oldest and most-potent conventions—the power of love to transform and redeem, and nowhere is the strength of that emotion more apparent than in Hal Ashby's *Coming Home* (1978), whose original script was written by antiwar activist Nancy Dowd.

   Coming Home is structured around a good old-fashioned love triangle compounded with a bit of feminism and some Vietnam realities for contemporary relevance. However, this plot outline is not meant to diminish this very popular and Academy Award-winning film but to underline the fact that by 1978, American audiences were hungry for direct references to the war—so much so that even relatively conventional representations were weighted with tremendous significance, probably far in excess of the real issues they raised.

   For many who were even mildly touched by the emotional and cultural changes wrought by the 1960s, a key to *Coming Home*'s particular resonance was the transformation of one part of the triangle, former cheerleader Sally Hyde (Jane Fonda), from a patronized, repressed, middle-class wife of gung-ho, tense, and ambitious marine captain Bob Hyde (Bruce Dern) into a sexually liberated and somewhat independent woman. Her metamorphosis is in no small part because of her love affair with the handsome, paralyzed Vietnam vet Luke Martin (Jon Voight), whom she meets while doing volunteer work at a local veterans' hospital during her husband's absence in Vietnam.

   Unfortunately, Sally's transformation seems unconvincing and mechanical, especially in the emphasis it places on her achieving orgasm (helped by the Beatles' "Strawberry Fields" on the soundtrack) while making love to Luke. By granting Sally little internality, the changes she undergoes are primarily stylistic shifts in dress and hairdo. Sally becomes somewhat more spontaneous and a bit bolder, but there is little sense of any genuine psychological or political transformation. In this, *Coming Home* unconsciously seems to affirm the shallow popular myth of the 1960s that equated changes in fashion and appearance with political and moral transformations.

   The film also constructs simplistic, poorly motivated transformations for Sally's lover and husband as well. Luke, for one, goes from an embittered, self-destructive, totally dependent cripple to a well-adjusted, empathetic, politically and sexually active handicapped person. So swift is his change to a caring, almost saintly figure that we get almost no sense of the length of time it must have taken or of the successes, failures, and profound frustrations that he must have undergone during the rehabilitation process.

   Even less successfully realized is Luke's emergence as an antiwar activist. The sudden conversion is supposedly caused by the suicide of Luke's war-tormented hospital buddy Billy (Robert Carradine), for whom he has been a father figure. Luke's act of protest—chaining himself to the gates of an army recruiting depot—is an act of individual existential protest without connection to an active antiwar veteran's movement. Of course, one can't prescribe how the film should handle antiwar protest, but in spite of Luke's pronouncement that the enemy is not the Vietcong but the Vietnam war itself, it shies away from a direct confrontation with the war's political and historical context. For example, when a naval intelligence unit (after Luke's protest) secretly photographs Sally and Luke, it almost appears as if they do it for pornographic reasons instead of it being another dirty political trick in an even dirtier war.

Facile Hollywood touches notwithstanding, there are moments when the film captures a great deal of the feel and texture of war's legacy. Scenes in the veterans' hospital of the crippled men besieged by nightmares, talking unself-consciously and often with black humor (i.e., Luke saying, "Thank God, now I can crawl again") about the war, about being sponged and fed and getting high, carry both authenticity and power. The hospital is no horror show, but the vets feel they don't get sufficient care or psychological rehabilitation. More important, they feel walled up and resent the fact that nobody really cares about them. They see themselves as either being objects of pity ("This isn't have a gimp over for dinner night, is it?") or as carrying too much of the war's reality for ordinary people to deal with.

The real nightmare of combat itself is left to our imagination and to whatever can be gathered from the pathological behavior and memories of Sally's returned husband, Bob. He is a man whose pathetic eagerness to go to war and become a hero turns into an extreme post-Vietnam sense of disillusion and disorientation. Although the discovery of his wife's adultery is the crowning blow, it is clear that his Vietnam experiences have already profoundly disrupted and undermined him: he feels he no longer has a place in the world.

Bob's recounting of Vietnam atrocities (e.g., the chopping off of the ears of dead Vietnamese by U.S. GIs) serves to produce less of a specific indictment of Vietnam than a sense that all war is hell. In a similar fashion, the accidental, self-inflicted wound that brings him home is not quite so much a symbol of his revulsion with the war as the subversion of his personal dream of heroism and a sign of his failure and impotence. Bob's self-hatred is so intense that it even defuses a potentially violent confrontation with Luke and Sally, turning it into nothing more than empty gestures, abusive language. He slinks away muttering the self-contemptuous "I'm not fit to be your husband."

Coming Home is a liberal and humane film that never quite gets to the heart of Vietnam. It knows that emotions like moral rage and the themes of moral and psychological transformation are clearly more accessible than a critique of the government and culture that sustained the war. The film turns the threat to society embodied in the returned vet from Hollywood's characteristically violent aggression into either acts of individual heroism or of self-loathing. Ultimately the menace of the vet is washed away by Luke's lump-in-the-throat, tear-filled, acknowledgement (in a debate with a recruiting officer before a class of high school seniors) of the terrible things that he did, that were done in Vietnam. And, as Luke expresses both guilt and revulsion with a war he finds hard to live with, there is some excessively neat cross-cutting to Bob, who carefully takes off his dress uniform and medals and, in suicidal anguish, drowns himself.

The schematic quality of this cross-cutting and the concluding images of Sally and Luke spending a joyous sunny day on the beach are characteristic of much of *Coming Home*. The film is almost devoid of moral complexity and is somewhat smug about the possibility of (despite Bob's suicide) turning the angry, resentful vets into symbols of postwar reconciliation. It's the understanding, loving, reborn Luke who has the final touching word, holding out hope for a better future.[36]

The overly strenuous efforts of film makers to dis-arm the returned vet only attested to the power he and the war had to disrupt the American imagination. In the view of American society, paraphrasing *New York Times* critic Vincent Canby, the Vietnam vet was a man who pretends to be like everyone else but lives in a small closet in the back of his soul—haunted, but ever alert and armed to the teeth![37] Moreover, no matter how Hollywood muted the bristling image of the spiritually or physically maimed Vietnam vet, he continued to evoke memories of a divisive, corrupting war. There were, of course, a range of veteran types and reactions to the war, but the personas of shattered, angry vets given to drug and alcohol abuse and unable to maintain a marriage or a job was the dominant one.

Furthermore, the image of the wounded Vietnam vet served another purpose. He at least whetted the audience's appetite for actual scenes of Vietnam and combat rather than mere indirect references or momentary flashbacks to it. With anti- and prowar passions cooling and almost as if applying its own version of a "decent interval" (Henry Kissinger's phrase describing the period between the signing of peace agreements, U.S. withdrawal, and a final settlement in Vietnam), Hollywood began to produce films that depicted front-line action during the late 1970s.

One of the earliest films to actually deal with Vietnam action was Ted Post's *Go Tell the Spartans* (1976), which had been shifted from studio to studio for eight years before it was finally made. Perhaps its production difficulties were brought about because *Go Tell the Spartans* examined in telling microcosm a number of the elements that ultimately undermined our efforts in Vietnam.

The title *Go Tell the Spartans* itself refers to Herodotus's account in *The Histories* of the misguided idealism, tactical blunders, and suicidal heroism at the Battle of Thermopylae, where its defenders left the message, "Go tell the Spartans, thou that passeth by, that here, obedient to their laws, we lie." *Go Tell the Spartans* tells a Vietnam varia-

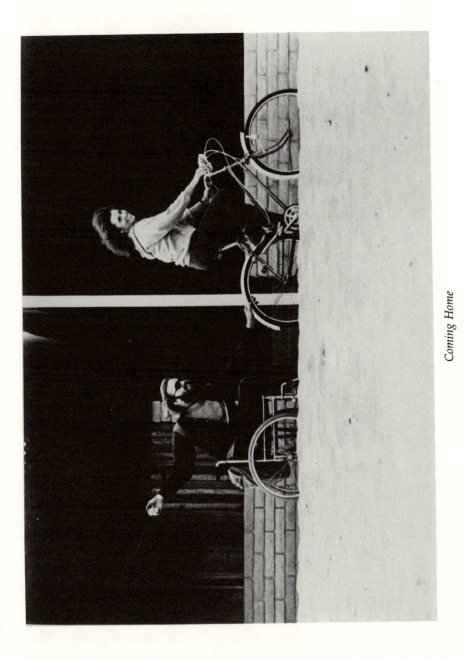

Coming Home

tion of the story and its tragic consequences and is replete with examples of what went wrong from the very beginning of the U.S. effort in Vietnam. The film provides a dark portrait of inept, poorly trained South Vietnamese soldiers; decadent and corrupt French-speaking province chiefs; and vicious, anticommunist South Vietnamese noncoms. In addition, we see U.S. tactical arrogance and personal pathology complete with generals functioning as military advisors who can't wait for the United States to come into the war with both feet: McNamaraesque, flow-chart, computerized warriors spouting technical and psychological jargon as well as ambitious, cynical junior officers, burnt-out noncoms, and drug-addicted medics.

Despite what seems to be a rather cluttered scenario, Post manages to create a tight, well-paced combat film by centering its action on the story of the doomed and futile attempt of a group of U.S.-advised Vietnamese troops to defend an abandoned and isolated Vietnamese village from Communist attack. The political focus of the film is the evocation of the differing attitudes toward the war, represented by its three main characters. The cynical, independent, powerful, and caring commanding officer Major Asa Barker (Burt Lancaster) sees Vietnam as an unreal war (the film is not pacifist—it sees World War II as a war worth fighting) and a "sucker's tour." Corporal Courcey (Craig Wasson) is an idealistic, compassionate draftee who innocently wants to see what the war is like. Finally, the inane, incompetent 2nd Lieutenant Hamilton (Joe Unger) understands nothing about the war except that he hates Communists, believes he's struggling for democracy, and knows that the United States can't lose a war.

Through these characters we begin to understand the inevitable, doomed consequences of the U.S. effort in Vietnam. Nothing of the capable professionalism that Barker brings to bear in the defense of the village seems able to overcome the corruption and ineptitude around him. Similarly, Courcey's undaunted and heroic ingenuousness and generosity makes it impossible for him to penetrate the protective masks of the Vietnamese or comprehend the implacability of the Vietcong. As a result, the death of Barker and the apparent mortal wounding of Courcey bear witness to the failure of both American know-how and idealism. By the end of the film, even Courcey feels that "it's their war" and country and that Americans have no place being and suffering there. In addition, the film foreshadows the quagmire yet to be by including a scene reminiscent of the fall of Saigon, where U.S. troops toss Vietnamese from the skids of their helicopter as they frantically withdraw from the village and leave their allies behind to die.[38]

Although *Go Tell the Spartans* is a small-budget, traditional action film lacking in a grand political or moral vision and populated with characters who are not much more than social or psychological types, it succeeds in conveying much of the futility and absurdity of the Vietnam experience. However, despite the authenticity of the film's texture, *Go Tell the Spartans* failed to capture the public's imagination. Part of the explanation for this is the limited distribution and publicity the film received. Additionally, because the film takes place a couple of years before the U.S. buildup, it does not directly reflect a time when the war was both a national trauma and a military nightmare. Shorn of its political implications, the film was viewed by audiences as merely a solid, gritty World War II film, devoid, of course, of the usual patriotic uplift.

Robert Aldrich's (*The Dirty Dozen* [1969]) *Twilight's Last Gleaming* (1977) also fits this mold. In it, Burt Lancaster, this time playing a deranged, messianic ex-POW air force general who breaks out of a military prison (he was railroaded there by the military brass) with some criminal-psychopath types and takes over a missile base. He threatens to launch nine atomic missiles and destroy the world unless the president reads on television a secret document revealing the "true facts" about Vietnam.

Like most of Aldrich's work the film is blunt and cynical. His villains are the cabinet members and high military officers who, in another administration, had argued that senseless slaughter in Vietnam was the only way the Soviets would know we meant business. The present cabinet and military are no better, although Aldrich is unable to breath any life into the pallid, solemn bunch. The president (Charles During) is an ordinary, decent man—a "working stiff" with power—who wants open government and is repelled by our gamesmanship with the Soviets. He is the only character capable of conveying even a moment of authentic feeling.

Twilight's Last Gleaming is basically an action film filled with images of elaborate missile technology and split-screen tension building. However, in its bold, reductive way, the film provides a direct and fairly cogent attack on U.S. Vietnam policy that almost no other Hollywood film of the time attempted. The essence of its critique is that U.S. policy is based on maintaining credibility by engaging in limited wars in a world where nuclear war is an impossible political option. This policy is seen as both homicidal and suicidal besides leaving the country ripped apart in its wake.[39]

Sidney Furie's attempt to depict Vietnam combat in *The Boys in Company C* (1977) provides a much more conventional attitude toward the war. Its World War II film clichés are carried even to the extent of following the adventures of a melting-pot platoon of young marines, updated for the 1960s to include a young, idealistic hippie (again Craig Wasson) and an urban black (Stan Shaw), from basic-training innocents to hardened combat vets.

Despite its predictability, certain strikingly realistic grace notes punctuate the film. It succeeds at moments in capturing the chaos of the war and the feeling that there is no defined pattern in Vietnam. One can be blown up anywhere—on rest and recreation in the towns and cities as well as on the battlefield. The film is also particularly unsparing in its indictment of South Vietnamese corruption and the duplicity and incompetence of the U.S. officer corps, who are either frantically obsessed with body counts and kill ratios or are willing to sacrifice American lives just so they can enjoy their liquor and food. The ineffectuality of the officer corps in *The Boys in Company C* creates an upsurge of insubordination, drug use, and fraggings, actions that in reality made McGeorge Bundy, an "expert," comment that "extrication from Vietnam is now the necessary precondition of the renewal of the U.S. Army as an institution."[40]

Aside from some realistic touches and its willingness to assert that few soldiers wanted to be in Vietnam, *The Boys in Company C* really doesn't analyze or have a coherent perspective on the war. The details are there, but they are never brought together. In fact, the main theme seems to evade and then negate the details, and it becomes in the end primarily a sentimental affirmation of the moral fiber of the men who fought the war.

Even if they use drugs and are insubordinate (the film holds that these are mere relapses) the young marines are really an utterly courageous, sturdy bunch, the sturdiest and most heroic of whom is Tyrone Washington (Stan Shaw). Initially depicted as an embittered, tough black from the south side of Chicago, he is alienated from the other members of the platoon and is seemingly only interested in setting up a drug network to Chicago once he gets to Vietnam. However, the horror of battle and the growing emotional support and respect of his comrades combine to soften him, and he becomes the leader and moral center of the platoon. Although his transmutation appears to be a product of a conventional liberal fantasist (since by most accounts white-black relations soured away from the front lines and even at times hovered on the brink of racial civil war), it underlines the film's basic belief in our marines' virtue and moral concern.

That moral force is reinforced by the *M*A*S*H*-style soccer game the company plays against a group of South Vietnamese. According to orders they must contrive to lose, in order to enhance South Vietnamese morale, or face returning to the front. Of course, given a choice between release from a war they don't like and their self-respect and pride, the Americans opt to win. The hardly subtle message here is that whatever the particular realities of the war, GI Joe is still a hero and winner.

It was just this question of moral fiber and the strength of the American will that seemed to take on an overriding significance in the final years of the war and in the postwar period. Richard Nixon was particularly candid about it when, in justification of the Cambodian invasion (and what was perhaps the first real revelation of the ultimate raison d'être of the Vietnam policy), he announced, "It is not our power but our will and character that is being tested tonight."[41]

Subsequently, the chaotic and unseemly departure of U.S. forces from Saigon in April, 1975, did nothing to add to the image of our strength of purpose (muscle-flexing episodes like the Mayaquez incident notwithstanding). Nor in the coming years was the U.S. image enhanced by our actions regarding Angola, Afghanistan, and Iran. Both the right and the left of the U.S. political spectrum began to share Nixon's concern with our national image. Liberal Senator John Culver (D., Iowa) remarked that "Vietnam has taken a mighty toll of the national will of the American people,"[42] while conservative Secretary of Defense James Schlesinger noted that "the world no longer regards American power as awesome."[43] This mood was perhaps best summarized by the *Newsweek* editorial that read, "The high hopes and wishful idealism with which the American nation had been best, has not been destroyed but they have been chastened by the failure of America to work its will in Indo-China."[44]

This preoccupation with the status of the national will paralleled Hollywood's search for an image or symbol of the war that would not merely rehash episodes and characters already seen on network news shows and in old World War II movies. The new symbol was supposed to reflect the American public's own profoundly ambivalent feelings toward the war and be able to touch upon its destructive and disturbing aspects without truly dealing with the political defeat of American aspirations. The figure that emerged was to be a "superman" character, who conveyed a real feeling for the war without revealing its true content.

A mixture of traditional American myth, European classics, and modern American literary sensibility, the superman first appeared in Karel Reisz's *Isadora* (1969), the film version of Robert Stone's 1974 prize-winning, feverish novel *Dog Soldiers* (the title refers to elite Cheyenne Warriors who operated outside of their tribe's martial conventions). Retitled *Who'll Stop the Rain?* (1978), the film uses the device of smuggling a few kilos of heroin from Vietnam into the United States by disenchanted journalist John Converse and his ex-marine buddy Ray Hicks as a metaphor for the war's corruption of American society.

Although the film depicts a decadent society soaked in alcohol, drugs, murder, and random noise, its prime focus is on the exploits of Ray Hicks (Nick Nolte). Hicks, described by his passive, self-destructive co-conspirator Converse (Michael Moriarity) as practically a psychopath, is depicted by Reisz as a martial arts expert, aspiring Zen cum Nietzschean *ubermensch.* Weaned on Nietzsche by his friend Converse, Hicks keeps a journal of Zarathrustra-like meditations containing such maxims as ''in danger all that counts is moving forward.'' When he kills three people with a forced overdose, he says, ''All my life I've been taking shit from inferior people. No more.''[45]

In *Who'll Stop the Rain?*, the Vietnam veteran appears for the first time as a man of action who tries to live beyond conventional values and even beyond time and history. Hicks is an angry, proletarian Nietzschean who believes he can will reality into any form he desires. For him the war is just a metaphor (Converse's description of elephants being strafed by helicopters is a symbol of the war's madness) whose importance exists only in an existential rather than a social or political category.

Although the film alludes to the war as a place where people find out who they are—a jungle where the big ones devour the little ones—there is little footage or discussion of the nature of the war. Vietnam is used as a metaphor for America's capacity for violence and self-annihilation. Its landscape is literally and figuratively a desert, a void where people lead vague, drifting lives or become vicious, murderous men. The United States, like Vietnam, is a country where killing has become as normal as eating.

Who'll Stop the Rain? is devoid of hope. The police are criminal, and the counterculture, even though once able to provide some warm moments of spontaneity and harmony, is not strong enough to grant sustaining or enduring values. The superman is a man accustomed to danger who sees life as war, and although he wants to preserve the idea of heroism, he can ultimately only destroy himself. He tells us little about the particularity of Vietnam, but he is a vivid, suggestive symbol of alienation and rage who succeeds in abstracting the war even further from its social and political roots.

In a similar fashion, the working-class hero of Michael Cimino's *The Deer Hunter* (1978), Michael Vronsky (Robert De Niro), takes on elements of the superman that help to distort the nature of the war. Michael is one of three Russian-American steelworkers from Pennsylvania who unthinkingly and enthusiastically enlist in Vietnam. (They understand and see nothing when they meet a morose Green Beret who has returned from Vietnam like a spectre of death, able only to murmur ''fuck it.'') He is an integral part of his community—a world that believes in God and country—and yet is detached from it. On one level, he is one of the boys with his hunting prowess, his daredevil exploits behind the wheel of a Cadillac Coup de Ville, and a profound loyalty to his more-extroverted and gregarious roommate Nicky (Christopher Walken) and such friends as the shy, mother-dominated Steven (John Savage).

However, on a more self-consciously symbolic level, he is part of that great American literary tradition stretching back to James Fenimore

5191-7581-15A   31

The Deer Hunter

Cooper: a man who carves out his identity in confrontation with nature. Like Cooper's *The Deerslayer*, Michael is chaste and given to the kind of purity of purpose embodied in his deerhunting gospel of the one-shot kill. Moreover, in the operatic long shots of his tracking a stag and in his naked dash from his friend Steven's wedding, we get a sense of a man confined by civilization who yearns for some form of transcendence. Michael is silent, stoic, self-controlled, and touched with the kind of inarticulate poetic yearnings that place him beyond the intellectual and emotional understanding of his friends. He is a super-man-warrior committed to a code built on loyalty and grace under pressure. Nevertheless, although not a reader of Nietzsche or a budding nihilist (he never plays with or pursues destruction for its own sake), there is part of Michael that is, as D. H. Lawrence describes Cooper's heroes, "hard, isolate, and a killer."[46]

These later elements of Michael's character emerge in Vietnam, and like Hicks in *Who'll Stop the Rain?*, Michael becomes an avatar of the will, projecting a sense of personal invulnerability and acting as father and protector for his friends. In the brilliantly and manipulatively edited Russian roulette scene, which is filled with powerful reaction shots, a heroic, unwavering Michael wills himself and his two friends to freedom as they slaughter their NLF torturers. In a sense, Michael is guilty here of the same hubris that helped project the United States into Vietnam in the first place. But in Cimino's terms, he is a superhuman hero merely doing what is necessary.

In contrast, the escape leaves the terror-stricken, traumatized Nicky drug addicted and psychologically destroyed. He is so numbed and suicidal that he becomes a star performer on Saigon's Russian roulette circuit (a conceit and metaphor based on nothing but Cimino's baroque imagination). Steven is left a despondent triple amputee who goes home to hide from his wife and child at a veteran's hospital, a place where he spends his days whirring around empty hallways in a wheelchair. Michael, on the other hand, remains physically whole but returns home disassociated and disoriented, ill at ease with his friends. He hides out from the homecoming party they throw for him by sitting alone in the darkness of a motel room moodily staring out at the town.

Even the hunting, a solemn and transcendent act for Michael, has gone sour. The first hunting sequence is directed with self-conscious grandeur by Cimino: Michael stalks a stag in the mountains amid falls and streams over a sound track pretentiously alternating between mystical silence and a heavenly choir. After Vietnam, when Michael captures a deer within his gun sight he shoots harmlessly into the air. For Michael, guns are now a matter of life and death, and he can neither indulge in his quest for the one-shot kill nor tolerate a friend's pathetic, macho gun games. He is both angry and anguished, and to purge himself of the despair, Michael makes one last attempt to bring his friends back together and re-create the community of "the boys" that existed before Vietnam.

The Deer Hunter's emphasis on Michael's will and heroism has the effect of making the Americans innocent and guiltless victims and the Vietnamese brutal aggressors in the war. In this, Cimino consciously or unconsciously (and one can't glean his intent from the film) inverts historical reality. Although Michael and his friends are clearly without direct guilt or responsibility for the war, they fought for a country that was the aggressor and the intruder in what was essentially a mixture of a civil and colonial war. The United States carpet-bombed and napalmed the Vietnamese—both innocent peasants and enemy soldiers—and adulterated and destroyed the social fabric of South Vietnam. Of course, one doesn't want to ingenuously affirm the innocence and purity of the NLF and the North Vietnamese, for they also tortured and butchered both civilians and enemy soldiers. Still, Cimino's depiction of Vietnam is dangerously naïve and morally obtuse in its emphasis on the guilt of the enemy without ever coming to terms with our country's primary responsibility for the extension and intensification of the conflict.

Consciously or not, *The Deer Hunter* is a consummate work of political amnesia and American ethnocentrism and racism. Cimino directed a film dealing with one of the most divisive wars in U.S. history and made it outside political and historical context. And though the film treats the war as primarily an arena where three innocent, apolitical steelworkers play out existential dramas of courage, fear, and breakdown, the film can't avoid having political resonance. The war is finally too charged and partisan a subject to be treated in ahistorical terms.

Nevertheless, Cimino has a gift for constructing scenes of great visual power and emotional immediacy. He brilliantly utilizes a handheld camera to capture the danger, terror, and uncontrolled violence and murderousness of Vietnam combat from Michael's point of view. There are no constraints; everyone is killed, blown up, burned alive, shot—civilians and soldiers, women and children. He conveys the sensation of desperate South Vietnamese crowds trying to escape by scratching and clambering over the U.S. Embassy walls amid the chaos of the abrupt U.S. withdrawal and Saigon's collapse.

Cimino's feeling for authentic texture extends from the combat scenes to the extraordinarily lengthy ethnic wedding sequence. Here he lovingly pans and tilts his camera around the ornate Russian Orthodox church filled with icons and mosaics. He captures the church ceremony and rituals and then dollies through the hall and shoots from floor level to evoke the joy, energy, brawling foolishness, and cacophony that characterizes the wedding celebration. The celebration uses natural sound, a great many nonprofessional actors, and the skillful improvisation of its professional actors to give the wedding an utterly authentic flavor.

Cimino also evocatively captures the communal rituals of "the boys": boozing; bowling; miming rock songs in a bar; engaging in beer and food fights; playing practical jokes and putting each other down; and even listening in meditative, melancholy silence while John (George Dzunda), the cuddly, warm bar owner, plays Chopin on the piano just before they're to take off for Vietnam. The rituals feel like natural extensions of their everyday lives rather than Hollywood constructions. The film, of course, remains absolutely fixed on male rituals and friendship, the women in the film being in the main merely giggling or supportive adjuncts to the men. Even Meryl Streep's sweet, sensitive Linda, Michael and Nick's romantic interest, is given little function other than to look delicate and soulful (sometimes a little too delicate for a supermarket cashier in a Pennsylvania steel town).

Nevertheless, despite the realistic flavor and detail that make up Cimino's portrait of this working-class community, his point of view is essentially a romantic one. The boys labor in an almost mythic, tranquil world wearing silvered, heat-reflective work clothes (sooty, sweating medieval knights). They work with gusto and pleasure in welder's sparks and blast-furnace flames that contrast sharply with the murderous flames of burning bodies in Vietnam. They express no job resentment or alienation and demonstrate no sign that they want to leave the seedy, industrial town they work in. It's true that Cimino's town emanates a feeling of back-slapping warmth, solidity, and full employment, and he augments those images with beautifully composed long shots of the silhouetted factory at dawn, a powerful monolith billowing smoke into an azure sky. It's a world characterized by meaningful work rather than drudgery (even though it took eight different locations to create a composite of the town and untroubled steel towns were far from the norm even in the late 1960s). Of course, the film's emotional effect is also heightened by contrasting (cutting abruptly without transition to a bloody Vietnamese battle) this relatively secure and warm communal world with the horrible intrusion of the war. Still, there aren't that many workers in the United States, even in Pennsylvania steel towns, untouched by American dreams of mobility and economic success and satisfied to stay put.

Cimino is able to give almost each of his male figures some nuance or dimension (particularly Stosh [John Cazale] an insecure, comic-pathetic and vicious ferret of a man), but the film is clearly uninterested in getting to the social and psychic heart of their lives. Cimino's interest lies rather in their behavior and the acting out of their rituals, but he views this world with an uncritical, even sentimental eye. Except for

Steven, the boys have no families, so male bonding becomes the central fact of their world. Cimino never cares to explore the adolescent nature of that bonding or how it shapes their relationships with women. (Much of their behavior reminds one of the more stylized cavalry films of John Ford). Nor does he explore the roles that ethnicity, class, the church, or the values of the industrial town play in their lives. Of course, Cimino is not a sociologist or a documentarian; he also does not have an analytic bent. Even much of Michael's mysterious, enigmatic behavior is left unexplored.

For example, it's clear from the wedding sequence that from the beginning Michael has an uneasy, unexpressed passion for Linda. He constantly passes intense, significant glances toward her and makes awkward, half-hearted gestures to embrace and touch her. But this love does not explain his celibacy. Is it sexual fear or, possibly, a fear of rejection? Cimino gives us no hint. Likewise his profound love and need for Nick are never explored. This is a love of such intensity that Michael is not only willing to return to Vietnam to look for Nick but also to sacrifice his life for him in one final game of Russian roulette. The problem is that Michael is both a figure in a realist film—a somewhat unusual steelworker—and an archetypal hero who is larger than life, existing beyond interpretation, quietly, courageously, ascetically and murderously doing what a working-class superman must do to keep his friends and world together.

In both its realistic and symbolic sequences, *The Deer Hunter* is built around an uncritical identification with Michael and his friends. For Cimino, these are men who have maintained a sense of loyalty and connection in a world where those values have gone out of fashion. A broken Nick still sends money from Saigon to Steven, who languishes at the veterans' hospital; and Michael is still capable of breaking through Nicky's death mask one last time to get him to tearfully react to memories of home and the one-shot kill.

But as stated previously, it's this identification with the world of "the boys" that makes for the film's utterly invidious and politically dangerous treatment of the Vietnamese. The Vietnamese are viewed almost uniformly as a repellent, savage people. They are conceived of as "the other," almost without exception either demonic or decadent variations of "the yellow peril." The grinning and diabolic Vietcong viciously coerce Michael and his friends to play Russian roulette for no other purpose than their sadistic pleasure and pen them like animals in bamboo cages under water with rats or behind barbed wire while waiting for the "game" to begin. The Russian roulette scene successfully arouses both an American audience's patriotic pride and its rage toward the Vietnamese. Roulette is also played in a different context by corrupt, callous South Vietnamese businessmen in Saigon, who gamble vast sums on Nicky and other suicidal stars of the circuit. There are some sympathetic scenes where frightened Vietnamese refugees are seen streaming along the roads with their sparse possessions, fleeing the war; they are victims of a conflict that has plunged their lives into chaos. But they are usually seen in a long shot, and in almost every instance that the camera gets sufficiently close to personalize, it sees evil and contemptibility.

The city of Saigon itself is depicted as a squalid, ominous living inferno either shot through red filters or saturated in blue-black, *film noir*-style darkness. The noise, filth, and decay (a prostitute beckoning Nick while her child cries in the next bed) contrasts sharply with the tired, humane streets of the Pennsylvania steel town. The Saigon images tend to self-consciousness: a trip with a decadent, cynical Frenchman (only the Americans are capable of innocence and virtue) in a small boat over a river with fires ablaze all around it—one more metaphor of Vietnam as damnation. And even though it's plainly no accident that the Saigon bars have go-go dancers and American names, not for a moment does Cimino try to suggest or point out that the hellish Saigon he has visualized is primarily an American import brought on by U.S. intervention and occupation.

The final scene of the film is a perfect illustration of the film's strengths and weaknesses. Michael and his friends sit in stunned, anguish silence as they gather for breakfast after Nicky's funeral. Suddenly, they all poignantly begin to sing in tremulous, muted voices the words of "God Bless America," affirming both the American will and their desire to reconstruct their own fragmented, small community. The film has no illusion that their singing can obliterate or repress the horrors of the war, but the song does affirm their belief in the United States and its future. One wants to believe that Cimino's intention is an ironic commentary on their continued patriotism, but there is no sign of it in the scene. The scene has emotional impact, but it's impossible to merely empathize with the characters' unambiguous belief in the country; after the terror and extremity of the film's Vietnam sequences, the singing feels absurd and pathetic. Cimino, however, never conveys what he himself feels about their affirmation, unless his emotional identification with their world can be seen as an endorsement of their values.

Of course, the power of *The Deer Hunter* does not lie in Cimino's capacity to get a handle on the war as a political and social phenomenon. Cimino is an intuitive director who knows how to capture for an audience the way war affected the psyches and lives of American GIs. In a searing close up of a silent, despairing Nick confronted with the inane, irrelevant questions of a doctor in an army hospital (surrounded by the mutilated and dying, coffins and body bags) he stunningly evokes the horrors of the war for American soldiers. Cimino also has a gift for utilizing a variety of camera angles and dazzling camera movements to create scenes that are both visually striking and emotionally affecting. What he lacks is the kind of governing intelligence that would give the audience more of a critical hold and coherent sense of what they are seeing and reacting to.

What is most disturbing about *The Deer Hunter* is that, despite its memorable frightening images of a horrific, chaotic war, it allows Vietnam to exist in a historical and political vacuum. Like most Hollywood films, *The Deer Hunter* personalizes history, with only the inadequate fusion of a pseudo-literary conceit and a Hollywood hero— the working-class superman—capable of bringing some order to the war's madness and some form of reconciliation at home.[47]

The apotheosis of the superman character appears in Francis Ford Coppola's *Apocalypse Now* (1979). The script for this film was loosely adapted from Joseph Conrad's novel *The Heart of Darkness*. Despite E. M. Forester's comment that Conrad was "misty" at his center, the novel's power to create a sense of the emotional and moral rot of imperialism was strong enough to have influenced both Robert Stone (who uses a quote for the same novel in the epigraph of *Dog Soldiers*) and Coppola.[48]

But Conrad's book is as much or more involved in evoking a permanently treacherous and ominous universe, a world "so hopeless and so dark, so impenetrable to human thought, so pitiless of human weakness." While it engages in a critique of imperialism, the river on which Conrad's narrator, Marlow, travels is deserted and still, an "implacable force" that seems to exist outside time and beyond history.[49]

In *Apocalypse Now*, Coppola deletes the earlier part of the *Heart of Darkness*, where Marlow contemptuously describes the trading company as a group of "sordid buccaneers" committed to grasping wealth from the land and littering it with goods of the West. Instead, Coppola emphasizes the section of the book that details the journey upriver and the final confrontation between Marlow and Kurtz (transformed from an ivory hunter who "had kicked himself loose of the earth" to a rogue Green Beret colonel who has set himself up as a god waging a brutal private war in the Cambodian jungle).[50] For Coppola (although it is obvious that he views the war as mad and murderous and the Americans as blindly impervious and unconscious of the environment they have been thrown into), it is the moral and existential rather than the political and social elements of the story that are the most seductive.

The book begins with a stoic, analytic man, described by Virginia Woolf as "sedentary,"[51] who faces in himself the same barbaric, primitive instincts that have shriveled and destroyed the moral conscience of Kurtz. Consequently, Conrad's story moves seamlessly from the world of the ordinary (London) to the realm of the existential and metaphysical (the Congo) and gains much of its impact from insight into how fragile and thin a barrier is European culture when confronting the horror that Kurtz perceives—a horror that exists in all men, not only those who choose to become diabolical gods.

However, Coppola doesn't bother with giving us a moral compass; he presents Vietnam as a given: a hallucinatory, surreal world and an absurdist epic. The film opens with the song. ''This Is the End'' on the sound track and superimposes images of apocalyptic flames over Coppola's Marlow, a sweating, unshaven drunken Willard (Martin Sheen). Willard is no respectable figure but a burned-out government hit man with six kills to his credit. He has the mad eyes and ravaged, haunted look of a man who has lived and seen too much, a man devoid of affect who can kill without guilt or hesitation. Coppola even has Willard directly inform the audience (through a portentous voiceover) that he is a man touched by a sense of nothingness who feels homeless and must have a new mission. The mission he's sent on is to terminate Colonel Kurtz's life.

Coppola's conception of Marlow is one of the less-sensational and more-realistic elements of a film comprised of spectacular set pieces evoking a world without moral center. The exhilarating, vertiginous ''Gotterdammerrung'' helicopter attack on a Vietcong village brings the audience directly into the experience of battle by filming from the point of view of the attackers in the air. The air mobile unit (a modern-day cavalry) is led by Colonel Kilgore (Robert Duval), who is an exaggerated version of General Patton. For Kilgore, napalm is the perfume of victory, and the purpose of destroying this Vietcong village (the Vietcong are at least given some dignity as ferocious defenders) is to discover the perfect wave for surfing. The swaggering, war-loving Kilgore is all blind, self-glorifying bravado, so obsessed with surfing and having a beach barbecue that he is impervious to the war raging around him. On one level, he's a suggestive symbol of American arrogance and ethnocentrism in his incapacity to believe that some small Asiatic people could hurt or even defeat his country or that there are other countries and people who have complex political and social interests and needs of their own. But on another level, this parody of American tunnel vision is lost in the brilliance of Coppola's cinematic effects and energy.

The film contains other set pieces that equally capture something of the war's chaos, incoherence, and sheer uncontrolled murderousness. As Willard and the boat's crew travel upriver to Cambodia and the Kurtz empire, they stop at an enormous supply depot in the middle of nowhere (one more attempt by the United States to reproduce American life in Vietnam) where a USO bump-and-grind show of undulating Playboy bunnies tittilates the sex-starved GIs until they rush the stage and must be tear gassed. Further upriver, the boat stops at the last U.S. outpost on the border between Vietnam and Cambodia, where an officer less platoon of sweating, anxious, drugged black soldiers shoot into the darkness at an invisible enemy in ''the asshole of the world.'' The whole scene is punctuated with bizarre atonal music, disembodied voices, and constantly burning fires and flares lighting up the sky and even hulks of planes lying in the water. It is a striking metaphor for a war without moral direction or sense, a war that feeds upon itself: the GIs are stationed there to build a bridge that is destroyed every night. What is problematic, as in so much of the film, is the excessiveness of it all—the light show makes the play of light, shadow, and sound more significant than the scene's political and moral resonance.

Coppola's Vietnam is basically hallucinatory, a war run by ''four-star clowns'' and built on drugs, despair, and death. There is barely even a glimpse of people at rest, unless the USO melee and riot can be considered recreation. Of course, one can't dictate what elements of the war Coppola should focus on. The problem does not rest with his notion of Vietnam as a surreal horror show but how he conceives of and realizes that vision.

Still, Coppola demonstrates that he is capable of getting to the heart of the war's madness with minimal cinematic display. As Willard's boat winds its way upriver, the GIs spot what looks like a suspicious Vietnamese fishing sampan. They board and turn it inside out looking for weapons but find nothing. One false move by a young Vietnamese woman sets the anxious, frightened Americans off and they mercilessly kill everybody in the boat. The scene captures directly and concretely the nature of a war where no rules or innocence exist and where everyone has become a possible enemy or victim.

There are other moving images and scenes, almost all found in the first two-thirds of the film. Those sections depict the boat's perilous trip while Willard obsessively puzzles over Kurtz' dossier and tries to understand his psyche. It's a deadly trip, permeated with a hysteria and sense of foreboding, the jungle oppressively surrounding them as they move further upriver. Although the GIs on the boat are neither mere symbols of American fighting men nor grotesques, they are not sufficiently complex creations to give much moral or psychological nuance and variation to the madness that fills every frame. They include a drugged-out, flower-child, clean-cut California surfer (Lance); a black street kid from the South Bronx (Mr. Clean), languidly jiving to Radio Saigon's broadcast of the Stones' ''Satisfaction''; a terror-stricken, pot-smoking cook from New Orleans (Chef) who just wants to go home; and their officer, the man who is given the most dimension, a wary, bitter, roughly paternal black navy professional (the Chief).

Neither the men nor Willard provide an oasis of repose, rationality, or moral balance in Coppola's Vietnam. What we see is almost unrelieved lunacy—a nightmarish Disneyland. As the boat moves into Kurtz's territory, its relationship to the war begins to recede and we see hallucinatory images of a plane and bodies stuck in a tree, the whole frame enveloped in mist. We've followed the river to the world of the damned, pervaded with bizarre effects: images of crosses, skulls superimposed over each other, dead bodies lying on shore, a painted tribe ominously watching Willard's boat while drums play on the sound track underlining the eerie silence.

All these gothic images and effects help make the final meeting between the empty, exhausted Willard and Kurtz anticlimatic. Conrad's Marlow is only moved after meeting Kurtz to "peer over the edge and then commit himself to Kurtz' vision rather than to limited, conventional perspectives of common-place individuals."[52] But both Willard's psyche and the whole world that surrounds him are so saturated in the apocalyptic that Willard is already cut off from the army and beyond the abyss when he meets up with Kurtz. So not only is there little possibility that Willard will be morally transformed by Kurtz, there is no real interaction between the two of them. In fact, the film becomes utterly static as an imprisoned Willard passively sits in the darkness and listens to the manic and pretentious remarks (quotes from Eliot's *The Hollow Men* and Frazer's *The Golden Bough* permeate Kurtz's monologue) of a bald, bulging, Buddha-like Kurtz, played without any sign of involvement by a mumbling Marlon Brando.

In Kurtz Coppola has created a metaphysical abstraction—the superman incarnate—who has gone beyond the bounds of acceptable military behavior set up his own kingdom in the jungle. Kurtz speaks of himself as transcending conventional opinion and morality, and Coppola heightens this exalted self-image by shooting Kurtz in chiaroscuro and soft focus and by giving Kurtz a temple littered with dismembered bodies (heads on pikes), altars, and pagan idols with drugged, painted natives milling about. (Coppola never questions the inherent racism of a white man turned into a god and king by dazed, servile Asiatics.) Kurtz also trades in gnostic tales of trained NLF cadres who have the strength of will to cut off the U.S.-inoculated arms of South Vietnamese villagers, demonstrating a "will which is crystalline in its purity." The moral of his tale is that the Vietcong are in tune with their "primordial instincts" and can kill without passion, feeling, or moral judgment. They have clearly become a collective supermen, a people worth emulating. Kurtz sees his own actions, his war against the North Vietnamese, Vietcong, and Cambodians, as a rejection of the U.S. army's tissue of lies. His is a war without rules and a genuine moral commitment to a clear, willed choice. He underlines this point with aphoristic comments such as "Judgment defeats us: we must make friends with moral terror," which comes very close to the Nietzchean "and whoever must be a creator in good and evil, verily he must be an annihilator of values."[53]

Apocalypse Now

Coppola's superman engages in the ultimate assertion of will: he wills his own death and that of his followers. He wants Willard to understand and bear witness for him and then kill him. He also leaves a manuscript that says, "Drop the bomb, exterminate them all." Nevertheless all his philosophic musings and his demonic and imperial posturing turn Kurtz into such a self-conscious symbol that the particularity of the Vietnam War disappears altogether, and a nebulous notion of civilization's madness takes its place. In a sense, both Kilgore and Willard, though a bit more concrete and less pretentious than Kurtz, are like him, men consumed by a love of killing and war. It's of course possible to see their destructive passion as a result of the Vietnam War, but *Apocalypse Now* isn't interested in exploring how the war has affected and altered the psyches of the participants. In fact, it universalizes and abstracts the war by making its terror part of the human condition rather than a result of specific social and political forces.

What clouds the connection between *Apocalypse Now* and the Vietnam experience even further is the insertion of Coppola's personal quest into the film. (In fact, one scene shows Coppola directing a television crew filming Kilgore and his air cavalry unit). In her book *Notes*, Eleanor Coppola (the director's wife) comments that while making the film, which went far over budget and had innumerable production difficulties and delays, Coppola had become both Willard setting off on his mission and Kurtz in his kingdom, both of these conceits helping to blur the distinction between fiction and reality.[54]

In fact, everything in Coppola's Vietnam is too hyperbolic, the character of Kurtz and the last section of the film most of all. There is not even a touch of irony in Coppola's conception of Kurtz; in fact, one feels an identification with, even exaltation of, Kurtz's megalomania. Thus, Dennis Hopper's manic 1960s photojournalist's adulation for Kurtz as a "great man," an archetypal figure who has his own "dialectic logic," is not so much parodied for the spaced-out, pretentious nonsense he babbles but seems to express much of Coppola's own sentiments and fantasies.

In constructing his own version of Kurtz, Coppola strains for significance, trying to sum up the highly charged and at moments overly spectacular imagery of the film's first two-thirds in one unifying symbol and idea. The problem, of course, is that Kurtz is a rhetorical figure, without psychological or political resonance, whose uttering "the horror, the horror" just before dying leaves one untouched both emotionally and politically; his notion of horror is too vaporous and stylized to have much connection to the particular terrors of the war. And since the relationship between Willard and Kurtz never develops, one never responds to what the murder must mean for Willard: the killing of the father, the purging of his alter ego. These are presumed interpretations, but they don't grow organically from the film's action.

There is a hollow core at the center of *Apocalypse Now's* fireworks, and the striking images can't in themselves prevent a profound sense of intellectual muddle. After killing Kurtz, Willard wanders through a labyrinth of caves and then, enveloped in smoke, confronts a mob of natives bowing down to him as the new "Kurtz." Willard refused to assume the role of the deity and takes off just before the whole compound is bombed by U.S. planes. (The film was given other endings, for Coppola was never clear about how he wanted it to conclude.) The meaning of Willard's refusal remains elusive. Has he had enough of imperialistic pretensions, be they Kurtz's tortured, egomaniacal ones or the U.S. government's complacent, traditional ones? Is Coppola suggesting that Willard's abdication means that America is trying to exorcise its sense of national invulnerability? The conclusion is blurred, lost in bloated superimpositions, shadows, and echo-chamber effects. Coppola may morally recoil from both Kurtz's and the war's embrace of and immersion in horror, but there is more than a touch of admiration for and identification with the excessiveness, extremity, and boldness of Kurtz and even of Kilgore (and, less consciously, with U.S. murderousness).

Apocalypse Now can also be seen as Hollywood's attempt to recover its position as a preeminent mythmaker in American culture. The film was eagerly awaited, as if it was capable of providing the emotional catharsis that would finally resolve America's moral and political dilemma about the war. *Apocalypse Now* and other Vietnam films were supposed to create a mythic fabric that would help the public comprehend the war and finally integrate it into the American imagination and psyche.

Clearly the two Hollywood heroes (antiheroes?) of the post-*Green Berets* Vietnam films—the wounded vet and the superman—from the basis of that attempted integration. Each of them provide a convenient symbol for a war that was impossible to deal with in the traditional Hollywood Manner. The vet's wounds and lost limbs express the rage and guilt that underlined the nation's anxieties, but the country's feelings were so volatile and confused that Hollywood often attempted to muffle and neutralize them within the confines of its traditional genre conventions and codes.

The creation of the superman gave Hollywood the opportunity to construct a character who could transcend most moral and social categories while helping obfuscate the war's connection to U.S. politics and society. The superman allowed the movie-going audience to view Vietnam as a war fought by men psychically and morally different from themselves, men whose internal lives remain unfathomable and live on a more-murderous and elevated plane of reality than other men. It allowed the particular political reasons for the war and the moral questions that the intervention and the fighting itself elicited to remain untouched. It also granted the public ideological and psychological comfort with the notion that the death and destruction had more to do with the human condition (or, in the case of *The Deer Hunter*, with some innate evil in the soul of the Vietnamese people) than with any concrete decision made by the U.S. government or any moral responsibility of the American public for actively supporting or passively accepting the war.

It's impossible to say if Hollywood's adoption of the superman figure was a conscious and subtle attempt to divert the public from the particular moral and political issues the war engendered. More likely, U.S. directors and the industry opted for what they felt personally and commercially most at ease with for films dealing with superhuman heroism or human destructiveness and corruption (e.g., *film noir*, the work of Sam Peckinpah) have obviously always been more a Hollywood staple than films that project a vision of historical, social, and moral complexity. It's always been more profitable to make films about corrupt, psychopathic, or nihilistic individuals than to explore the dialectical relationship between individual consciousness and behavior and social and cultural values (like Polansky's *Force of Evil*) or to analyze the ambiguities inherent in making moral and political choices (as in Kazan's *Wild River*). The outlines of films built on a vision of human corruption are bolder and simpler, and if the perspective is not utterly nihilistic, the forces of good (a Michael Vronsky [*The Deer Hunter*]) can at least struggle against the forces of evil (the Vietnamese). In films of this sort, the American desire to see political conflict in personal and moralistic terms (rather than historical and ideological) is reinforced and sustained.

Nevertheless, whatever Hollywood's logic for using the superman symbol, movie makers had difficulty making Vietnam films that would give the public some solace and satisfaction. Although the majority of the 3 million soldiers who served there did not become politicized, many of them (as well as a large percentage of the public) knew that U.S. power and will were defeated in Vietnam. An even smaller number understood that the war was degraded, inhuman, and genocidal. While the public did not clamor for films that dealt with the war, it was also true that images and symbols created by Hollywood weren't sufficiently complex and resonant to provide a true catharsis. Vietnam was so nightmarish and obscene a conflict that it would be extremely difficult for any director, however politically and morally incisive and imaginative, to encapsulate it. Both Cimono and Coppola were bold and ambitious enough to attempt films that might get to the heart of Vietnam. Nevertheless, scale itself was insufficient in conveying the complex political and moral issues of the war. In fact, both often confused effect with substance, overwhelming the audience where simplicity (not simplemindedness) would have been truer and more effective. Hope remains, however, that the new cadre of film makers created by the Vietnam War could someday go beyond their predecessors' remarkable images, striking metaphors, and (in Cimino's case) emotionally striking scenes to penetrate the moral and political heart of darkness that was Vietnam.[55]

PART III

Hunter-Heroes
and Survivors

On April 28, 1957, 18 years and two days prior to the stunning victory of the North Vietnamese armies in South Vietnam and their entry into Saigon, Senator Joseph R. McCarthy entered Bethesda Naval hospital as a patient for what would be his final illness. Although these two dates have no direct link, they do have more than a passing connection. McCarthy's rise to power was, to a large extent, based on his gift for discovering scapegoats who would provide a confused, disturbed American public with the answer to Who lost China? McCarthy built his career on the supposed Reds, pinkos, and liberals he found in institutions like the army and the Department of State (until he overreached himself by attacking President Eisenhower). After 1975, however, in the wake of the occupation of Saigon, there was not a hint of the kind of controversy or agonizing that followed the Communist victory in China. No one even bothered to raise the question of Who lost Indochina? In fact politicians, journalists, and the American public all seemed in a rush to forget about the longest war in U.S. history.[1]

Despite this conscious effort at collective amnesia, the consequences of the war could hardly be avoided on either a public or a private level. The war caused vast cracks in the bipartisan foreign policy of interventionism that had governed U.S. global strategy since the end of World War II. As a matter of fact, shortly after the final U.S. troop withdrawals from Vietnam, Congress passed, over a presidential veto, the War Powers Act (1973), which expressly forbid the president from engaging U.S. troops in any area for more than 60 days without congressional approval. Indeed, as the decade wore on into the 1980s, so deeply ingrained had this suspicion of foreign intervention become that President Reagan found it increasingly difficult to win legislative approval for economic and military aid against Communist-dominated governments and insurgent movements in Central America.

Onto the scrapheap, along with the concept of a bipartisan foreign policy, went the myth of American omnipotence. If further evidence was needed after the North Vietnamese occupation of Saigon, it was provided by the protracted hostage crisis in Iran and by the 1983 loss of 241 U.S. marines (and our subsequent withdrawal from Beirut, Lebanon) after a series of suicide attacks by Shiite terrorists.[2] Even devoted hawks like Secretary of Defense Casper Weinberger noted that

Recent history has proved that we cannot assume unilaterally the role of the world's defender. So while we may and should offer substantial amounts of economic and military assistance to our allies in their time of need and help them deter attacks against them—usually we cannot substitute our troops or will for theirs.[3]

Echoing this sentiment and effectively summarizing this mood were the comments of another well-known conservative, former Secretary of Defense James Schlesinger, who said, "The United States has lost preeminence. While it remains the leading nation on the international scene, its power which earlier was indisputable, is now very much disputable."[4]

Not even the short, swift, and triumphant U.S. invasion of Grenada dispelled the grip of Vietnam on U.S. policy. The veil of censorship that descended over the invasion smacked of the lessons learned in Vietnam (and to some extent the brief, victorious campaign of the British in the Falklands), wherein correspondents were prevented from roaming freely over the battlefield and from filing dispatches that might conflict with official versions of events (the so-called credibility gap).

The war's terrible toll was manifested less dramatically in the public realm than in the private lives of those who served in combat. Here, the 58,000 killed, over 300,000 wounded, and the 100,000 returning with partial disabilities were merely a part of the continuing human cost of Vietnam. For many survivors of the 2.6 million Americans who served in Vietnam (1.6 million in combat zones), the war seemed hardly to have ended. Of course, there were always the well-publicized vets who adjusted to post-war American life (as exemplified by Jeremiah Denton, a former POW; Bob Kerry, a wounded Navy Seal; and naval Lieutenant John Kerry, a leader of Vietnam Veterans against the War, all of whom built successful political careers based upon their war records. But countless others live not only in bitter, frustrated, and disillusioned pain, they live in constant anxiety about their health and the genetic consequences to themselves and their children from exposure to Agent

Orange. Many more are psychologically crippled by the destructive effects of what became known as post-traumatic stress syndrome—the obsessive recollection of the traumatic events of the war.

It was this latter problem that figured most prominently in the post-war image of Vietnam vets in the American mind, endowing them with traits of psychological disorientation and potential violence. Certainly that war veterans suffered from anxiety, depression, nightmares, emotional withdrawal and repression, and alcohol and drug abuse was not new. In World War I and World War II these symptoms had come to be known collectively as "shell shock" and then "battle fatigue." The poet-novelist Robert Graves, himself a World War I trench-warfare veteran, noted in his war memoirs, "I was mentally and nervously organized for war, shells used to come bursting on my bed at midnight, even though Nancy shared my bed with me; strangers in the daytime would assume the faces of friends who had been killed."[5] However, despite the fact that veterans of other wars also experienced trauma, the special kind of war fought by the Vietnam vet and the postwar atmosphere he confronted compounded the intensity of its effects.

The Vietnam era soldier was relatively younger than his World War II counterpart, his average age being approximately 19 compared with 26 for the World War II vet. As a result, the Vietnam vet lacked the worldly experience that might have supplied him with the ego strength to withstand the stresses of combat. Additionally, the policy of limiting service in Vietnam to a tour of one year had widespread and damaging effects. Adopted with the progressive intent of avoiding the feeling of hopelessness that had undermined GI morale in World War II (they served for the duration or until wounded), this policy ironically increased rather than decreased the amount of time spent in combat. In contrast, for example, to the battle-scarred marine division that took the island of Tarawa in World War II, which in its three years in the South Pacific never saw more than a total of 60 days on the front line, a marine in Vietnam could be exposed to as much as 80 days of continuous service in the field (without the benefit of the long periods of R-and-R enjoyed by the World War II GI in Australia or New Zealand). In addition, seasoned men who had acquired the kind of skills necessary to survive in Vietnam were removed from the line. By the same token, it also encouraged so-called short-timers to avoid combat, creating for some a sense of guilt for having left buddies behind.

The special circumstances of the fighting in Vietnam exacerbated these problems. Instead of the liberated towns and territories of World War II and the Korean War, Vietnam was characterized by guerrilla-style warfare with no fixed positions or battle lines, where the smiling "mamasan," the street urchin, or the seemingly indifferent peasant plowing a field in the daytime could become the remorseless "Charlie" of the night. Similarly, the hill that had been taken with so much blood-shed one day might have to be evacuated the very next and then retaken on the third when it was reoccupied by the Vietcong. What remained, therefore, was a war with no real victories, just a terrible battle of attrition whose sole yardsticks were body counts ("If it's Vietnamese and it's dead, it's the enemy"), search-and-destroy missions, free-fire zones, and the deadly technology of napalm, herbicides, helicopter gunships, and millions of tons of bombs.[6]

Perhaps most significant in undermining the morale of the Vietnam vet was his homecoming itself. Fraught with a great deal of anxiety and potential for disruption even under the best of circumstances, his transition to civilian life was totally mismanaged. Thus passage from the war zone to home might take no more than 24 hours, resulting in the veteran suddenly finding himself walking down a peaceful street in his home-town, where only hours before he might have been engaged in a vicious and bloody firefight. Gone, unfortunately, was the time of transition permitted by the slow-moving troopships of World War II and the Korean War that despite the boredom and the frustration they caused, provided the veteran with necessary time for decompression and reflection.

Even more profoundly upsetting to the veteran was the treatment he received when he arrived home, particularly the lack of respect, honor, or even interest in his experiences. In fact, instead of being stood to drinks by admiring friends and strangers, having his pick of the prettiest hometown girls, or being watched with envy by the 4Fs and draft dodgers, the veteran was often treated like a pariah. Such was the antiwar climate fostered by years of antiwar agitation that there were no victory parades for the veteran, and he was seen at best as a fool or dupe for going to war or at worst, a possible war criminal. No wonder that many Vietnam vets referred to themselves as "the unwilling working for the unqualified to do the unnecessary for the ungrateful." In turn, much of the American public saw the Vietnam vet as a man whose resentment and bitterness turned him into a threatening figure whose rage could explode at any time.[7]

Unfortunately, the latter did happen and the stereotype was enhanced by usually well-publicized events wherein former vets, some of whom were highly decorated, committed suicide, criminal acts, and even murder. Nevertheless, slowly and imperceptively after 1979 there began to be a change in the image of the vet and the legacy of Vietnam. Interestingly enough, in view of the comments of the fictional GI in Tim O'Brien's *Going After Cacciato* about making the war into a movie, the change owed some of its impetus to the movies, and its most notable initial moment came at the Academy Award ceremonies of 1979.

In that year, Jon Voight and Jane Fonda won best acting awards for

Coming Home while *The Deer Hunter* and its director Michael Cimino won for best picture and director. The following day, the *Los Angeles Herald-Examiner* proclaimed exultantly in banner headlines, "The War Finally Wins." In addition, the latter half of the year saw the opening of Francis Coppola's much-ballyhooed version of the war *Apocalypse Now*. Taken together, these events created a feeling that somehow Americans had finally put the war behind them.

Of course, the fact of America granting itself an Academy Award for its role in the war is suffused with irony and is almost reminiscent of Senator George Aiken's scenario for ending the war: the United States clears out and then declares itself the victor. However, for some Vietnam veterans, these films were at best an equivocal acknowledgment of their experience; they sometimes merely served to awaken terrible and long-repressed memories. One veteran recalled that

The Deer Hunter was the first Vietnam movie that I have seen. I went with a young lady. I said, "Let's go to the flick. Let's go see this picture *The Deer Hunter*. It's about Nam." I'm walking in there thinking that this is an ordinary picture, like *The Green Berets* with my man John Wayne that I saw on TV. That wasn't no Nam. I laughed about it. But *The Deer Hunter* was a different story.

There's one part in there where two white guys are hanging on the skids of a helicopter, scratching for dear life to get on it. One dude fell off because he was weak. The other dude said to hell with it, jumped off and ran through the water after him. That was the Nam I knew. I put myself there. I was sick to my stomach. I got cold and sweated. I tried to fight it. It was like a drug addition. The girl thought I was flipping out. All of a sudden they are in a firefight on the screen and if I had a gun on me I would have started shooting.

I'm serious, I came apart. I crouched down behind the seat and crawled up the aisle of the theater and out into the light on my hands and knees. I didn't know that it was a movie anymore. I was back in the war and that was what I had to do.[8]

Other veterans saw these films as so distorted as to be treated with contempt. As one said, "You see movies like *The Deer Hunter* and all that . . . ain't close to what it was really like over there. They don't tell you what really happened over there."[9]

However, the comments of a black GI on the film *Apocalypse Now* perhaps puts the purpose of these films in their proper perspective.

I don't like movies about Vietnam 'cause I don't think that they are prepared to tell the truth. *Apocalypse Now* didn't tell the truth, it wasn't real. I guess it was a great thing for the country to get off on, but it didn't remind me of anything I saw. . . . By making us look insane, the people who made the movie was [sic] somehow relieving themselves of what they asked us to do over there. But we were not insane. We were not ignorant, we knew what we were doing.[10]

By contrast, neither ambivalence nor a mood of philosophical reflection marked the reaction of Vietnam vets to the outburst of almost hysterical patriotic fervor that greeted the homecoming of the Iranian hostages in January, 1981. This outpouring of sympathy, parades, and awards had the ironic effect of goading vets into forcing some sort of acknowledgement of their own sacrifice. Although the extreme reaction of ex-marine Gary Cooper (who went berserk and was killed by his hometown police in Hammond, Indiana, after the return of the hostages) was an anomaly, many vets certainly felt that the time was now ripe to communicate their experiences.[11]

Symbolic of this changing atmosphere was presidential nominee Ronald Reagan's August 1980 campaign-speech reference to Vietnam as a "noble cause."[12] While it may have been pleasing to a certain segment of the American public, this remark's major significance was that it signaled the fact that an atmosphere now existed where it was possible to talk about the war. The December 1981 special edition of *Newsweek* entitled *Charlie Company: What Vietnam Did to Us* lifted the lid on the experiences of the men in a company of the Big Red One infantry division and soon spawned a whole slew of oral histories about the war (e.g., *Everything We Had, Nam, Bloods,* etc.)

The culmination of this resurrection of collective memory occurred at the unveiling of the Vietnam War Memorial in November 1982. Despite criticism from both the right and left that the monument lacked heroic stature (a statue was added in November 1984, across from the long, low, marble wall with its list of the 57,692 war dead) and that it failed to even mention Vietnam (making it seem, as the *New Republic* charged, that they might have died in some "monstrous traffic accident"), the memorial was embraced by both the vets and the public at large with enthusiasm and almost religious awe.[13] In fact, at the time of this writing, it had become second only to the Lincoln Memorial in yearly attendance by tourists in Washington, D.C.

With the tenth anniversary of the end of the war approaching, both newspapers and television picked up on the war and the legacy of Vietnam. The Public Broadcasting Station (PBS) broadcast a 13-week documentary history of the war that won six Emmy Awards in 1984. This was soon followed by a series in the nation's largest-circulation newspaper, *The Wall Street Journal,* titled "Vietnam Legacy."[14] Most important of all in stirring up renewed interest in the war and to some extent vaguely reminiscent of the daily media reports from the battlefields of Vietnam were the almost daily communiques from the press and television on the progress of the courtroom battles in the case of General William Westmoreland v. CBS.

The Westmoreland controversy actually began in January 1982, when *CBS Reports* broadcast its documentary *The Uncounted Enemy: A Vietnam*

Deception, which charged that General Westmoreland, the former U.S. armed forces commander in Vietnam, had deceived President Lyndon B. Johnson and the U.S. public on the level of enemy strength in Vietnam. This charge prompted Westmoreland to institute a $120 million libel suit against CBS.

After an 18-week trial in 1985, Westmoreland ultimately dropped his case. Although there were numerous ambiguities involved (Westmoreland's own lawyer had been an antiwar activist), the two-year legal battle resulted in the court appearances of the "best and brightest" of the era (e.g., McGeorge Bundy, Robert McNamara, Walt Rostow) and forced them to comment publicly and for the record on issues they hadn't spoken of since the late 1960s. The lawsuit also aroused barely hidden acrimony that still smoldered—years after the war's end. In fact, the publisher of at least one major U.S. magazine felt that the purpose of the trial was not to restore the general's honor, but to vindicate the war in the eyes of the American public. Thus, John R. MacArthur, the publisher of *Harper's* magazine, which was the first to publish the story of Westmoreland's alleged deception, wrote,

The pathetic dénouement of the Westmoreland trial suggests that the General's financial backers withdrew their support when they realized their ideological adventure was about to end in failure. It was certainly their call, since the lawsuit had little to do with Gen. Westmoreland's honor. From the beginning the trial was about politics and represented a crude attempt by ideologues to rewrite the history of the Vietnam war.[15]

One striking example of the United States' newly found ability to deal with the war's legacy was the welcome-home parade for vets in New York in May 1985. Not interested in engaging in political debates or rewriting Vietnam history, it was intended to convey public warmth and support for the vets, not for the war. Twenty-five thousand vets marched down Broadway in a traditional shower of ticker-tape, and perhaps a million people cheered, applauded, and even wept watching them from the sidewalks. The participants ranged from General Westmoreland to vets in battle fatigues who did not wish to see the war romanticized. For one day, at least, these men who fought in Vietnam received a belated homecoming.

The Vietnam legacy has led to a rich body of historical revisionism that owed as much to events as to scholarship and that rendered the wartime assumptions of both the political right and left, the hawk and the dove, null and void. Thus prowar advocates who had argued that the North Vietnamese were merely pawns of the Chinese Communists were undoubtedly confounded by the swiftness with which the Chinese and the North Vietnamese engaged in polemics and then outright armed struggle in the war's wake. Also adding to their chagrin was the ease with which the United States and Communist China achieved a diplomatic, economic, and military rapprochement in the postwar period.

The same dubious fate awaited the domino theory. Although Laos and Cambodia did come under North Vietnamese domination, the presumed danger to Thailand, Indonesia, and Malaysia failed to materialize and they in fact emerged more stable and prosperous than ever before. Moreover, their prosperity and relative freedom provided a vivid contrast to the drab, bloody, and impoverished societies of postwar Vietnam, Laos, and Cambodia.

On the other hand, the left's romanticization of the NLF and the North Vietnamese faded when faced with North Vietnam's indulgence in Stalinist tactics and policies. As a matter of fact, the speed with which the North Vietnamese moved to integrate South Vietnam into a united Vietnam and to quash any opposition to its rule (e.g., Buddhists, ethnic Chinese) belied the political fables and fantasies of a part of the antiwar movement. These groups had held that the NLF were an autonomous South Vietnamese organization and that the North Vietnamese were nothing more than freedom-loving, anticolonialist, peasant revolutionaries.

Still, not every event in the postwar period served to debunk these beliefs. Far outdoing in reality the most Grand Guignol fantasy of the right—the bloodbath theory—was the massacre of millions (not, however, in South Vietnam) in Cambodia. Here, Pol Pot and the murderous Khmer Rouge sought to transform the society by slaughtering an estimated 1-3 million Cambodians after the fall of Phnom Penh.[16]

Events like this served to provide a receptive audience for the message of neoconservative intellectuals like *Commentary* editor Norman Podhoretz, who offered facile rationales and justifications for the war. Podhoretz explained that our defeat in Vietnam was the result of trying to fight the war on the military, political, and strategic cheap. In addition, he pointed to the totalitarianism that had descended on South Vietnam following the Communist victory as proof that whatever the corruption and limitation to the democracy and human rights that existed under the Thieu government, it was preferable to the iron dictatorship of a Communist regime.[17]

In contrast to Podhoretz's polemical style, more academically detached scholars also challenged basic assumptions about the war and the Vietnamese. Their revised analysis of the nature of the South Vietnamese peasant saw him less as a Confucian villager than a capitalist small soldier, while others held that the Tet offensive, far from being a total disaster for the United States, was actually a military victory (albeit a political defeat). In the same vein, James Pinckney Harrison's *The Endless War: Vietnam's Struggle for Independence* concluded that the 50-year struggle (1925-75) of the Communists in Vietnam had turned the peasantry into such "iron fortresses" of anticolonialist and anti-imperialist consciousness and organization that only genocide could have eliminated them.[18]

Less overtly contentious but probably more profoundly influential on American culture was the literature inspired by the war. Here, after some initial hesitancy, the novels and memoirs swelled to floodlike proportions. The early memoirs and novels set a tone that was closely akin to the profoundly disillusioned and ironic poetry and prose of the World War I era. Although the Vietnam literature did not have a Siegfried Sassoon, Robert Graves, Wilfred Owen, Rupert Brooke, Alan Seeger, John Dos Passos, Ernest Hemingway, or e.e. Cummings, journalist-novelist Philip Caputo (who served from 1965 to 1966 and then returned just before the fall of Saigon) wrote eloquently that

War is always attractive to young men who know nothing about it; but we had also been seduced into uniform by Kennedy's challenge to ask, "What you can do for your country," and by the missionary idealism he had awakened in us. America seemed omnipotent then; the country could still claim that it had never lost a war, and we believed that we were ordained to play cop to communist robbers and spread out political faith around the world. . . . So when we marched into the rice paddies on that damp March afternoon, we carried along with our packs and rifles, the implicit convictions that the Vietcong would be beaten and that we were doing something altogether noble and good. We kept the packs and rifles; the conviction we lost.[19]

In a much more visceral and emotional manner, Ron Kovic, a marine paralyzed from the waist down in Vietnam, wrote in his memoir of the war and his return to it,

It reminded him of the time in church a few Sundays before, when Father Bradley had suddenly pointed to him during the middle of a sermon, telling everyone he was a hero and a patriot in the eyes of God and the country for fighting the Communists. "We must pray for brave boys like Ron Kovic," said the priest. "And most of all," he said, "we must pray for victory in Vietnam and peace throughout the world." And when the service was over, people came to shake his hand and to thank him for all he had done for God and his country, and he left the church feeling very sick and threw up in the parking lot.[20]

From Norman Mailer's 1967 parody of American macho *Why We Are in Vietnam*, whose main character D.J. ends his manic, novel-length monologue with the comment, "We're off to see the wizard in Vietnam . . . Vietnam, hot damn") to Tim O'Brien's Cacciato walking west and home from the war in the 1981 *Going After Cacciato*, the frequency with which the novels and memoirs return to the themes of alienation from and profound disenchantment with the United States clearly illuminates what the war had wrought.[21]

The desire to write about the war resulted in so many novels with so many similar scenes and themes that they moved novelist C.D.B. Bryan, himself the author of one of the earliest and best books about the war, *Friendly Fire*, to comment that there now existed a "Generic Vietnam War Narrative."[22] This novel, according to Bryan, had as its obligatory hero a young white male who is patriotic even though somewhat alienated. After basic training he is assigned to a unit in Vietnam consisting of characters like Daytripper, a perennially stoned soldier, and Rebel, a crazy white guy who likes to kill. Then come incidents like the first patrol, an atrocity scene, dope scenes, helicopter assaults, and battle scenes. Summarizing the theme of these novels, Bryan wrote that the "Generic Vietnam War Narrative" charged "the gradual deterioration of order, the disintegration of idealism, the breakdown of character, the alienation from those at home, and finally, the loss of all sensibility save the will to survive."[23]

Bryan was not as much attempting to denigrate these novels, the quality of which he insisted was quite high overall, but to argue that their consistently similar narratives, characters, and themes were part of the need to make sense of the Vietnam experience. Unfortunately, none of them, except perhaps a handful of nonfiction works (e.g., Michael Herr's *Dispatches* and Dr. Ronald J. Glasser's semifictional *365 Days*), had, according to Bryan, really come close to accurately depicting the war.

If this was considered true of the novels, many thought it was doubly so of the films on Vietnam. Although a number of them, particularly the 1979-80 trio of *Coming Home*, *The Deer Hunter*, and *Apocalypse Now* had been highly acclaimed and may indeed have contributed to something of a national catharsis, they had hardly met with unanimous acceptance as accurate reflections of the war. Along with some of the veterans we have cited, critics like Vietnam journalist Gloria Emerson (*Winners and Losers*) and Ward Just (*In the City of Fear*) found the films not only lacking verisimilitude, but also lacking any larger grasp of the meaning of the war. Linking both fiction and films to this failure, Just wrote that "Vietnam was such a spectacular netherworld that the writers of fiction and the makers of film have a difficult time improving on it; it has not been reinvented, so remains largely out of sight, except, of course, for the survivors."[24]

Obviously, criticism of the Vietnam novels and films indicate a strong feeling that somehow creative imagination in the United States had still failed to take the full measure of the war. On the other hand, as much as Bryan, Just, and others might hope for novels and films that would eschew clichés and stereotypes and provide some insights into the moral and political insignificance of the war, it is precisely clichés, stereotypes, conventions, and evasion and displacement that are the life blood of popular culture, particularly the movies. Consequently, it must have been enormously galling to many in Hollywood to find that after years of being charged with evasion, its first major attempts to deal with the war directly had failed to satisfy the critics or still their criticism. Perhaps even more irksome to some movie makers (those a bit less concerned with critical approval and more concerned with box-office grosses) was the fact that the cautiously evolved Vietnam symbols and protagonists of the 1970s (the wounded vet and the superman) had only partially filled the need for acceptable and accessible Vietnam metaphors. As a matter of fact, instead of supplying a satisfying basis for any kind of Vietnam genre, their attempts succeeded in only confusing the audience—sometimes even inspiring remorse, guilt, and anxiety—and in stifling further cinematic consideration of the war.

Of course, metaphor constituted only part of the problem. With the 1980 Reagan victory and the conservative trend it supposedly heralded, as well as the initial economic hard times it spawned, in Hollywood there was a conspicuous turning away from films with serious social and political themes toward movies stressing entertainment and escapism. Moreover, the prospects for films about Vietnam dimmed even further when *The Deer Hunter* director Michael Cimino's epic western *Heaven's Gate* proved to be a colossal flop. This disaster prompted Hollywood studios and producers to scurry for the cover of safe film properties like sequels and bankable star vehicles. As a result, a number of interesting films (some contemplated for production, others even already in release) were unceremoniously shelved or yanked from the theaters by panicky producers. Except for the timely intervention of perceptive United Artists executives, Ivan Passer's unconventional but revealing study of a Vietnam vet and post-Vietnam America *Cutter's Way* (1987), (initially entitled *Cutter and Bone*) might have met the same fate.

The panic inspired by the *Heaven's Gate* disaster, however, was not the only reason why *Cutter's Way* failed initially to get much recognition. Just as significant was the fact that it suffered by comparison with big-budget films like *Coming Home*, *The Deer Hunter*, and *Apocalypse Now*. Not ony did it lack big name stars like Brando, De Niro and Fonda, as well as important directors like Hal Ashby or Francis Coppola, its director Ivan Passer was considered a failure in some industry circles. Despite being one of the luminaries of the Czech film renaissance of the 1960s (with scripts for Milos Forman's *Loves of a Blonde* [1965] and *The Fireman's Ball* [1967] and the direction of the small masterpiece *Intimate Lighting* [1965] to his credit), Passer's previous American directorial efforts *Born to Win* (1971) and the inchoate *Law and Disorder* (1974) had not done well critically or at the box office.

Nonetheless, in *Cutter's Way* Passer developed the character of a Vietnam vet (Alex Cutter [John Heard]) who is neither a spaced-out psychotic nor a Sir Galahad in jungle combat fatigues. He is a Vietnam vet who simultaneously seems to be both wounded vet and superman. Indeed, he is a character of such complexity that it is his psyche and relationship to his best friend, the Ivy League stud and beach bum Richard Bone (Jeff Bridges), which becomes the centerpiece of the film, much more so than their bungled attempts to capture a ruthless tycoon whom they suspect of having committed a particularly grisly murder. As a matter of fact, their Hardy boys' notion of crime solving is merely a throwaway, hardly sustaining narrative tension, excitement, or interest. It is useful only to the extent that it allows Passer to also evoke the mood of post-Vietnam, postcounterculture America, a world of cool, detached power wielders and those so lost that there is little but self-immolating rage or apathy left to vent.

Here the abrasive, raspy voiced Cutter is the key. Played with manic intensity and sometimes cunning eccentricity by Heard, Cutter is an alcoholic, cynical Vietnam vet who has lost his eye, arm, and leg. He is filled with the venomous desire to revenge himself on those in power who sent him off to that horror without themselves being touched by the war. Nevertheless, Cutter is far from a committed radical member of the Vietnam Veterans against the War. He is portrayed with all the feeling for nuance and ambiguity (though more violently and fiercely) that Passer evoked in his self-important, foolish, and complacent Czech petty bourgeoisie. For intance, in one of the film's early scenes, Cutter's racist baiting of a group of blacks in a pool hall almost brings them to the point of using his head as a cueball only for them to back off when Bone utters the magical explanation that "he was in Nam." It is a beautiful example of Cutter's continued use of his Vietnam wounds to shrewdly manipulate and exploit those around him. He is a man who can alternately be both grandiose and grand, someone who moves seamlessly between moral vision, literary allusion, bombast, slyness, incisive wit, and paranoia. And underneath it all there rests a core of pathos. Heard's performance captures both an edgy, self-destructive nihilism and a need for the heroic affirmation inherent in Cutter's character.

Passer, however, never sentimentalizes or projects heroic virtues onto losers like Cutter and Bone. But it's clear that his sympathies rest with them rather than with an affluent, sterile southern California, characterized by a self-conscious ethnic parade complete with grotesque floats filled with costumed Indians, Mexicans, and mock cowboys and an empty, bleak, steel-and-concrete Los Angeles cityscape where oil rigs stand in the distance, ominously dominating the Pacific. In a similar fashion, the villain and putative murderer, Cord (Steven Elliot), is an oil millionaire who is seen in low-angle shots astride his horse as he acts as marshal of the ethnic parade or as he calmly officates at a polo match. In fact, Cord seems nothing less than a direct descendant of Edward Arnold's steely, forbidding tycoon in *Meet John Doe*. But *Cutter's Way* has no "little people" to arouse or Christian, humanitarian, and democratic principles to invoke against Cord. There is only the striking image and fluid, exciting tracking shots of Cutter riding a white horse; charging through tables of hors d'oeuvres; smashing up Cord's posh lawn party; and with a shout of exhilaration, plunging through a window to his death. A vainglorious and suicidal gesture, but the only choice left to be made in Passer's America.

Unquestionably, Cutter's symbolic ride is more emotionally liberating than it is intellectually illuminating. *Cutter's Way* contains no real political critique, just a loony, surreal image of Cutter's Ahab-like quest for justice and his struggle against an evil oil baron. Cord supposedly personifies the destructiveness and corruption of the U.S. power structure, and the film (in the usual Hollywood manner) finds it sufficient to evoke the image personalizing American corruption without making any connection between the tycoon and the social system that spawned and shaped him.

In contrast to the facile nature of the film's politics, Passer displays a surer, more-subtle hand when dealing with the relationship between Cutter and Bone and, to some degree, the posthippie life-style they lead. Passer captures well the feeling of lives adrift and alienated, lived from day to day without much direction or drive to define them. In addition, he subtly catches the essence of the symbiotic relationship between Cutter and Bone of crazed self-destructive idealism and moral apathy. Cutter needs the tanned, handsome, blond Bone's passivity, emotional detachment, and physical wholeness just as Bone in turn needs Cutter's mad aggression and energy. *Cutter's Way* gets to the heart of the subtle sadomasochistic mutual need that underlies many relationships and friendships. Cutter baits Bone constantly for his amiability, but Bone, played with quiet, understated intelligence by Bridges, nevertheless remains loyal and protective of him. The deepest bond and the one profound commitment they both have is to each other, and it is exemplified by Bone merging with and fulfilling Cutter's desire to shoot Cord at the film's climax.

Unfortunately, Passer is less sure of himself when dealing with the film's female characters. The murder victim's sister does a quick turn as a hip blonde who wants to help in the plot against Cord, but she comes off as no more than a pert, banal, oddly affectless cheerleader type and is suddenly dropped from the film. Cutter's wife, Mo (Lisa Eichorn), is an alcoholic depressive who masochistically loves Cutter but is also clearly attracted to Bone, as he is to her. (There is one subtle, quiet moment in the film where Mo and Bone dance in the darkness and silently and gently communicate their mutual desire.) But if Mo is able to give us a sense of her feelings of incompleteness, there is something too elliptic and underdeveloped in her characterization. We never really know what the basis of her commitment to and passion for either man is about. Despite being psychologically knowing and sharp tongued, she remains a melancholy, brooding, numbed victim, more an addition to a gallery of crippled outsiders than a person in her own right.

In spite of these flaws, *Cutter's Way* succeeds in managing to touch upon the tortured Vietnam and the ambiguous counterculture legacies without indulging in sentimental clichés or egregious stereotypes. The film takes the Vietnam metaphors developed in the films of the 1970s and deepens them by creating a more complex synthesis of them. Consequently, as evoked by the character of Alex Cutter, the wounded vet no longer resembles the passive victim of earlier Vietnam films, to be either pitied or feared, nor in his moments of grandiosity is he touched by the superman romanticism that surrounds Michael Vronsky in *The Deer Hunter* or the metahistorical Kurtz in *Apocalypse Now*.

In Cutter, Passer created a wounded vet who defies reduction to a category or a symbol; he is so rich, subtle, and specific a character that he almost leaps off the screen. Of course, this is not to claim that Passer's film is the definitive statement on the war. As stated previously, Passer's strength lies in characterization, not in political or social analysis. Nonetheless, the self-destructive rage and quixotic idealism of Cutter, the diffidence, sensitivity, and indolent sexuality of the drifting Bone and even the cartoonlike power of Cord provide a suggestive way of viewing how the Vietnam experience connects to American culture and the social system as both cause and effect.[25]

Unfortunately, it was a step that film makers and the public seemed reluctant to take. Hollywood's examination of the domestic results of the war, particularly the political, social, and cultural upheaval it caused, remained myopic. Although there had been some insightful films about this era in the 1960s and 1970s (*Medium Cool, Alice's Restaurant*) as well as Brian De Palma's independent films (*Greetings, Hi! Mom*), these were far outnumbered and outweighed by films such as *Getting Straight, The Strawberry Statement, R.P.M.,* and *The Magic Garden of Stanley Sweetheart,* which trivialized and exploited the period, or by films like *American Graffiti,* which avoided it altogether by concentrating on the more-tranquil 1950s.[26]

Of course, one might excuse the earlier films with the explanation that they were still too close to the era to put it in proper perspective. Clearly, this explanation is less justifiable for a film like *A Small Circle of Friends* (1980) which was made more recently. The product of director Rob Cohen and writer Ezra Sacks, this film might have been expected to provide a more-subtle and more-complex picture of the decade, since its creators had experienced the 1960s first hand. What they produced instead was a breathless tour of a number of leading 1960s political and cultural landmarks. They depict bloody student protests against the war, raucous parties celebrating Johnson's announcement that he wouldn't run for a second term in 1968, bookstores turning into head shops, and straight academic types becoming sitar-playing Hare Krishnas, all of which serve to embellish a tale that might better have been titled *Jules and Jim Go to Harvard*.

Although modeled after Truffaut's brilliant 1961 work about pre- and post-World War I bohemians and their romantic, tragic ménage à trois, *A Small Circle of Friends* is both intellectually and formally in a different league. Cohen's film is permeated with adolescent hi-jinks and angst rather than the lyricism and genuine anguish of *Jules and Jim*. Nor does his heroine Karen Allen as Jessica Bloom (Cliffie), with her apple-cheeked, clear-eyed beauty and straight-from-the-shoulder acting style, have the mystery, luminosity, or ambiguity of Jeanne Moreau's Catherine. It's her love affairs with two Harvard men—the brash, self-absorbed, self-styled "new journalist" Leonardo Da Vinci (née Rizzo), played by Brad Davis, and the stolid, responsible, WASP pre-med student Nick Baxter (Jameson Parker), Leo's best friend—that is at the core of the film. Nothing in the relationships, even the film's penultimate dramatic moment when the three go to bed together (off camera), is meant to truly delve into questions about personal loyalty, responsibility, and freedom. Rather, the relationship is primarily an excuse for allowing the trio to become involved in activities like student occupation of university buildings and feminist consciousness raising. The film merely exploits these events and movements without exploring their nature or linking them to a larger social world.

Criticisms notwithstanding, one critic noted that *A Small Circle of Friends* was at moments "probably the most intelligent exploration so far of the disruptive Vietnam years."[27] That this has a touch of truth is owed less to any of the major characters than to secondary characters like the rural, southern-born Eagle Scout Haddox (John Friedrich), radicalized by events into a Weather Underground fugitive terrorist, who dies in a Greenwich Village-style bomb blast, or the feminist activist Alice (Shelly Long), Jessica's best friend. Both suggest some of the commitment and often misguided idealism of the era. In a similar fashion the film captures what another critic saw as the "euphoria and desperation of the sixties" in its depiction of responses to the first draft lottery: bursts of applause when high numbers are drawn and shrieks of despair when low numbers are picked.[28]

There is a tendency in this film to make it seem that the Harvard students, who in reality operated in comparative safety from the draft and war, were the most tragic victims of Vietnam. To be fair, the film does in passing give us glimpses of a patriotic black cook whose son went off to Vietnam and of working-class high school graduates from Boston who died there.

Artistic and intellectual limitations aside, *A Small Circle of Friends* strikes home with its presentation of dress, hair styles, character types, events, ideas, and moral and political dilemmas that characterized the 1960s. There is no depth to any of it, but the film gives us true-to-life images of anxiety-ridden draft physicals, Nixon's declaration of victory in 1968, women's Karate classes, and hair and beards growing longer with each passing year.

Its realistic touches alone place *A Small Circle of Friends* in a somewhat different category from other 1960s films made in the 1980s. In Arthur Penn's *Four Friends* (1981) and Lawrence Kasdan's *The Big Chill* (1983), the 1960s serve more as backdrop or exist as a nostalgic moment where the characters lived supposedly richer, more deeply committed, caring, and fulfilling lives. In *Four Friends*, the 1960s are merely a setting for the picaresque adventures of the son of East European immigrant steel-workers who tries to come to terms with his roots and romantic fantasies, defining his identity in the process. *The Big Chill* speaks to the common historical experience of a generation confronting success, settling down, and selling out in the 1980s, although it is difficult to believe that any of its characters had any more connection to the 1960s than to grow long hair, smoke dope, or attend a political rally. A third film, *The Return of the Secaucus Seven* (1980), directed by independent film maker-novelist John Sayles, succeeds in conveying the consciousness, humor, language, and concerns of 1960s activists who try to maintain some of their political commitments as their lives become more settled and bourgeois. However, in none of the three films do the moral and political dilemmas and consequences of the Vietnam War play a significant role. (A scene depicting all of the characters in *The Big Chill* at a 1960s antiwar rally was even cut from the film's final version.)

Contrary to its apparent invisibility in films about the 1960s, that Vietnam still exercises a very strong hold on the imagination of many 1980s film makers can be seen in Walter Hill's production of *Southern Comfort* (1981). Hill's penchant for turning action-adventure films into stylish allegory had already been recorded in *The Warriors* (1979), in which a New York street gang reenacts the Greek General Xenephon and his soldiers' fourth-century BC march to the sea. It isn't hard to find echoes of the Vietnam War in *Southern Comfort*'s tale of nine weekend Louisiana national guard warriors who provoke Cajun bayou inhabitants into guerrilla warfare. By using Louisiana's Atchafalaya Basin's marshlands, hanging cypresses, giant oaks, mist, and Spanish moss, Hill and cinematographer Andrew Laszlo, backed by a weird blues score composed by Ry Cooder, create a grey-green primordial world that is quite literally a quagmire from which the protagonists can't escape.

Nor do the parallels to Vietnam stop here. With bows to literary and film antecedents such as William Stryon's *The Long March*, James

Dickey's *Deliverance*, Agatha Christie's *Ten Little Indians*, and John Ford's *The Lost Patrol*, the film uses the incidents and skirmishes in the swamp as metaphors for the war. The guardsmen blunder onto alien terrain without any real sense of what they're doing; running in circles in the swamp, their confusion and fragmentation powerfully parallel the U.S. GI experience in Vietnam. However, many of the particular details and incidents in the film are less suggestive. For example, there seems to be little connection between the adolescent pranksterism that initiates the conflict (the guardsmen steal a few Cajun boats, fire on the Cajuns with blanks, and in the return fire, see their leader and the only professional soldier among them killed) and the real policies and complex power politics that got us involved in Vietnam. In a similar fashion, the mad guardsman who sees himself as an avenging angel in blowing up a Cajun house is a rather contrived equivalent to our heedless, futile escalation of the war. And the Cajuns themselves, although rural, alien, and somewhat outside mainstream American culture, can't really serve as effective surrogates for the Vietcong, who were ideologically committed men taking part in a revolutionary struggle. Neither does the film's explanation (one that is indebted to Norman Mailer's *Why Are We in Vietnam?*) that the war was caused by the United States' insane, gun-obsessed machismo get close to the heart of the conflict. Machismo clearly played a contributing role in U.S. intervention, but a social-psychological explanation that exists in a political-historical vacuum is reductive and simplistic. The film also seems to be contributing to the whole ethic of machismo by the care and pleasure it takes in portraying the violence.

Nevertheless *Southern Comfort* succeeds and is at its most resonant in its depiction of the gradual disintegration of the squad. In contrast to Hill's previous films (*The Warriors* and the James gang western *The Long Riders*, where group pride, solidarity, and survival were portrayed as the highest virtues), *Southern Comfort* presents us with a group that is riven with social tension, backbiting, and contempt. Part of the burden for that conflict is borne by the two upper-middle-class characters in the squad, Lee Spencer (Keith Carradine), a witty banker's son, and a dour, secretive, upwardly mobile chemical engineer, named Charles Hardin (Powers Boothe). Both hold themselves aloof from the others (the angry, violent Hardin in particular, since he has raised himself from redneck roots) and look down on the rest as a bunch of ignorant louts. And although Spencer and Hardin are portrayed as more intelligent and skillful than the others—Carradine especially grants his character an engaging, breezy self-confidence—there is no doubt that their detachment and superciliousness, particularly their constant second guessing of and carping at the clumsy, military-manual-style leadership of Corporal Claude Casper (Les Lannem), contributes as much to the destruction of the squad as the rage, dimness, and murderous attacks of its other members.

More than anything else, however, the breakdown of the group gives Hill ample opportunity to contrast their lack of unity and the ruinous effect of their fragmentation and anomie with the communal cohesiveness and solidarity of the Cajuns. This contrast is most vividly rendered in one of the film's final sequences, in which Hardin and Spencer, the last survivors, reach what they think is the safety of a village at the edge of the basin. Here, again echoing Vietnam, Hill uses the scene to make a neat comparison to how American GIs must have felt not knowing friend from foe in the alien environs of Vietnam. As the guardsmen tread warily through the village, Hill contrasts the solitariness and paranoia of the two soldiers with the Cajuns' enjoyment of the warm, communal pleasure of a folk festival complete with food, wine, songs, and dances.

It is *Southern Comfort*'s depiction of this divisiveness, egoism, and privatism coupled with the overwhelming sense of being caught in an incomprehensible conflict that is the film's most striking aspect. This is not to say that the film provides a coherent critique of the war and the U.S. entry into it. *Southern Comfort* is clearly more interested in action sequences and tension-building cross-cutting than in illuminating the Vietnam conflict or its characters' moral and social values. Still, it's able to suggest that a key factor in our loss of the war was our lack of cohesiveness and control—both our inability to subsume class, racial, and value differences while waging a war against a common enemy and each individual soldier's lack of self-discipline. However, *Southern Comfort* does not then take the leap and declare that if not for all the carping, we could have won the war. Its tone is implicitly antiwar, separating it from a number of other 1980s films that begin from a prowar perspective to offer explanations for our defeat.

These later interpretations revealed, at least superficially, a striking similarity to the "stab in the back" thesis of the Nazi attack on the Weimar Republic. Of course, this is not meant to imply that these films' covert message hinted that the United States should make haste to move down the road toward fascism. Instead, they seemed to disclose a growing sense of frustration and powerlessness among Americans in the face of an increasingly complicated world. Murderous terrorist attacks and revolutions in the Third World against regimes allied with us stimulated the search for scapegoats on which to blame the loss of the war. These targets were less specific than the usual Vietnam whipping boys like the hostility of the media; the wishy-washy, impotent attitude of Congress; or the supposedly almost treasonous conduct of some left-wing intellectuals. By contrast, this new thesis bore a remarkable resemblance to the message of the Walt Kelley's comic strip *Pogo*, which declared, "We have met the enemy and he is us!'' Not the least of the implications for this comic-strip version of our defeat in Vietnam was the opportunity it gave to movie makers to successfully revive another of Hollywood's Vietnam metaphors—the superman. This time, however, they presented a superman shorn of any of the ethnic-communal or personal ties of a Michael Vronsky in *The Deer Hunter* or the pseudo-oracular profoundities of Kurtz in *Apocalypse Now*. Instead, he seemed to spring like a dragon's tooth from the war, combining the contradictory qualities of a John Wayne with the neurasthenia and alienation of Travis Bickle. He's a character whose first embodiment in the 1980s was the former Green Beret and Congressional Medal of Honor winner John Rambo (Sylvester Stallone) in *First Blood* (1982).

The paradox of John Rambo as superman (although he certainly conforms to the archetype) is that on first inspection, unshaven and with unkempt shoulder-length hair, he seems to be just another of your average hippie losers. As a matter of fact, the errand that brings him to the peaceful, snowcapped mountains of the Pacific Northwest countryside is nothing less than a reminder of the wounded vet. He immediately finds out that the man he was planning to meet, the last surviving member of his Vietnam combat team, has died of a cancer linked to Agent Orange (''He got killed in the war, and didn't even know it''). However, from Stallone's overdeveloped Mr. Universe physique and his smoldering, silent gazes, we know that he is no mere counterculture wimp. As fast as you can say post-traumatic stress syndrome, he has been picked up for vagrancy by the overzealous sheriff of the ironically named town of Hope (''It's a quiet little town . . . but that's the way we like it, and I get paid to keep it that way'') and brutalized by sadistic deputies to such an extent that he has flashbacks to his torture by the Vietcong. This treatment turns him into the ultimate fighting machine, with whom no amount of police, national guardsmen, helicopters, antitank weapons and even Doberman Pinschers can cope.

Transformed into a superman, Rambo is the definitive guerrilla warrior, displaying jungle skills that would be the envy of a Tarzan. One of the police ostensibly trying to bring him to ground says that ''we ain't huntin' him, he's huntin' us.'' His remark literally comes true as Rambo turns on his pursuers and launches a one-man war that turns the town of Hope into a burnt-out, napalmed, no-man's land.

This is the ultimate revenge fantasy of every Vietnam veteran who was ever humiliated by the homecoming reception he did or didn't receive. Moreover, in the few bits of dialogue he mumbles (Stallone acts mainly with his pectorals), especially in a concluding, sobbing, almost psychotic monologue directed at his former Green Beret commander, Colonel Trautman (Richard Crenna), Rambo makes clear the rationale for his rampage. For him, there are no ''friendly civilians'' and, delivering his nebulous version of the "stab in the back" thesis, says "Somebody didn't want us to win." The audience may begin to agree with Rambo after viewing this cartoon portrait of a neon-lit, wasteland town complete with stupid sheriff and bungling, ineffectual national guardsmen. Here is a corrupt, homefront world that seems incapable of providing support for any coherent project, let alone the war in Vietnam.

Despite this message, however, the really wondrous impact of *First Blood* lies not in its creation of a superman hero with marvelous survival skills (he can minister to his own wounds and kill wild animals for meat) and almost magical abilities as a warrior (Stallone can rout a helicopter by merely throwing stones at it) but in the protean way in which Rambo reconciles and synthesizes so many of the war's contradictions. It's an accomplishment that had audiences flocking to see the film in such numbers that it rivaled even *E.T.* as the leading U.S. box-office attraction. The film was particularly successful among white working-class audiences for whom Stallone held a special status because of his identification with the working-class hero in *Rocky*. Among other things, the character of Rambo combined the twin 1970s movie metaphors of the wounded vet and the superman in the same persona without any hint of contradiction or irony. By making Rambo simultaneously into a hippie-drifter and a misunderstood patriot, the superman united the external characteristics of those who dissented from the war with those who fought in and supported it. Finally, Rambo's attacks on a complacent and conformist society placed the long-feared Vietnam vet in the company of other gentler, more-reflective American movie heroes (e.g., Capra's Mr. Smith) who fought lonely and individualistic battles against the shallowness and corruption of established social and political institutions.

However, in this film the individual is a fighting machine, a trained killer who can do nothing else in life. And though Rambo's behavior has supposedly been shaped by the war, the film clearly takes pleasure in his murderous skills and gives no sign that he has ever any different. In turning this mentally unconscious figure (or physique) into a new American hero, one senses a whiff of fascism (unconscious, of course) in the air. In addition to its homage to psychopathic behavior, the film turns the roving Green Beret Colonel Trautman (Richard Crenna), Rambo's former commander, into the voice of reason—the only man who can control him ("I didn't come here to rescue Rambo, I came here to rescue you from Rambo"). Transforming one of the war's most destructive symbols, the Green Berets, into peacemakers and symbols of benign power is just one example among many of Stallone's utter disregard of history.

In contrast to the supposed sanity manifested by the Green Beret colonel, the local people and authorities are xenophobic, belligerent, and seem to be the main stumbling blocks to the Vietnam vet's smooth reentry to society. By extension, one could begin to blame the conduct of the war on the people rather than the state, although it's doubtful Stallone meant to give the film an antipopulist twist. Stallone's aim, however, was to exult in the Vietnam vet, attack the ''maggots'' (the antiwar demonstrators and those who had no respect for or subverted the vets), and allow the Reagan administration, with Trautman as its representative, to stand beyond criticism. (Of course, this notion could not stand much scrutiny since aside from rhetoric and symbols the Reagan administration had systematically undercut or destroyed almost all programs that attempted to aid the Vietnam vet's readjustment.)

That this notion of the federal government hardly sustained much faith even among film makers is evidenced by the depiction of the returned black Vietnam POW Eddie Keller, played by Richard Pryor, in Michael Pressman's film of James Kirkwood's novel *Some Kind of Hero* (1982). Originally written about Kirkwood's Korean War homecoming, the film nonetheless turns the character of Eddie Keller into a timeless, slapstick Job. He's a victim who, upon returning to the States after six years of internment as a POW in Vietnam, finds that his wife has left him for another man, whom their daughter now calls ''daddy,'' and that they have lost all his money in the interim. This throws Keller into bankruptcy and renders him incapable of aiding his mother, who is about to be evicted from her nursing home. Eddie is unable to help her because he can't collect his Veteran's benefits, the army considering him practically treasonous for signing a confession while a prisoner (an act committed after numerous refusals, and then only because he wanted to get medical attention for his dying cellmate).

To some, this plague of problems and distress might seem excessive and pure Hollywood. Compared, however, to the real life of black fighter pilot Colonel Fred V. Cherry, who spent seven years as a POW and returned home to find that his wife had left him and had borne a child to another man and that his two sons had enlisted in the army and who finally had to sue the army for $150,000 in back payments because of their negligence, it might even be considered mild.[29]

Whether or not Colonel Cherry's ordeal was a case of life following art is not really as relevant to our concerns as the fact that *Some Kind of Hero* is another example of Richard Pryor's enormous talent again triumphing over either totally inept or mediocre material. The victim of a long series of junk movies (e.g., *Stir Crazy* [1980], *Bustin' Loose* [1981]), Pryor's serio-comic gifts enable him to achieve an extremely subtle performance despite a script that includes a whore with a heart of gold (even here, however, Pryor and his costar Margot Kidder, as Toni the high-priced Beverly Hills call girl, succeed in creating one of the screen's rare inter-racial affairs that is casual and unselfconscious) and a tedious, overly extended episode where he outwits the mob.

There are a number of truly comic and satiric moments in the film as, for example, Pryor complains to his North Vietnamese captors that they have steamed his roaches instead of sauteeing them the way he likes them. In a more socially pointed scene, which takes place upon Eddie's arrival back in the States, a media crew alternately prods and coaxes a reluctant but disoriented Pryor into kissing the ground and stumbling over a few absurd, upbeat words about the prison experience making him a better person. There is also a depiction of the callous military bureaucracy throwing up legal roadblock after legal roadblock (which even a friendly officer, Colonel Bowers [Ron Cox] can't circumvent) to hinder Eddie in his quest to obtain the benefits that are rightly his. Finally, in the tradition of *The Best Years of Our Lives*, Eddie tries to get a bank loan but in this instance is rejected. Through it all, Pryor invests Eddie with the kind of physicality that effortlessly conveys feelings of nausea and hysteria, tears and laughter, without skipping a beat.

Unfortunately, despite the virtuoso nature of the performance that almost succeeds in papering over some of the film's major flaws, there is still a void at its core. This becomes especially evident when one remembers that Pryor is black and that the film quite consciously seems to avoid almost every opportunity for dealing with the special problems of the black Vietnam vet. Rather than even attempt to flesh out some of the grim statistics that dog the black Vietnam vet or to treat them in a mildly satiric form, given the comic talents of Pryor, the film either dodges them completely or, where it can't, buries them under gobs of sentiment. Thus Eddie is said to have owned a bookstore before he was drafted. This fact hardly squares with the situation of the mass of black GIs who joined the army to escape unemployment and life in the streets. By the same token, there is hardly a mention of the high rate of black combat deaths during the war (25 percent in 1965 and 12.5 percent for the war overall) or that the rate of postwar unemployment, divorce, drug addiction, and imprisonment among black vets was likely to be twice that of whites. But so expertly and coolly is the supposedly hapless Eddie able to outwit the sharks of organized crime—combining the professionalism of a Raffles, the cracksman, with the daring of a James Bond—that we feel the closest he might have come to post-traumatic stress syndrome is the Sunday crossword.

Also, although Eddie's cellmate Vinnie (Ray Sharkey) is initially portrayed as a rather mild racist (a trait that gets swiftly shunted aside by their mutual prison ordeal and Vinnie's tragic death), the film does not give any real sense of the level and extent of the racism and racial tension and conflict that existed in Vietnam. While possibly submerged in combat under the slogan "same mud, same blood," behind the lines these powerful emotions often resulted in race riots and racially motivated fraggings. They produced tensions so great that one black GI remembered, "When I heard that Martin Luther King was assassinated my first inclination was to run out and punch the first white guy I saw. I was hurt. All I wanted to do was go home."[30]

These omissions (undoubtedly made in the effort to foster Pryor's crossover box office appeal) transformed the character of Eddie from one who might have had some relevance to the experience of the black Vietnam vet into a bleached-out and comic version of a contemporary Candide. As a result, it is rather hard to see any parallels between this character and the superman Rambo. Nonetheless, they do exist and, as a matter of fact, reveal some interesting changes in the perception of the Vietnam vet. The most significant of these is that both are shown as returning to a society that is hostile to them and that both must become outlaws in order to survive and to maintain any semblance of self-respect.

When this is added to the realization that the audience not only identified with these heroes but revealed in their victories (particularly wallowing in the physical destruction dished out by Rambo), a sense that something new was afoot in the image of the Vietnam vet began to emerge. What is clear is that the vet in these films is a far cry from the passive victim or deranged psychopath of earlier Vietnam works. Indeed, the Vietnam vet here assumes the guise of a character who is alternately to be feared, not a little bit envied, and even admired.

The growing sense of respect for the Vietnam vet was hardly restricted to the mass audience. A number of intellectuals and writers, former opponents of the war, now spoke and wrote of the Vietnam vet as having become a better person for his wartime experience. James Fallows, former presidential speech writer for Jimmy Carter, *Atlantic Monthly* editor, and a draft resister during the war, said, "It's probably true that the ones who went—who had to cope with permanent irreversible situations in a personal sense—were strengthened and became more mature through the experience."[31] Even stronger and more controversial were the sentiments expressed in a 1981 *New York Times* article by former draft resister and poet Michael Blumenthal, who wrote,

To put it bluntly, they (the Vietnam vets) have something we haven't got. It is to be sure, somewhat vague, but nonetheless real and can be embraced under several headings; realism, discipline, masculinity (kind of a dirty word these days), resilience, tenacity, resourcefulness. . . . I'm not sure they didn't turn out to be better men in the best sense of the word.[32]

Dubbed "Vietnam guilt chic" by some critics,[33] these feelings nonetheless represented a new vision of the Vietnam vet. When combined with the comments of *Newsweek* magazine editor and Vietnam marine officer William Broyles that "it's an amazing discovery to find men putting their hands on the levers of American business, politics and media, who were there (Vietnam)'', it seemed like something of a sea change was at work in American culture.[34] One anecdote told by a Vietnam vet best sums up the new state of affairs. Listening to a young man and woman in a restaurant arguing about the war, he heard the young man talk about his wartime experiences. Something about them rang false. He interrupted and then, after a "heated debate" with the young man, the couple left. Later, however, the young man returned and apologized, explaining to the vet that "you were right. I didn't go to Vietnam, but those stories are the best way to score with girls."[35]

Although one would be hard pressed to find a film to match the unabashed opportunism of this remark, a cinematic footnote to it was provided by the film *Americana* (1983). Despite being released in 1983, it was produced in the mid-1970s and provided one of the earliest glimpses of the more-positive image of the Vietnam vet in film, thus it historically anticipated the heroes of both *First Blood* and *Some Kind of Hero*.

Produced, directed, and starred in by David Carradine, *Americana* deals with a silent, inexpressive returned vet on his way cross-country finding a broken-down carousel in a rural Kansas hamlet in the middle of the wheat fields. He decides to stay and fix it. Met at first by indifference and then hostility from the loutish townspeople, he nonetheless succeeds in rebuilding the carousel, an act motivated by either postwar contrition or a need to affirm some notion of community. In the end, the town forgets its anger (for the moment) and gathers around the carousel.

Unfortunately, the film is given to a leisurely pace and long takes that reveal little; it is so muted and understated that its point becomes imperceptible. The characters in *Americana* are equally inexplicable. Barbara Hershey plays an enigmatic, sexually loose plains nymph, complete with worn housedress, who flits in and out of the frame for no particular reason. And Carradine's alienated Vietnam captain, who has been so traumatized and repelled by the war that he doesn't pick up his disability checks, gives us little but moody, sullen silences.

The film does have a nice feel for the flat Kansas landscape during a relentlessly hot summer, but the behavior of the townspeople, like that of the main characters, doesn't quite make sense. They're destructive and sadistic, enjoying cock fights and taking savage pleasure in Carradine's fight with a killer dog. One supposes their sadism and brutality have something to do with the way the American public responded to the Vietnam vets, but it's all rather inchoate and was done more successfully (*Americana* never had much of a release or run) by *First Blood* and *Some Kind of Hero*.

Whatever the success of *First Blood*, *Some Kind of Hero*, and *Americana* in refurbishing the image of the Vietnam vet, they were hardly isolated examples of the American Cinema's Vietnam War revisionism. Another, perhaps potentially more-significant trend toward revisionism actually sought to reverse the results of the war—at least in the American imagination. In a series of films that capitalized on the war's one remaining cause célèbre and, in the process, also unsuspectingly tapped a rich supply of unconscious national cultural mythology, there was nothing less than a rewriting of history wherein America won the war (albeit only in the movies).

Paradoxically, the tragic situation of the families of GIs missing in action was the immediate source of inspiration for this bit of solace to the nation's self-esteem. Of the reported 2,500 MIAs, many were presumed dead but their bodies never recovered. Another number (and here the count varied) were considered by many to be alive and held captive by the Vietnamese, a belief sustained by numerous but totally unconfirmed and unofficial reports.[36] These reports were cited by anguished relatives and their supporters to justify an aggressive and sometimes strident campaign to force the U.S. government into obtaining their release or at least an official accounting of these men.

By no means, however, was the campaign to free the MIAs limited to conventional approaches such as petitioning and lobbying. In November 1982, a former Green Beret colonel, James B. Gritz, and a group of his followers were foiled on their attempt to launch a raid into Laos intended to free the Americans reported to be held captive there. The raid, whose most noteworthy achievement was its theatricality, was hardly diminished by the fact that it was partially financed by two Hollywood stars, William Shatner (*Star Trek*) and Clint Eastwood (*Dirty Harry*), both of whom wanted the rights to the story should the raid prove successful.

Needless to say, even the failure of the raid didn't deter Hollywood, as it could always recoup and succeed on the screen. Within six months of the affair, violence-loving director-producer John Milius (*Conan the Barbarian*), *First Blood* director Ted Kotcheff, and scriptwriter Joe Gayton turned the ill-fated Gritz raid into a film called *Uncommon Valor* (1983).

Taking its title from Admiral Chester W. Nimitz's World War II comment that "uncommon valor was a common virtue" among the marines at the battle of Iwo Jima, the movie opens with a stunning, slow-motion (Vietnamese music on the sound track) sequence.[37] This scene not only serves as the basis of the film's narrative but also functions as a metaphor for U.S. abandonment of both the fight in Vietnam and those still missing in action. In it, an ambushed U.S. patrol rushes pell mell through rice fields to escape in a helicopter sent out to rescue them. In their flight, a number of the marines are shot and wounded, and at least one marine stops to pick up a wounded buddy and carry him to the helicopter. Disregarding the agonized pleas of his buddies, the panic-stricken pilot takes off and the marine is left behind despite frustrated attempts to reach out to him. The scene remains frozen in time and in the memory of Marine Colonel Jason Rhodes (Gene Hackman), the father of the forgotten man. It becomes Rhodes's obsessive quest to find and free his son regardless of government indifference, discouragement, even outright opposition and Asian treachery and violence.

To accomplish this task, Rhodes enlists some of the members of his son's former platoon: the bronzed, beach bum-surfer cum explosives expert Blaster (Reb Brown); a nightmare-ridden, Vietnam tunnel rat turned postwar sculptor, Wilkes (Fred Ward); two former helicopter pilots, the apathetic Charts (Tim Thomerson) and upwardly mobile black hospital administrator Curtis Johnson (Harold Sylvester); a drug-blasted, grenade-carrying ex-Hells Angel, Sailor (Randall "Tex" Cobb); and a mysterious young man who never served in Vietnam but whose father, it is subsequently revealed, is MIA. It's a dirty half-dozen who join Rhodes out of feelings of guilt; the sheer need for exuberant adventure and risk; and most powerfully, their inability to purge the war from their minds.

Also enlisted are our memories of war films ranging from *Bataan* (1943) to *Bridge on the River Kwai* (1957), since the film evokes those multitudes of platoons who trained for hazardous, even suicidal missions and in the process achieved almost transcendental levels of professionalism and camaraderie (with a rite of passage into manhood for one or two of their number thrown into the bargain). Seen in these terms, *Uncommon Valor* is a concordance of war-movie themes, enlivened and energized by the fluidity and tactical skill with which Kotcheff stages the training, attack, and action sequences. (They are so well done that they actually breathe life into the nearly moribund genre.)

If *Uncommon Valor* suggests old war movies in its use of shoot-'em-up action, its mood reflects more the recent phenomenon of right-wing populist pessimism about the United States. The film skillfully presents an us-against-them portrait of a profoundly linked group of Vietnam vets against a fearful government without the will to rescue the MIAs. Coupled with this portrait is more than a hint of disgust and distrust for the U.S. socioeconomic system, since Rhodes implicitly contends that the callous postwar treatment of Vietnam vets stems from the fact that they committed one of capitalism's most unpardonable sins—"You lost, that's a little like going bankrupt." Of course, this doesn't prevent him from accepting financial backing from high-handed oil magnate MacGregor (Robert Stack), who shares with Rhodes a son missing in action and a contempt for politicians. Finally, there is a not-so-subtle jab at the antiwar movement in Rhodes's comment that this time, "no one can dispute the rightness of what we're doing." All in all the film adds up to a sharp indictment of an ineffectual government and a callous, uncaring society plus a retrospective affirmation of a war whose only limitation was that we didn't win.

Nevertheless, the film's makers are too much in love with action for its own sake—helicopter attacks, exploding bridges, and commie killing—to seriously pursue the antigovernment line of the film to its logical, antidemocratic conclusions. Although he is made the spokesman for these ideas, Hackman's Colonel Rhodes is characterized by such stoic restraint that he prevents the film from degenerating into a fascist rant. A former marine himself, Hackman injects none of the machismo or chauvinism of a John Wayne into his performance. Instead, Hackman's Rhodes, a man with a family military tradition that stretches back to Gettysburg, hides his pain and feelings of loss behind iron self-control. His is a steely discipline breached only in his dreams (one especially of his son as a child entering his room at night to ask for his protection) and in a brief, affectionate parting recitation to his men, on the eve of the raid, of some lines from Shakespeare's *Julius Caesar*.

> And whether we shall meet again I know not.
> Therefore our everlasting farewell take:
> For ever, and for ever, farewell. . . .
> If we do meet again, why, we shall smile;
> If not, why then, this parting was well made.[38]

Although this bit of classicism seems to stand out rather curiously in a film so otherwise zealously devoted to action, the script is actually replete with references to classical myths such as Jason and the Argonauts and epics like *The Odyssey*. Nevertheless, despite its suggestion of old war films, the film's most significant debt was to John Ford's 1956 western *The Searchers*. It was a debt openly acknowledged by the film's producer John Milius who, besides claiming to have seen the film at least 60 times and naming his son after its hero, Ethan Edwards, also said that "there is a *Searchers* reference in all my films."[39]

However, more important than this film's references to *The Searchers* (which even included the quote, "We're going home, buddy") or the Ford film's influence on contemporary film makers was *The Searchers'* unique applicability to the Vietnam and post-Vietnam era. As one critic noted, "It is no accident that the critical re-evaluation of *The Searchers* proceeded during the Vietnam war."[40]

Ford's film tells the story of the frontiersman and ex-Confederate soldier Ethan Edwards (John Wayne), who searches for years for his kidnapped niece, only to find that with the passage of time she has grown to accept and even love her Indian captors. It is a dark, powerful narrative filmed in luminous images that dealt with U.S. racism and colonialism in ways that have special relevance to the Vietnam War. In the same vein, in the post-Vietnam period, the film's embodiment of one of America's oldest and most-enduring archetypical forms—the captivity myth—rendered it perfectly suited for dealing with the MIA issue.

Initially created by the Puritans, captivity narratives told of pure, virtuous white men and women taken prisoner by devilish, ogrelike Indians who tempted them into sinful practices of the flesh and spirit. In so doing, the narratives incorporated the Puritan fear that the American wilderness, a world of chaos, would corrupt them spiritually and thus undermine their religious mission in the New World. The Indians, however, don't succeed in subverting the piety of their captives. In fact, captivity is a means by which the prisoners rediscover God's will and move toward a greater inner discipline, controlling the fragmentation of values that often accompanied emigration.

As these tales evolved, there eventually emerged the figure of the fearless, stoic hunter-hero (e.g., Daniel Boone, Hawkeye) whose intimacy with the wilderness and insight into the Indian ethos gave him the ability to fight the Indians on their own terms. This precursor to Rambo remained linked to white social values but could still survive the wilderness after being reduced to barest essentials. Most important, he succeeded through his violent ordeal in wresting the savage land away from the Indians and projected into the future a white man's agrarian Arcadia. This assumption of the culture's destiny and virtue is the justification for our expropriation of the wilderness and for what historian Richard Slotkin called a "regeneration through violence."[41]

The power of this cultural archetype was evident in the rhetoric of the Vietnam War years. In his 1965 Johns Hopkins University speech, Lyndon Johnson used images that might literally have been lifted from the captivity narratives. Painting a picture of families assaulted by the dark forces of savagery, he said,

And it is a war of unparalleled brutality: Simple farmers are targets of assassination and kidnapping. Women and children are strangled in the night because their men are loyal to the government. And helpless villages are ravaged by sneak attacks.[42]

In fact, one need only substitute the words *red Indian* for *Vietnamese reds* in these sentences to hear echoes of the Boone tales' creator John Filson's line that "the innocent husbandman was shot down while cultivating the soil of his family's supply."[43] Likewise, in comments like those of the U.S. officer who announced during the Tet offensive that "we had to destroy the city in order to save it," there is more than a mild suggestion of this "regeneration through violence."[44]

Aside from its title, *The Deer Hunter* is filled with references to the hunter-hero and obliquely to the captivity narrative; for instance, Michael's return to Saigon to rescue Nicky from his self-imposed imprisonment. Intimations of the archetype can also be seen in *Apocalypse Now*'s Captain Willard, who journeys upstream to terminate the jungle-crazed Colonel Kurtz.

Uncommon Valor leaned even more heavily on the captivity theme. Milius applied these seemingly neglected archetypal notions to the Vietnam War and used them to structure the film's narrative, thus placing it within the popular culture tradition of "redemptive violence." These classic American myths provided a basis for future films about the war and also allowed the public to perceive for the first time our involvement in Vietnam as both just and victorious (something that earlier films about the war [with the possible exception of *The Green Berets*] was unable to accomplish). *Uncommon Valor* projected a number of popular fantasies that fit neatly into the Reaganite temper of patriotic self-congratulation and assertions of the national will that dominated the spirit of the 1980s. In essence, the film tries to finally convince the American people that the Vietnam War was indeed a noble cause.

In attempting to tack the myth of redemptive violence onto the Vietnam experience, *Uncommon Valor* falls short of its goal, because nowhere in the film is there a parallel to the character so central to the mythic paradigm, the hunter-hero. Hackman, for all the quiet power and dignity of his performance, portrays Rhodes as too much the stoic professional soldier (even to the film's stiff-upper-lipped conclusion, when he watches the rescued POWs' joyous reunion with their families with the painful knowledge that his own son died in captivity) to allow much room for such a character to take shape. The closest he comes to the legendary model—who retains his hold on civilization while adopting the skills of the Indians to defeat them—in his use of the guerrilla-raid stratagem to free the POWs. In addition, the film's focus on the group's interdependence and the revival of the men's wartime bonds provide very little opportunity for a character of such dimension to emerge.

Hollywood, however, had a stereotype conveniently close at hand to match the character of the hunter-hero. Indeed, the Vietnam superman, with his ability to survive the moral and psychic wilderness of Southeast Asia, seemed a ready-made counterpart to the hunter-hero. Nor did Hollywood lack for aspirants to the role. Still, it did come as something for a surprise that the first film star who successfully grafted the character of the superman onto an updated version of the captivity narratives was not someone from the front rank of Hollywood's macho elite (Bronson, Eastwood, Reynolds, etc.), but the karate-champ idol of the 42nd Street murder-and-mayhem circuit, Chuck Norris.

Upon reflection, however, Norris seems an almost perfect choice for the role. His half-Indian parentage links him to the half-primitive, half-civilized element in the character of the legendary hero, and his mastery of the martial arts (acquired during a stint as an airman in South Korea and later parlayed into a world middle-weight karate championship) fulfills the tradition of the hunter-hero, who adopts the skills of the natives in order to defeat them. Furthermore, by applying the advice of his screen mentor Steve McQueen to let his fists and feet do the talking for him, he had already established the screen persona of a mild-mannered, taciturn loner who singlehandedly puts to rout a whole host of sleazy villains (*Force of One, Lone Wolf McQuade*). Sharing the ideology of yet another film idol, John Wayne ("I'm a conservative a real flag waver"), Norris allowed little room for any of the ambiguities of the earlier superman, which made him ideally suited to lead a victorious assault against a different sort of barbaric foe—the Vietnamese commies.[45]

Strictly speaking, the films *Missing in Action* (1984) and *Missing in Action 2: The Beginning* (1985) weren't Norris' first foray into Vietnam. In his first starring role in *Good Guys Wear Black* (1979), Norris plays John Booker, a former Vietnam commando turned (unbelievably) professor, who uncovers the plot of a power-hungry diplomat (James Franciscus) to set up a Booker-led CIA rescue mission of POWs so that it would fail. As Secretary of State, the diplomat later systematically kills off the mission survivors in order to cover up his wrongdoing. Despite the fact that the film has some striking flashback battle scenes (shot in darkness) and even contains the themes elaborated upon in subsequent Norris films about Vietnam of weak-kneed, alcoholic, corrupt, sometimes even criminal U.S. government officials (they even collaborate with the North Vietnamese) who hindered our war effort, the film is still very much a domestic thriller.

In contrast, *Missing in Action* and its sequel take place in Vietnam and Southeast Asia, and they are filled with references to the war, the captivity narratives, and the myth of redemptive violence. Norris (Colonel Braddock) is fully at home in the role of the inexpressive, individualistic hunter-hero as Vietnam superman and hardly needs much prompting to adapt the hunter-hero's tactic of using the enemy's stratagem of guerrilla combat and his skill in the martial (as well as every other military skill) arts to achieve his goal of freeing the POWs. Except for the beginning of the first film, when he initially gives the impression of being something of a wounded hero complete with bad dreams and flashbacks to his torturous internment, there is hardly a moment when he isn't wreaking havoc on the Vietnamese.

In the 1984 film, once he hears of a congressional delegation that is going to Saigon to investigate the MIA situation, Braddock quickly jettisons any feelings of postwar guilt and alienation and springs into action. When he arrives in the renamed Ho Chi Minh City, he hears himself denounced as a war criminal by the Vietnamese. This hardly stops him from making a dramatic and dangerous solo nighttime reconnaissance expedition (leaping acrobatically from roof to roof) around the city in an attempt to locate the prison camp where the MIAs are being held. Pausing only long enough to round up his wartime buddy Tuck (M. Emmet Walsh) and some sophisticated military gear in Thailand, he proceeds to liberate the MIAs at the expense of literally hundreds of Vietnamese soldiers, whose bodies he leaves littering the landscape. Instead of heading home, he rushes the former MIAs into a conference chamber just as the Vietnamese make the announcement (with the U.S. delegation in seeming passive agreement) that there are no POWs left in Vietnam.

Through all these heroics, Norris (like all previous Vietnam supermen) remains invulnerable and imperturbable. Clad in black (reminiscent of his *Good Guys Wear Black* and, coincidently, of the Vietcong's battle attire of a black pajamalike outfit) or dressed in a camouflage suit, he roams Vietnamese cities and countryside alike with the freedom of any practiced hunter-hero who can just as easily carry out a successful guerrilla raid as he can dispatch a Vietnamese with either a karate chop or a grenade.

Contriving, however, to create a character who is both Vietnam superman and hunter-hero, an honest man who has no use for diplomacy or bureaucratic rules, is hardly *Missing in Action*'s only distinction. Like *Uncommon Valor*, *Missing in Action* also uses the terrible plight of the U.S. captives and the cruelty of their Vietnamese captors to reverse history and turn the Americans into victims and the Vietnamese into stock World World II B-movie vicious and duplicitous Jap villains. They are given to such sick, savage, and reprehensible actions that the film creates and justifies the context for another version of a regeneration through violence. In this version, the killing of hundreds of Vietnamese aims at something more than Norris pandering to the blood lust and love of action of his audience. Although the film does not pretend to be a serious political work, the violence suggests that the U.S. fighting man is still formidable and, if given a second chance and freed from government constraints and weakness, would have won the war.

Missing in Acton 2: The Beginning (1985) adds very little to this fantasy. Hundreds more Vietnamese are dispatched in all manner of ways from garroting to plastique, all of which undoubtedly seem a welcome evening of the score to the audience, since the cruelty of the Vietnamese (who flout all of the Geneva conventions in this film) might make even the Marquis de Sade wince. In one particularly heinous act of torture devised to make him confess his alleged war crimes, Braddock is hung by his heels and his head covered by a bag that contains a rat. Of course, Braddock expertly kills the rat with his teeth.

Instances of improbable action here surpass all bounds. For example, the prison camp where Braddock and his fellow Americans (not to mention a substantial number of Vietnamese) are being held is supposed to be located in an isolated jungle fortress. In reality, it seems to be right off a main highway near Hanoi. A number of visitors pass through, including a smooth French mercenary, who arrives by helicopter with whores. The mercenary is a partner in the opium trade with the insidious, sadistic, riding-booted prison commander, who behaves more like a war lord than a North Vietnamese Communist ideologue. Another guest is a nervy, foolhardy Australian journalist, who turns up looking for a story on MIAs and gets his brains blown out for his troubles. Nobody appears concerned about the logic of these incongruous characters turning up, all of them seeming to have wandered in from another action-adventure B film.

The center of the film remains Braddock's escape and subsequent revenge. Still, the film takes a perfunctory stab at social significance by creating an alter ego to the loyal, unwavering Braddock—a black POW officer who collaborates with the Vietnamese to get favorable treatment for himself and because he feels the U.S. government has written the POWs off. But since he's balanced by a loyal, malaria-ridden black officer who is burned alive by the demonic Vietnamese camp commander, and because he himself finally turns against the Vietnamese, all of it adds up to merely another plot wrinkle; there is no real suggestion here that the Vietnamese could have used black grievances and resentments against U.S. society to sow dissension among the prisoners.

Firmly disposing of this unwelcome thought, the film can get on to its major order of business: Braddock's one-man demolition of the Vietnamese. He accomplishes this task with his usual cool, methodical efficiency and concludes with a slam-bang, crowd-pleasing karate contretemps between him and the brutal camp commander. The fight reduces the ideological differences to a one-on-one power struggle where, of course, the Vietnamese is beaten to a pulp and blown up in payment for all the evil that he has done.

Their obvious and painful shortcomings aside, both *Missing in Action* and its sequel had interesting, although unintended, consequences. By fusing into one identity the characteristics of the Vietnam superman and the hunter-hero and by placing him within the context (originated in *Uncommon Valor*) of a contemporary version of the captivity tales, these films took a giant step in the creation of a set of conventions for the Vietnam War film. Even though it had long eluded Hollywood directors (one major reason so few films were made about the war during its active military phase), there now seemed a way to tie the Vietnam War to the codes of the traditional war film. The films provided a rationale for the loss of the war (irresponsible or corrupt politicians), a popular war-film hero, and a perfidious and demonic enemy. They also reversed the tactical and historic roles of the Americans and Vietnamese—it is the Americans who are both the victims and the guerrillas here—while ignoring the real circumstances of the war. No mention or images of carpet bombing, the use of Agent Orange, search-and-destroy missions, or strategic hamlets disrupt the familiar war-film heroics of these works. And the films had no difficulty gaining popularity with audiences, since they guaranteed plenty of exciting and bloody action, little extraneous dialogue, and even the illusion of a final glorious victory. Theirs was a success that hardly diminished with repetition.

If nothing else, both *Missing in Action* and *Uncommon Valor* might seem to have served as warm-ups for what was acknowledged as the apotheosis of this budding cycle, *Rambo: First Blood Part II* (1985). Intended to some extent to answer those critics who claimed that Sylvester Stallone couldn't succeed in anything but the role of Rocky, Rambo was soon elevated from the realm of mere box-office success ($57 million in the first two weeks) to that of a political byword. Helping it to attain this exalted status was undoubtedly the oft-repeated references to it by President Reagan. Renowned for lacing his speeches with snatches of "ordinary Joe" screen dialogue and for defining political conflicts in the simple Manichean terms of Hollywood genre films, Reagan first referred to *Rambo* in an angry polemic against a group of Arab terrorists who had hijacked a U.S. passenger plane in the Middle East ("Boy, I saw *Rambo* last night; now I know what to do next time").[46] Later, in his drive to get Congress to enact tax-reform legislation, he said, "In the spirit of Rambo, let me tell you we're going to win this time."[47] In a similar fashion, the film turned into something of a cause célèbre when it and *Rocky IV* (in which the Italian Stallion defeats a villainous Soviet superheavyweight champion in a bout billed as "World War III" in its advertisements) were denounced by the Soviets as "warnography."[48]

In comparison to *Rambo*, with its crude Russophobia, high-decibel murder and mayhem, and narcissistic camera worship of Stallone's glistening, nautilus-crafted body, the original *First Blood* seems an almost pastoral idyll. In fact, with its long shots of Pacific Northwest coastal mountains and rich green forests, its skillful blending of both Vietnam superman and wounded hero stereotypes in the character of Rambo, with just the right touch of counterculture alienation and working class patriotism, and its ultimate plea for tolerance and under-standing for the Vietnam vet, *First Blood* mutes some of its climax's more hysterical rhetoric. With its minimal body count (only one particularly sadistic cop dies, and even the bullheaded sheriff who initiates the trouble suffers nothing more than a deep flesh wound), the film could be mistaken by someone with cataracts as being about a natural man's struggle to survive in the wilderness.

Despite the differences between the two films, in the sequel Rambo still sustains some lingering traces of the qualities that marked his debut. Unlike the red, white, and blue patriotism of Norris's Colonel Braddock or the cool professionalism of Hackman's Colonel Rhodes, there remain residues of the original character's alienation and nihilism in Stallone's noncom patriot. In fact, despite his vaunted declaration at the film's conclusion that the only thing that he and the MIAs he had rescued wanted was for "our country to love us as much as we love it," there is a strong feeling that America's sudden affection and concern may be too little and too late. As a result, there is inherent in Rambo's manner (and by extension for many other Vietnam vets) a touch of insubordination; a defiant stance that seems to hold congressmen, military officers, and even other Americans in only slightly less contempt than the Soviets and Vietnamese. Rambo, like the poet whose name he bears and sensibility he lacks, projects the feeling of a man who, having spent a "season in hell" (a fact confirmed by his commander Colonel Trautman's statement that "what you choose to call hell, he calls home") will never be the same again.

Almost as if *Rambo* aspired to a conscious imitation of Rimbaud's line, "Among the shipwrecked you chose me," the film opens with Rambo's rescue from a prison stockade stockpile where he was consigned after his *First Blood* rampage. From that moment on, after deciding to accept a secret mission into Vietnam and photograph the MIAs to prove their existence, the film degenerates into a rant against the U.S. government. From Rambo's mildly sardonic comment, "do we get to win this time?" to Colonel Trautman's agonized protest, "It was a lie like the whole damn war," the film becomes nothing less than a full scale *J'accuse*. It lashes out with particular venom against the opportunistic government bureaucrat Murdock (Charles Napier), who both inspires the MIA mission and wants it to fail so that the whole politically embarrassing issue would be buried once and for all. The treacherous Murdock is seen as a cartoon symbol of a soulless and impotent government that betrayed its own troops because it never had the will to win.

Coupled with this populist, superpatriotic backlash is a revival of the Red (Soviet) menace. In cold-war terms that would do credit to Herbert ("I Led Three Lives") Philbrick, the Soviets, led by an arrogant and sadistic military advisor, Colonel Podovsky (Steven Berkoff), have all the flair of Nazi SS villains—to the extent of viewing the Vietnamese in racist terms as "yellow scum." It is the Soviets, rather than the dim and suicidal Vietnamese rushing headlong into Rambo's gunfire (seemingly forgotten are the North Vietnamese military tactics that resulted in Dien-Bein-Phu and Tet), who are the real enemy in the film. In addition, the

Soviet torture of Rambo on a contraption that is part inner-spring mattress and part electric waffle iron (hardly a credit to the imagination and efficiency of the KGB inventors of psychiatric imprisonment) results in depicting the spreadeagled Rambo in an almost Christ-like fashion. Thus, after his inevitable escape, he is "resurrected" as both superman and hunter-hero.

It is more than a simple superman, however, who is resurrected. Stallone turns Rambo into a working-class echo of Brando's Colonel Kurtz. That is, whenever he can unlock his jaws, Rambo's mumbling dialogue consists of Kurtz-like Zen utterances such as, "To survive a war you must become a war," or "I've always thought the mind was the best weapon." Besides his variation on Kurtz, Rambo also shares the invincible warrior qualities (a "pure fighting machine") and sexual purity of Michael Vronsky. In fact, while destroying the enemy singlehanded-ly, he has a sexually chaste encounter with a woman guerrilla, Co, which amounts to nothing more than the exchange of a few shy but highly charged romantic words and glances. But before this relationship develops and undermines the warrior's strength and purpose, she is conveniently killed.

All of this pales, however, before the projection of Rambo as the hunter-hero or perhaps, in terms of Stallone's conception and performance, a scowling, statuesque noble savage. Once he's escaped from Soviet captivity and freed of all sentimental connection with the woman guerrilla, Rambo can get down to the really serious business of killing. Indeed, in these scenes Rambo strikingly veers from the traditional image of the hunter-hero figure who occupies a middle ground between savagery and civilization. Back home in the jungle, Rambo is stripped to the waist and of all restraint, a talisman from his dead love bound around his forehead, resembling nothing less than a primitive warrior. He carries an arsenal consisting of explosive tipped arrows and a serrated Bowie knife the size of a small shovel, coming closer to the image of an Indian brave on the warpath than to such mythical hunters as Daniel Boone, Davy Crockett, or James Fenimore Cooper's Hawkeye. Unlike the patriotic Braddock or the spartan Rhodes, with their proud nonviolent contempt for politicians, Rambo is not inclined to mute his rage when he has his most insidious enemy, Murdock, the government bureaucrat who set him up, cowering before him.

Nevertheless, it is Murdock's computers rather than his scalp that feel Rambo's final fury. In an uncontrolled Luddite-style outburst, he uses a machine gun to destroy Murdock's data-processing center. It is a seemingly senseless and futile act, but it has a great deal of symbolic effect. Rambo acts for all the ordinary Joes who feel oppressed by a cold, inhuman bureaucracy and experts who want to manipulate, rationalize, and abstract all sense of moral outrage and action. In this case, they are the bureaucrats who supposedly betrayed Rambo, the MIAs, and all those who fought in Vietnam. And for Stallone, the only proper response is the most primal one: armed revenge.

With this image of the insidious bureaucrat, *Rambo* goes one step beyond films like *Uncommon Valor* and *Missing in Action,* whose primary goal was to create the illusion of victory in Vietnam and might only in passing point an accusing finger at a politician. *Rambo,* however, not only nurtures the same illusion of victory in Vietnam but metes out symbolic punishment to the bureaucrats, and politicos, and by extension the system that sustains them.

The crowd-pleasing effect of these violent actions aside, there may have been some in the audience to whom this final act of retribution might, upon reflection, give pause. It's true that Rambo's act of vengeance successfully tapped populist resentment of the bureaucracy, but the film's being in touch with popular emotion did not require that it be dangerously simplistic in its search for scapegoats to explain what occurred in Vietnam. There is an underside to Rambo's supposed moral superiority to the politicians: an implicit feeling that he will never receive justice from the government and that his only possible alternative is destructive rage. It is the kind of festering nihilistic feeling that his poetic namesake Rimbaud wrote of a century before when he exalted in blood and denounced the idea of justice.[49]

This is not, however, the dominant strain in the film and never really undermines the otherwise unrelenting portrait of the United States triumphant in *Rambo.* In fact, in *Rambo,* the regeneration through violence begun with such spectacular results in *Uncommon Valor* and then carried forward with so much energy in *Missing in Action* came full cycle. The film's bloody cinematic humiliation of the Vietnamese and the Soviets and its freeing of the MIAs turned Rambo into a pop symbol for ordinary Americans and Reagan and a synonym for a resurrected feeling of American pride, power, and unabashed aggression.

Nevertheless, by adding a touch of primitivism to the archetypes of the superman and the hunter-hero, Stallone succeeded in connecting the character so closely to his own persona that he left little room for other directors to work out new variations on the character. As a result, although Stallone was able to add another Hollywood mythic hero to his personal pantheon of America Redux, alongside his working-class "great white hope" Rocky, he also brought the MIA cycle to a momentary (hopefully permanent) standstill.

It was a situation that time and events conspired to achieve, since there was a distinct possibility that the MIA problem might be on its way to a solution. Desiring better diplomatic and economic relations with the United States, the Vietnamese began to permit U.S. inspection teams to

Rambo: First Blood Part II

search for the remains of the missing, and they even admitted the possibility that a few Americans might be still held captive in areas remote from government control. This of course was not the sort of behavior that militant patriotic fantasies could be built around. In this case, the sadistic Communist devils turned out to be too rational and pragmatic for the rhetoric of both right-wing politicos and their cinematic counterparts.

None of this prevented Vietnam from becoming firmly established as background material in other genres and mediums. In television it became almost de rigueur for a cop or private investigator (e.g., *Miami Vice, Magnum P.I., Simon and Simon, The A Team*), perhaps to add weight to the characters, to have spent time in Vietnam. By the same token, one Hollywood production company decided that Vietnam would be an apt setting for romance, granting it an added psychological dimension. In *Purple Hearts* (1984), Vietnam seems at times to exist solely for the purpose of playing a role in the eternal triangle that usually keeps screen lovers apart.

In this case the conventional romantic duo is Dr. Don Jardine (Ken Wahl), a handsome, rebellious, but expert marine surgeon, and a beautiful, efficient, idealistic navy nurse, Debbie Soloman (Cheryl Ladd). What initially keeps this tough-talking boy separated from this insipid girl are not the horrors of war, but Hollywood's version of the old *Arrowsmith* dilemma. That is, after the Vietnam War, Jardine plans to become a rich and prominent surgeon, which leads Solomon, disillusioned by her own doctor father's intense commitment to the bottom line, to treat him like a leper. Of course, love and the accidents of war combine to overcome these and other contrived obstacles.

From the beginning, Jardine strikes one as a concerned, committed doctor who is willing to risk military punishment to take a wounded black GI to a Da Nang hospital and in battle even attempts to treat the enemy wounded. So it's predictable that by the film's conclusion they both end up dedicated to doing good works at a veteran's hospital unsurprisingly called American Hospital.

Purple Hearts is not only dominated by this romantic soap opera, but it provides an utterly sanitized image of the U.S. soldiers fighting in Vietnam. The GIs who appear in the film are drug free and fully committed to and uncritical of the war. Their officers are, for the most part, caring, paternal figures, and black and white soldiers live and fight against the common enemy in absolute harmony with each other. However, amid this inflated heroism and sense of community, the horrors of the war occasionally intrude. When it does, the film succeeds in constructing remarkably close reproductions of wartime situations. For example, when Jardine is shipped off for disciplinary reasons to the Khe

Sanh-like marine outpost under siege by the North Vietnamese, he is so emotionally ravaged seeing the dead scattered all about that he contemplates suicide.

It is in these moments that the Vietnam War, despite director Sidney Furie's (*The Boys in Company C*) best efforts to contain it within the confines of romantic soap opera and heroic melodrama, springs desperately to life. In short, no matter how much a film like *Purple Hearts* may have demonstrated the new-found adaptability of Hollywood formulas to the Vietnam War, a moment that awakened memory of an actual event like the siege of Khe Sanh could still suggest something of the harrowing quality of that experience. Therefore, whatever the skills Hollywood film makers exhibited in manipulating and evading the painful truths of the war, the victory of genre could never be fully complete. As long as this sort of event and other experiences like it appeared in film, they possessed the potential to subvert those Hollywood fantasies and stereotypes that were utilized to mask the nature of the war.

There is no more cogent reference to the limits of these conventions than a snatch of self-reflexive dialogue that occurs in one of the best Vietnam films (its Cambodian locale notwithstanding) of the 1980s, *The Killing Fields* (1984). In the scene, former *New York Times* Cambodian correspondent Sydney Schanberg (San Waterston), after having just received a prestigious journalism award for his Cambodian coverage, is confronted by his wartime colleague, freelance photographer Al Rockoff (John Malkovitch). Rockoff accuses Schanberg of doing nothing to rescue his Cambodian assistant Dith Pran (played by Dr. Haing Ngor, a Cambodian refugee and a nonprofessional actor), whom he was forced to abandon to the not-so-tender mercies of the Khner Rouge revolutionaries when he left Cambodia. Schanberg, tortured by his own sense of guilt over the affair, replies angrily (partially trying to justify himself) to Rockoff that "this is not a fucking forties movie; you can't just get on a plane and make the whole damn world come out right." And although the statement is essentially meant to convey something of Schanberg's frustration over his inability to help his friend, the remark also unintentionally highlighted the difference between *The Killing Fields* and the vast majority of Hollywood war films.

The goals of *The Killing Fields* are more ambitious and intricate than most other films. It not only attempts to evoke the wartime experiences of Schanberg and Pran, it tries to capture the tone and texture of the genocidal gulag that Cambodia (a.k.a. Kampuchea) became after the Khmer Rouge takeover in 1975. To achieve these ends, a group of Englishmen—producer David Puttnam (*Chariots of Fire*) former documentary director Roland Joffé, and screenwriter Bruce

Robinson—turned to an approach that Puttnam dubbed "operatic realism"[50] fusion of the gritty, documentary realism of *The Battle of Algiers* with the baroque grandeur of an *Apocalypse Now*.

Despite being stylistically powerful and original, the film doesn't quite achieve this grand formal fusion. Its most substantial flaw is its tendency to tilt dangerously in the direction of the male weepie when what it really wants to do is portray male bonding, particularly in the melancholy Schanberg's continuous, breast-beating, "Did I do right" mea culpas after he leaves Pran in Cambodia and Pran's dreamy-eyed interior monologues addressed to Schanberg from captivity. It also does not help matters that Waterston plays Schanberg as a stolid man, without personal tics beyond a mask of dignified seriousness, who shows almost no signs of an inner life. In fact, the ravages of war depicted here are viewed through an impersonal camera eye rather than filtered through the eyes and personality of Schanberg.

In the same manner, Schanberg and Pran are also depicted less in the mold of some crack newsteam of equals than as a reporter and his tag-along sidekick out on the trail of the big story. Despite both Pran's protestation that "I'm a newspaperman, too" (when Schanberg offers to help him leave the country with his family) and his dignified behavior and heroic action throughout the film, the relationship between Pran and Schanberg never gets beyond that of a loyal, self-sacrificing Gunga Din and a white colonial officer (without the comedy). It's a limited conception of Pran, exposing only his saintly side and excluding the practically gonzo-journalist part of his relationship with Schanberg, complete with smoking pot, bribing officials, and braying at the moon, that Schanberg described in the 1980 *New York Times Magazine* piece, "The Death and Life of Dirth Pran," that served as the basis for the film.

The film's bow to old Hollywood conventions and its inability to convey the nature of the Pran-Schanberg relationship are more than offset by the graphic, fast-paced, sometimes hand-held camera work of cinematographer Chris Menges, who tracks relentlessly through streets and hospitals capturing with great immediacy, the fires, chaos, blood, mutilation, and death that permeated Cambodia. There are also brilliantly composed images, like the one of four helicopters appearing suddenly like ominous giant insects in a clear blue sky, and a powerful, painful sound track filled with the shrieks of frightened people and the roar of rockets bursting all over the landscape. In fact, *The Killing Fields*'s gift for vividly recreating a disintegrating world demonstrates the capacity of fictional cinema to create imagistic correlatives of actual events that could convey both the emotional intensity and moral-political dimension far better than most other mediums.

Except for a few moments of photojournalism and documentary coverage of the war, there was relatively little else, until then, that

The Killing Fields

compares with *The Killing Fields*'s evocation of the wanton, callous nature of U.S. military power in Southeast Asia, the veil of secrecy it sometimes tried to draw over its actions, and the personal and political consequences of that policy. There is probably nothing that bears better witness to these themes than the close-up of an abandoned, terrified, and sobbing child amid the physically devastated, corpse-laden landscape of the accidentally bombed noncombatant town of Neak Luong. Nor is there any greater testimony to the bitter stonewalling and manipulation of U.S. officialdom than the bureaucratic stumbling blocks (not to mention the physical dangers) faced by Schanberg and Pran when they try to ferret out information about the tragedy and report it. Finally, nothing captures more completely the utter bankruptcy of U.S. policy in Southeast Asia than the noisy, tense scenes, without dialogue, of anxious Cambodians crowding around the U.S. embassy gates in an attempt to seek refuge from the Khmer Rouge takeover. Their flight takes place among whirring and careening helicopters sent to rescue U.S. officials and a select number of Cambodians. To accentuate the sense of debacle, we are presented with the desolate face of the U.S. ambassador's aide (Spalding Gray) as he sits sprawled on the floor of his office staring forlornly into space (pondering the disaster that surrounds him) while the chaotic and unceremonious evacuation proceeds.[51]

Along with these moments, *The Killing Fields* provides us with one of the few portraits of the horrific world that Cambodia became after the Khmer Rouge's totalitarian bamboo curtain closed upon it in 1975. Run by a secret elite referred to as Angca (High Organization), and led by the messianic (perhaps mad) revolutionary ideologue Pol Pot, the Khmer Rouge were responsible for the deaths of millions (some estimates range as high as 3 million) of Cambodians in their effort to destroy the cities and expunge all Western and intellectual influence and transform the country into one peasant commune. Nonetheless, their initial reception by a large portion of the people of Phnom Penh was a mixture of joy and relief that the war was finally over, and the film even pictures Dith Pran running to greet them shouting, "Paix! Paix!" That initial feeling of exhilaration would shortly turn into terror as the prepubescent, coke-guzzling revolutionaries of the Khmer Rouge, some no older than 13, were turned loose upon the populace to indulge themselves in an orgy of antiurban violence and destruction. It was a reign of terror that did not even exempt foreign journalists. In one of the film's most harrowing scenes, Schanberg and a number of other foreign journalists are held captive and menaced by a group of Khmer Rouge, until the equally terrified (but patient and humbly persistent) Dith Pran finally succeeds in negotiating their release.

But even these frightening moments are nothing compared with the film's evocation of "Cambodia Year Zero," the Khmer Rouge's crude and bloody attempt to totally transform Cambodian society by literally tearing it up by its roots and starting over again. Beginning with riveting images of long columns of refugees being brutally herded by the Khmer Rouge from the city of Phnom Penh to the countryside, the film captures the anxiety and barely submerged hysteria of people inhabiting a political nightmare. In addition, there are scenes of the desperate but ultimately futile efforts of the seemingly indefatigable Al Rockoff to forge a passport photo of Dith Pran to prevent his falling into their hands. The film also doesn't shy away from reminding us that what happened in Cambodia bears a striking resemblance to what occurred during the holocaust and in the Stalinist gulags.

It is these monstrous events that the film invokes in its second half, when depicting Dith Pran's experiences as an inmate in a reeducation camp in postrevolutionary Cambodia. In these camps, amid loud-speakers constantly drumming revolutionary slogans, back-breaking labor in the rice fields, public confessionals, continuous beatings, summary executions (using plastic bags over the heads of the victims to suffocate them), and starvation, the Khmer Rouge tried to create the new Kampuchea. They see themselves as building a society where every expression of individuality is eliminated and where the nuclear family was to be eradicated with the same ease and swiftness a child erases a diagram of it from a reeducation camp blackboard. In this society built on hate, the Party is all-powerful, demanding total obedience and moving young peasant revolutionaries to act like killer dogs sniffing out the slightest hint of counterrevolutionary sentiment or a concealed bourgeois past among the inmate-workers.

Throughout all these months of repression and dehumanization, Dith Pran maintains an indomitable will to survive. Staving off starvation by eating lizards and scorpions and sucking the blood of a still-living water buffalo while hiding his past behind an impenetrable wall of silence and feigned ignorance, he manages to stay alive while constantly thinking of ways to escape. Finally succeeding, he picks his way through actual killing fields of petrified vegetation (funereal music on the soundtrack) where the barely buried and sometimes just-scattered skulls and bones of the thousands who died in the Khmer Rouge bloodbath suffuse the landscape—a stunning metaphor for this revolution. He is recaptured, but this time his captivity is rendered a bit more humane, for he is protected by an older, urbane, English-speaking Khmer Rouge leader who is himself repelled by a revolution whose ideological commitments have turned into genocidal madness. The leader, knowing that he will be killed by the Khmer Rouge for questioning their policy, entrusts the care of his infant son to Pran and helps him plot his escape to Thailand just as the 1979 Vietnamese invasion of Kampuchea takes place.

This brief portrait of a sophisticated, sympathetic Communist is unique, since it is the first to appear in any of the films about the war. The leader is seen as a man who is repelled by the killing and fears for the future of his country. He speaks in the tones of a populist and patriot, not an ideologue, as he tells the silent Pran (still feigning non-comprehension): "I love my country. I have sacrificed everything for it. My wife died for the revolution. But the leaders of Angca no longer trust the people. Therefore, I can no longer trust them." These words suggest that even the Khmer Rouge, despite their barbarism, cannot be viewed only as some demonic monolith; that their revolution, like all revolutions (including the Vietnamese), encompasses a variety of personalities and ideological commitments—a historical reality that only *The Killing Fields,* of all the Vietnam films, even bothers touching on.

Given the film's unwillingness to turn Cambodia into a simple, Manichean world where there are good guys and bad ones, figures as divergent as archconservative speechwriter (for Nixon and Reagan) and political columnist Pat Buchanan and a sharp, English critic of U.S. policy in Cambodia, journalist-author William Shawcross *(Sideshow: Kissinger-Nixon and the Destruction of Cambodia)* could both discover aspects of *The Killing Fields* they could praise.[52] These reactions weren't too difficult to figure out, since in Buchanan's case the film's depiction of the bloodbath and gulags following the Khmer Rouge's takeover confirmed the direst predictions of conservatives about the nature of a Communist takeover of power. In a similar mode, moments in the film like Schanberg's angry response, "Maybe what we didn't estimate was the insanity that $7 billion worth of bombing would produce," and a reporter's question attempting to link responsibility for what happened in Cambodia to his and other journalists' underestimation of the brutality of the Khmer Rouge (Schanberg also evenhandedly admitted to underestimating their capacity for destruction) fit neatly into Shawcross's complex explanation of what took place in Cambodia.

Despite the fact that the film's primary aim was not to vindicate the bloody fantasies or the political analyses of the right or left, it did nonetheless, to paraphrase Czech novelist Milan Kundera, aid us in the struggle of memory against forgetting,[53] an act that is an integral part of the struggle of men against arbitrary and repressive power. The film's richly detailed evocation of a world that has become a gigantic abattoir reminds us (at least those of us who still see ourselves as part of the left) to reflect back on time when the Khmer Rouge were viewed as just one more Third World revolution against imperialism whose every horrendous act could be rationalized and absolved. It was a position that exemplified the worst of 1960s left sentimentality: romanticizing every Third World revolution as if their reality was no more bound by contradiction and ambiguity than a work of heroic poster art.

Of course, the film doesn't leave the right unscathed either. In one scene, a mournful Schanberg watches a television documentary about Cambodia filled with poignant reminders of the crimes and failures of our foreign policy. The documentary shows then-President Nixon justifying U.S. policy in Southeast Asia and ordering U.S. troops into Cambodia. That image of Nixon arouses memories that wash away the recent resurrection of his reputation among intellectuals and academics (owing in some degree to the invidious contrast his quasi-Metternichean foreign-policy triumphs like the opening to China make with the curious mixture of confusion and vagueness about decision making; the aggressive, patriotic rhetoric; and the preemptory military action that characterize Reagan's foreign policy). We cannot forget that Nixon (the duplicitous villain and not the statesman of détente) was the man who between 1969 and 1973 systematically expanded and intensified the war so that 20,553 Americans, 107,504 South Vietnamese, and an estimated 500,000 North Vietnamese lost their lives. And most important, in light of the film's depiction of U.S. bombings, it reminds us that it was the Nixon government that approved and perhaps even instigated Lon Nol's coup against Prince Sihanouk and the subsequent secret B-52 bombings (without congressional approval) that helped destabilize the previously neutral country and precipitated its slide into absolute chaos.[54]

However, the political and historical logic behind the actions of both the Khmer Rouge and the United States is merely implied. What the film makers want to primarily explore is neither ideology nor history, as much as they want to affirm the values of decency, loyalty, and liberty and to oppose those people who were willing to sacrifice human life to the cold necessities of ideology or program. There is one moment in the film that this affirmation begins to feel saccharine. In its final scene, the full tragedy of Cambodia-Kampuchea (a tragedy without a foreseeable end, which has added to its cast the North Vietnamese, the Chinese, and the Thais and still includes Pol Pot as a main actor) is too neatly submerged in the warm hugs, tears, and friendship of the reunited Schanberg and Pran.

Nevertheless, despite the embraces and the inflated sound of John Lennon's utopian "Imagine" on the sound track, the film's searing images of a landscape dominated by death linger on. *The Killing Fields* may have only sketched the ideological and political basis behind the Cambodian struggle, but it succeeds in providing an emotionally power-ful treatment of a war where U.S. impersonal contempt for the people of Cambodia combined with the more intimate and lethal murderousness of the Khmer Rouge to thoroughly shatter a whole society. The film achieves this without resorting to the outsized archetypes and stereotypes—the wounded vet, the superman, and the hunter-hero—that marked Hollywood's usual depiction of the war. Of course, this was as much an English film as a Hollywood product, which may help explain why the film was able to develop in Dith Pran a more human-sized and realistic symbol for the war. Pran's character in the film may have lacked psychological depth, but in his will to survive the most perilous and soul-destroying experiences, he demonstrates one of the few victories for the human spirit to come out of the charnel house of Cambodia and Vietnam.

Although hardly an entirely new phenomenon (there were already suggestions of this theme present in both *The Deer Hunter* and *Coming Home*), the survivor image and implications connected with the movie audience, especially in the cultural context in which it now appeared. This new climate of opinion was generated by the memorials and parades that offered a belated but cathartic homecoming to the vets. The well-publicized celebrations clearly signified the remarkable degree of emotional and intellectual reconciliation that had gone on between American society and the Vietnam vets.

No less revealing of this seismic change in American culture was the transformation of the vets' own attitudes toward the war. Thus, ex-Vietnam officer and ex-*Newsweek* editor William Broyles, Jr., returned more than a decade later to Vietnam and wrote *Brother in Arms: A Journey from War to Peace* (Knopf, 1986), a book about his visits to former enemies and old battlefields. Broyles's Vietnam War was not primarily built on madness and nihilism; he saw it almost disingenuously as "a great challenge" that gave him keen insight into his own "physical and emotional limits."[55] Still, he didn't close himself off totally from the war's agony, and he wrote that in Vietnam, "the war won and kept on winning."[56] However, his return there did not leave him filled with rage toward either the Vietnamese or our own government's policies but provided him with an intense feeling of solidarity with all those who fought in the war. He now understood that he "had more in common with my old enemies than anyone except the men that fought at my side."[57] There were other, more strident responses to the established canon about the war experience. Some veterans condemned the use of Vietnam by many of their fellow vets as an explanation for all their postwar problems as a con game. And one U.S. film director carried his revisionism even further by concluding that the Vietnam veteran, "because he lost the most, because he did it seemingly for nothing—will become the most romanticized war hero in American history."[58]

This prophecy clearly has not yet been fulfilled, but it does underline the significance of the survivor image. Here was a symbol that made it possible to portray the Vietnam veteran in a totally different manner. It opened up the possibility of depicting him in terms that were far less aberrant and extreme than the gallery of crazed outsiders, avenging angels, and supermen that dominated the Vietnam films of the past decade. The emotions and experiences of these individuals could not be depicted in terms far more realistic than the bloody, murderous fantasies that permeated films like Stallone's *First Blood*.

It is within this context that the French expatriate director Louis Malle made *Alamo Bay* (1985), a film whose major source of conflict was not the Vietnam War (although it can clearly be traced to it) but the economic struggle that took place between American (Anglo) and Vietnamese refugee fishermen in Galveston Bay from 1979 to 1981. After an initial tranquil period when at least 100,000 Vietnamese—some of whom became active in the fishing business—settled in Texas (some of the more than a million ''boat people'' who left Vietnam after the war), the economy turned sour, intense competition ensued, and the original welcome turned to bitter hatred and violence. The level of rancor became so intense that the Anglo fishing community became fertile ground for Ku Klux Klan organizers and resulted in one death.[59]

The film's focus is on that struggle, even though its most vivid aspect is the rekindled love affiar between Glory (Amy Madigan), the feisty daughter of a crusty fish processor, and her former high school sweetheart, brooding ex-Vietnam vet Shang Pierce (Ed Harris). The affair is a passionate, open one (their slow, almost sexually graphic barroom dance has an erotic quality almost unmatched in recent Hollywood films), it is nonetheless both hopeless and increasingly destructive. Shang is trapped with three kids in a bitter, loveless marriage to a dim slattern, and as economic hard times force him to lose his beloved fishing boat (portentously named American Dream Girl), he turns into a violent racist. He strikes out angrily at Glory, whose father has committed the unpardonable sin of buying fish from the Vietnamese and who herself befriends them, and the Vietnamese themselves, whom he blames about equally for his troubles.

The power of the film's sexuality notwithstanding (Malle's contributions to screen eroticism go back to *The Lovers* [1958] and include such explorations of unconventional sexual relationships as incest in *Murmur of the Heart* [1971] and child prostitution in *Pretty Baby* [1978]), the film's emphasis is on Shang and the Vietnamese refugee Dinh and through them examines the current state of the American Dream. It's a theme that Malle, himself a new immigrant to the United States, dealt with before in his evocative *Atlantic City* (1981).

For Malle, Shang and Dinh represent two different aspects of that dream. In fact, it is the eternally smiling Dinh, the survivor who ate grass in order to keep from starving after the Communists attacked his village, whose hard work and ambition (''In America everybody gets rich'') embodies the innocent, optimistic side of the dream. Dinh believes in the United States as a country of infinite possibility, where becoming an American is as easy and unself-conscious as playing baseball with the children of the Vietnamese family he lives with. He is so without guile that he casually strolls into an Anglo bar and orders a Lone Star beer, completely unaware of the racist resentment and violence (he is roughed up and thrown out) that he is bound to arouse. In his Stetson hat and cowboy boots, he almost fits Glory's half-humorous description of him as the "last cowboy left in Texas." It's a title that he tries to live up to by joining Glory in resisting the KKK's attempt to stop the Vietnamese from fishing, even announcing in his best John Wayne manner that "I don't like people who try to scare me." However, Dinh is so sexless and lifeless that he subverts Malle's desire to make him the ironic embodiment of the American Dream.

Although Malle doesn't get much closer to Shang's internal life, Harris's ability to grant his character physical grace, a macho swagger, and a sense of pride and rugged individualism give him the surface attributes of the traditional American hero and make him a much more striking figure than Dinh. Of course, Shang is no hero. He is an ordinary and somewhat mean-spirited man who lives in a worn fishing town (whose physical texture is captured by Malle's tracking camera) where time not working is spent in a seedy, neon-lit bar bearing the pathetically ironic name Zanadew. It's a parochial world where even the nearby more-worldly and liberal city of Corpus Christi is a place where office workers dress up and play act as cowboys on their night off. Malle views this world from a distance, with a bit of condescension and contempt, most of his small-town Americans being redneck louts who have turned their failure to realize the Dream into racist resentment and violence. He is even further removed from the Vietnamese, who, except for breaking the fishing laws in pursuit of the dollar, project a powerful feeling of community and a great deal of filial piety. They also work hard and clearly will make ideal U.S. citizens. It's an abstract, romanticized portrait that conveys little of their particularity as people.

Malle is too subtle a director to make the Anglo fishermen and Shang into mere Hollywood villains. In *Alamo Bay*, he explores within an American context the same theme—the banality of evil—that he examined to so much acclaim in his 1974 French film *Lacombe, Lucien*. In that film, after being rejected by the French Resistance, a bland and brutal peasant youth joins the Vichy police, not from any ideological commitment but out of a need to gain self-esteem. In a somewhat parallel situation, Shang joins the KKK not for any ideological or economic reasons (although he clearly resents the fact that the Vietnamese are competing with him for fish), but out of feelings of jealousy and pique toward Glory.

Malle makes his point about the banality of evil even stronger by depicting the KKK as a ragbag collection of inarticulate, frustrated resentful fishermen who merely want to remove the competition. The

Klan organizer is an uncharismatic figure who is conscious of public relations, wears a ten-gallon hat and spouts the usual hate-filled lines about the Catholic Church and the Communists. He also indulges in threadbare epigrams like "History is with the white race" and talks without irony about learning organizing tactics from Martin Luther King. The fishermen themselves need no philosophy to justify their cross burning, but this modern-day Klan has neither the grandeur of D.W. Griffith's saviors of the white race nor the one-dimensional villainy of Hollywood's socially conscious *Black Legion* (1936).

In fact, this Klan of "good old boys" only becomes ominous when a flotilla of KKK-manned fishing boats rides out to intimidate the Vietnamese fishermen. In this scene, the rifle-toting Shang is in the vanguard of a well-armed contingent of Klan members, some in traditional regalia, others wearing T-shirts bearing the inscription, "Secret Member of the KKK." Accompanied by banners proclaiming "Death to all Gooks" flies an upside-down U.S. flag. The episode reverberates with the sensation that the Vietnam War is once again being reenacted—except this time the Americans are out to destroy Vietnamese Catholic anticommunists who fought on their side. Of course, Americans in Vietnam often found the situation so morally and militarily confusing that they were unable to distinguish friends from enemies, viewing them all as a "yellow peril."

Throughout most of the film, however, the war remains in the background. References to it are made by a friendly Vietnam vet truck driver who picks up Dinh and remembers with affection the drugs and women of Vietnam. The Vietnamese themselves are remarkably free of rersentments about the war, and, except for Dinh's matter of fact allusion to the attack on his village, what they desire most is to successfully establish themselves in the United States. However, the boat flotilla scene and especially the climactic attempt by Shang and friends to burn Dinh's boat and Glory's office and shed with Molotov cocktails (in what has all the trappings of a search-and-destroy mission) bring the war home. The attack forces Glory to kill Shang (whom she still loves) before he murders the defenseless Dinh, leaving the audience with a long close-up of a stunned, agonized Glory. On the one hand, the whole sequence is merely a tense shoot-out in the darkness, like the conclusion of a conventional action film. On the other, it acts as a muted metaphor for the murderous complexity of the war. It reminds us of the difficult and tragic choices that Americans faced during the war, and the scarred, immutable legacy Vietnam left on American consciousness and culture.

To the extent that *Alamo Bay* dealt with Vietnam, it became one of the few films to view the war's aftermath with a quiet intelligence and without recourse to extensive murder and mayhem. In Shang, Malle also created a character who is much more than a solitary, mad vet seeking revenge on society for some ineffable trauma suffered in Vietnam. He is obviously an angry, muscle-headed racist, but at the same time he is a working-class man deeply connected to his work and community. All he really wants to do is fish, have sex with Glory, and pursue his portion of the American Dream. The closest he comes to an expression of bitterness toward the war is the remark he makes to the official who has just turned down his bank-loan extension: "We defend everybody in the world, but there's no protection for an American. And that ain't right."

Still, after his boat is repossessed, his surliness turns to brutishness and we sense that some of his violent, destructive behavior has its roots in Vietnam. In *Alamo Bay* Malle not only touches on the nature of the Vietnam legacy but deals with the banality of evil and the chronic tendency of Americans to define the American Dream in exclusive and racist terms ("America for Americans") while throwing in a sexually charged love affair as well. In fact, too many themes inhabit the film, and with the survivor Dinh being a character devoid of human juices, the theme of survival is barely conveyed. For all its intelligence and realism, *Alamo Bay* lacked the dramatic tension and energy to cause much of a stir, and it disappeared very quickly from circulation.[60]

A somewhat better fate awaited the survivors in Alan Parker's (*Fame* [1980]) film version of William Wharton's gentle, lyrical novel *Birdy* (1984). Well known for his use of adolescents and children, ranging from the prepubescent gangsters of *Bugsy Malone* (1976) to the shamelessly career-oriented high school students of *Fame*, Parker once again directed a film that works with adolescent fantasy and feelings of apartness from and anger toward a drab and cruel world.

In *Birdy*, the source of these themes is the relationship between two working-class, South Philadelphia adolescents, Al Columbato (Nicholas Cage) and his friend Birdy (Matthew Modine). On the surface, Al is an ordinary Joe, interested in girls and wrestling, while Birdy is an asocial solitary, obsessed with birds and flight to the point of eroticism and, ultimately, madness. However, the connection between them is a profound one: Birdy needs Al's groundedness and capacity to live everyday life as ballast to keep him from going over the edge, while Birdy's dreams and obsession provide an escape for the part of Al that resents authority and feels caged by the dreary world he inhabits.

Told mostly in flashback and through the interior monologues of both characters, the film traces their friendship from their initial encounter and adolescent adventures to the moment when Al, wounded and disfigured—a Vietnam legacy—is brought to a military hospital by a literal-minded, jargon-spouting army psychiatrist in an effort to try to snap Birdy out of his catatonic state. Like Al, Birdy has also been a victim of Vietnam (changed from novel's World War II setting), missing in action for over a month after his helicopter had been shot down.

Even though the film is not centered on Vietnam, there are repeated flashbacks to the war traumas both continue to experience: a close-up of Birdy, his helicopter downed, screaming hysterically while surrounded by flocks of birds ominously flying about, followed by the camera's rapid tracking over a napalm-charred Vietnam landscape; Al slogging through the mud and rice paddies only to have his face blown up. In the hospital, Al still smells the sweet odor of burning flesh, and he speaks about the war: "Funny, in any other war we would be heroes. Oh, man we didn't know what we were getting into with the John Wayne shit, did we? Boy were we dumb. We were always dumb." If this isn't sufficient to get his point across, director Parker heavy-handedly depicts the psychiatrist's noncom secretary spitting compulsively because he's had a bad taste in his mouth ever since he was in combat.

In *Birdy*, the war is the ultimate cruelty in a world that to both Al and Birdy feels imprisoning. However, there is an inherent shallowness in placing the horrors of the Vietnam War seemingly on the same moral level with Birdy's shrewish mother, who poisons his pigeons; Al's father (the garbageman), a belligerent bully who can only insult his son; and a greedy South Philly neighbor who captures dogs so they can be slaughtered for meat. In addition, the film is burdened by the simplistic Laingian notion that madness is the realm of those pure of heart (Birdy lies Christ-like on the floor of his hospital cell) who rebel consciously and unconsciously against injustice and repressive authority.

Nevertheless, such is the power of the film's depiction of Birdy's mania with birds and flight that at moments *Birdy* turns into a poetic, magical work. Birdy's dreams transform his seedy working-class world of worn frame houses and weedy vacant lots turned softball fields into a world of avian mystery, wonder, and even danger. (The scene where the family cat steals into Birdy's room to attack his beloved canary Pertha has all the tension of a Hitchcock thriller.) We are also so drawn into Birdy's obsession with capturing and taming pigeons—wearing a suit made of their feathers, trying to fly off a gas tank, and attempting to learn canary language—that we are not surprised by anything he does. So it doesn't seem outrageous, after a night spent in a melancholy sexual encounter with an awkward, frightened girl that Birdy should lie naked in an almost erotic embrace with his pet canary, bird sounds filling the sound track, silhouettes of birds on the wall. In a similar fashion, it doesn't seem at all absurd that in a subsequent moment of transcendent fantasy, he becomes a bird and, through the cinematography of Michael Seresin's swooping, soaring camera and accompanied by Peter Gabriel's throbbing music, takes an exhilarating flight through his neighborhood over clotheslines, roofs, backyards, and junkyards.

In addition, Modine (who must have spent hours observing birds for the role) is utterly convincing as the psychically maimed Birdy, who in his catatonic state has literally taken on the physical characteristics of a bird. Thus, whether seen from an extreme low or overhead angle crouched beneath a sink in the corner of his hospital cell looking with fierce birdlike suspicion at Al or perched nude on his bedpost looking off into a heavenly blue light that comes through a barred window, he actually resembles nothing less than an immense, grounded bird.

Equally moving is Nicholas Cage's portrayal of the more-practical and more-social Al. In his protective and sensitively caring attempt to reach Birdy and bring him out of his psychotic state, we see and feel how much they mean to each other. Al sees Birdy's withdrawal as a reflection of his own lack of will and his anxiety about fitting into the world with a face that looks like a "freak mask" or a "medium-rare cheeseburger," and he views Birdy's recovery as a symbol of his own fate.

The film concludes with a bit of contrivance when, out of nowhere, Birdy miraculously breaks his silence to interrupt Al's sodden, angst-laden monologue about how he feels like an oppressed dog that nobody wants, saying, "Al, sometimes you're so full of shit." This leads to a final break-out from the hospital and one more seemingly suicidal but unscathing try at flight by Birdy. It's a sentimental climax, but even this unsubtle metaphor provides a moving image of the indomitability of the human spirit, of man's capacity to survive through adversity with some notion of freedom intact.

Birdy added a new dimension to the survivor. In films like *The Killing Fields* and *Alamo Bay*, this symbol took a peripheral place to an exploration of the political agony of Cambodia or an evocation of the dark side of the American Dream. In *Birdy*, however, Al and Birdy's psychic and physical wounds and their ability to ultimately transcend them become the film's central themes. Of course, Birdy needs no Vietnam to set him dreaming and fantasizing. Still, his dreams give him the strength to survive the war.

The returning vet's need for dreams hardly originated in *Birdy*. In Ethiopian-born Hale Gerima's independent *Ashes and Embers* (1982), the dreams and nightmates of a black vet exist on both a personal and ideological level. Unlike *Some Kind of Hero*'s conventional and glitzy Hollywood version of the problems of a returning black vet, *Ashes and Embers* eschews traditional narrative for a jaggedly edited, nonlinear depiction of a black vet's psychological problems and his attempt to resolve them by linking himself to the radical black tradition.

The film opens with a racist Los Angeles cop pointing his gun at the back of a spreadeagled black Vietnam vet, Ned (Chuck) Charles (John Anderson) for violating a minor traffic regulation and then flashes back to his first experiences upon returning home from Vietnam. It was a time when he was obsessed by Vietnam memories (a montage of newsreel and fiction) and lived in such a perpetual state of guilt, anxiety, and alienation that he slept with the lights on. He was also incapable of relating to another person, including his girlfriend; her son, a benign, literate television repairman who offers him work and friendly counsel; and even his beloved, feisty, rural southern grandmother. It was a period best summed up by his own anguished comment that ''I'm still not back from the war yet.''

Throughout he's a virtual volcano of rage, capable of erupting at any moment. Many of the film's most powerful scenes are just such explosions. For example, goaded by his girlfriend's leftist study group's simplistic anti-imperialistic clichés about the war and its atrocities, he screams, ''I can't even begin to tell you what was done to me and what I done to others.'' He tells them their talk has no context, that it's abstract, that when you are out there ''you're left with your instincts.''

In a similar fashion, when he opens up to his terrified but practically mesmerized girlfriend about his war experience, it's hardly, as he sardonically labels it, ''your sweet smell of napalm in the morning'' Hollywood version of Vietnam. His war is a relentless, horrific account of deadly firefights, body bags, murdered women and children, and the image of the headless torso of a buddy spurting blood on him that continues to haunt his days and nights.

Ashes and Embers, however, isn't solely limited to conveying the psychic destruction wrought by the war. Displaying some of the same insight he exhibited toward ghetto life in his 1976 film about a black welfare mother in Watts, *Bush Mama,* Gerima demonstrates that he is equally perceptive about other aspects of black life. He takes a telling shot at the black bourgeoisie in the person of a buttoned-down real estate man who salutes Chuck with the comradely ''blood'' as he calmly prepares to manipulate Chuck's tax-ridden grandmother (Evelyn Blackwell) out of some of her land. For Gerima, the gap-toothed, innately dignified grandmother is a fount of sturdy folk wisdom whom Chuck must begin to understand so he can deal ''with all the contradictions that we experience everyday.'' It's on her farm among the flowers, trees, and rich soil that Chuck finds his only solace, and in one of the film's most memorable flashbacks, he identifies his grandmother with the Vietnamese film cutting between her stooped, conical-hatted figure and that of a Vietnamese peasant woman.

The relationship between the grandmother and Chuck is also the subject of the film's most lyrical scene. Here Chuck gives in to her desire that he be baptized, and they affectionately march arm in arm in stately processional to a church, backed by an ancient gospel hymn. This act is, however, so filled with terror for Chuck that he flees the church: "I'm not with nobody." It throws him into such a severe tailspin that it lands him wandering homeless and totally disoriented through the streets of Washington D.C. This state of acute despair only begins to lift when Chuck hears his friend Jim, the television repairman (Norman Blalock), schematically invoke and lecture on the spirit and example of the "great black warriors of the past," who are not African tribal chieftains but men like Paul Robeson, with a voice like a beautiful booming "freedom bell", and W.E.B. Dubois. According to Jim, both of these men singlehandedly fought the government to a standstill and are powerful models of black defiance of the white power structure.

All this leads to move Chuck out of his near madness and exemplifies Gerima's obsession with the development of consciousness—with the awareness of the intellectual processes that lead to the transformation of the world. That consciousness moves Chuck beyond nationalism to a form of Marxist analysis that allows him to declare that "being black is not enough" (though Gerima never denies the significance of blackness).[61]

Unfortunately, this message functions more as a didactic point than as a light that might be shed on the condition of the black Vietnam vet in postwar America. In fact, hurriedly and willfully turning Chuck from a raging nihilist (a variation on the wounded vet of other Vietnam films) into a Marxist ideologue adds little to our understanding of the black vet's problems or to the applicability of a Marxist analysis to his situation. So a scene where the penniless and emotionally bankrupt Chuck is suddenly dunned for $1,585 in back benefits by an indifferent Veterans' Administration misses the opportunity to get to the heart of the system the film constantly rails against. Instead of providing insight into how blacks were sent off to bleed and die in disproportionate numbers in Vietnam and were then frustrated and abandoned once they returned home, Gerima offers another tired indictment of the callousness of the bureaucracy (a phenomenon not unknown in Communist countries).

In the same vein, although sensitive to how inadequate clichés about imperialism are for an understanding of the anguished complexity of the Vietnam experience, Gerima concludes the film with equally tired oratory and iconography (posters of Angela Davis and Malcolm X are omnipresent) about class warfare and the evils of capitalism. As a result, if a Marxist analysis is at all helpful in providing a solution to the economic and social problems of black Americans it's lost in *Ashes and Embers* in declamatory rhetoric. Consequently, what remains most memorable in this repetitive, overheated, and chaotic work is not its ideas, but its images of black rage, stoicism, and nobility, images closer to black nationalism than to Marxism.

Nevertheless, Gerima's Marxism, despite its heavy-handedness, does try to take the problems of black and, by extension, white veterans as well out of the realm of the personal and give them a political context. In a sense, *Ashes and Embers* placed ideology at least on par with Hollywood's traditional faith in the power of love (a solution facilely displayed in the 1985 film *Cease Fire*, where a Vietnam vet played by television star Don Johnson is saved from the ravages of his guilt-ridden war memories by a loving wife and a supportive Vietnam veterans "rap" group). Thus Gerima's ideology and vision of a heroic past become one more element besides Dith Pran's belief in friendship and family; Birdy's mad, visionary dreams; and Dinh's and Shang's commitment to different sides of the American Dream with which these survivors are able to sustain themselves against the terrors of the war and the dilemmas of peace.

The variety of survivors' dreams is one sign that the Vietnam War film has grown more complex and mature. It's of course true that a film like *The Deer Hunter* was a powerful and visually striking evocation of working-class GIs traumatized by the war, but its conception of the war itself is muddled and simplistic, reassuring the public that despite the war's capacity to destroy lives emotionally and physically there are supermen who can sustain America's will and power. *The Killing Fields* offers in turn a clearer, sparer, and more intellectually and politically compelling version of a Vietnam whose roots lay in particular U.S. foreign-policy decisions rather than in a corrupt and demonic human nature.

Still, the superman was the first metaphor to give the American public a sense of the surreal, nightmarish quality of the war. However, when severed from the unique cinematic imagination of Cimino and Coppola and linked through genre conventions to American historical archetypes like the captivity myth and the hunter-hero or the notion of redemption through violence, the superman becomes the central figure in a cinematic revisionist history of the war. In these versions the Rambos and the Colonel Braddocks project the image of a United States that could have triumphed in Vietnam had our troops not been constrained by flaccid bureaucrats and corrupt politicians.

Oddly, this comic-strip vision of Vietnam may have had the indirect effect of contributing to the production of films that attempted to portray the war in a more realistic fashion. The box-office success of *Rambo* put to rest the argument that the audience would not "pay to sit there in the dark and have it brought up."[62] And the simple-mindedness and gratuitous violence of these cartoons may have pushed at least the adults in the audience to seek an antidote in films that could provide a more authentic depiction of the war.

The returning vet probably provided the most-powerful impetus for Hollywood's decision to treat Vietnam in a more-realistic fashion. In the

1970s, film makers turned him into the symbol of the wounded vet, whose rage reflected the anxiety felt by the public about the effect of the war on both our soldiers and the society. However, as passions cooled the wounded vet was used less to symbolize a character potentially dangerous and destructive to society than as a man whose anger was more likely to be directed at himself, and he emerged as a person in need of compassion and empathy rather than a disruptive and threatening figure. By the 1980s, though many had still not adjusted to civilian life, a number of vets had achieved visible leadership roles in U.S. society (e.g., Senator John Kerry of Massachusetts) and their psychic and physical wounds seemed more a source of moral strength and courage than scars that elicited pity. As a result, the wounded vets were transformed into survivors whose means of survival were as diverse as the characters themselves. And whatever victories they experienced testified more to the capacity of the human spirit to endure than to any Ramboesque heroics.

The arrival and relative success of *The Killing Fields* signified that U.S. audience were about ready to confront the painful reality of the Vietnam War directly on the screen. Films could now be made that, paraphrasing C.D.B. Bryan about Vietnam War fiction, might finally allow us to make sense of it all.[63]

PART IV

Confronting Vietnam

Almost from the moment the last U.S. troops withdrew from Vietnam in March of 1973 came the clamor that the war should no longer be allowed to distract us, that we should "put the war behind us." Perhaps that feeling was most definitively expressed by President Ford in his speech at Tulane University two years later (just before the fall of Saigon): "Today Americans can regain the sense of pride that existed before Vietnam. But it cannot be achieved refighting a war that is finished."[1] However, Ford's call to move on with the nation's business did not purge the memory of Vietnam from the American imagination.

In supposedly famous military victories like the invasion of Grenada or the bombing of Libya, one can sense the government seeking an escape from the Vietnam syndrome as well as particular strategic and political ends.[2] Of course, these "triumphs" did not lay to rest the ghost of Vietnam. Striking this same vein is Olvier Stone's Academy Award-winning *Platoon* (1986), the cathartic aspect of the film clearly contributing to its success. Obviously, one film could not completely purge the traces and memories of Vietnam from our national consciousness, but as John Wheeler, president of the Center for the Study of Vietnam Generation and chairman of the Vietnam Veterans Memorial Fund said, "The Vietnam memorial was one gate our country had to pass through. *Platoon* is another; it is part of the healing process."[3]

Oliver Stone's background and career provided almost ideal preparation for writing and directing *Platoon*, and in some ways his experiences were representative of many young men of his generation. Born in comparative affluence, he was a Yale dropout who dreamed, like the grunt James (Cherry) Chelini in John Del Vecchio's Vietnam War novel *The 13th Valley*, of the "lands and wars of Hemingway and Mailer."[4] Stone's literary model was Conrad's *Lord Jim*, which was one factor that moved him to go to Vietnam as a teacher and to subsequently enlist. While there he was both wounded and decorated in combat. Then, like so many other ex-GIs who were psychologically undermined by the war, he returned home to brushes with drugs and jail until he pulled himself together at New York University's film school. This led to an extremely successful Hollywood career: an Oscar for the screenplay of *Midnight Express* (1977) and a long list of writing credits (*Scarface, Year of the Dragon*), culminating in a widely praised directorial debut in the edgy, atmospheric *Salvador* (1986).

During much of his post-Vietnam years, Stone carried with him a script based on his war experiences. Turned down by every major Hollywood studio, the small British production company Hemdale advanced him a shoestring $6-million budget for the film. Stone gathered a group of relatively unknown Hollywood actors and some off-Broadway veterans and put them under the tutelage of a former Vietnam marine officer who initiated them to a semblance of the Vietnam experience with a two-week quasi-boot camp. The result was a semiautobiographical film that recreates much of the war's daily agony and resembles in some ways the best World War II films, like *Walk in the Sun* (1945) and the *The Story of GI Joe* (1945).

Indeed, the film's greatest strength lies in its social realism—its feeling of verisimilitude for the discomfort, ants, heat, and mud—of the jungle and brush: the fatigue of patrols, the boredom and sense of release of base camp, the terror of ambuses, and the chaos and cacophony of night firefights. Filmed in tight closeup and medium shots, this powerfully evokes the murderous immediacy of the world into which the GIs were thrust.

Platoon, however, isn't all gritty war cries and horrors, rockets and mines exploding, and bodies strewn across the landscape. These vivid images and sounds are an integral part of a somewhat classic meditation on what war does to people, but this is seen less in anger than in sadness. And like the wind that unobtrusively whips the plastic coverings off the dead bodies of GIs in the film's opening sequence, *Platoon* tries, with some success, to be lean and honest and to convey the war's painful realities without becoming hyperbolic.

From its opening credits' quote from *Ecclesiastes* ("Rejoice, O young man in thy youth") and the blowing away of a curtain of dust to reveal a cargo plane filled with raw recruits, among them the film's eponymous hero Chris Taylor (Charles Sheen), the film constitutes an act of remembrance and mourning and is a classic coming-of-age work about the transformation of a young, innocent GI. What follows are a series of traditional war-film scenes, though given richer texture and depth by

Platoon

Stone. The confrontation of the green, innocent recruits with the cynical, contemptuous vets, the first anxious patrol, the terrifying night attack, and Taylor's initiation as one of the boys by turning on at base camp—all of these rites of passage conceived with the sombre recognition that Vietnam was a continuous nightmare that could only possibly end when you got on the helicopter to begin the trip home.

The events are conveyed through both Taylor's eyes and the voiceover narration of his self-consciously literary letters back home. Taylor, like Stone, is an upper-middle-class Yale dropout and patriot who has absurdly come to Vietnam to discover a truer, more-authentic life than he could find in his comfortable world back home ("Maybe from down here I can start up again and be something I don't see yet, learn something I don't yet know"). What he does discover, besides the horrors of Vietnam, are the anonymous, working-class and underclass bottom dogs of U.S. society, a gallery of characters that are given a bit more nuance and treated less stereotypically and sentimentally than is the norm in Hollywood war films. Stone gives us the baby-faced, beer can-crunching Bunny (Kevin Dillon), who loves war and killing and is a perfect illustration that the most savage thing on earth is "an 18-year-old American with a gun"; gum-chewing Sgt. O'Neill (John MacGinley), whose obsequious attempts to arbitrage anxiety into safety only lead him into more danger; and a group of blacks of whom the earthy, wise, and decent King (Keith David) is balanced by the perpetually whining and malingering Junior (Reggie Johnson). In fact, though the blacks share a wariness of their white counterparts and exhibit a degree of solidarity among themselves, Stone grants them just enough individuality to avoid turning them into characterless abstractions even though the film's prime focus, as in most Vietnam films, is on the experience of white, not black soldiers.

Like Stephen Crane's *The Red Badge of Courage,* the film seems to focus around a young man's initiation into war, especially as Taylor panics on his first night in battle and mistakes a scratch for a mortal wound. Stone, however, has other things in mind as well, for the film begins to take on other dimensions after the massacre episode. That incident is handled by Stone with such chilling power that in another war film it might have been the penultimate moment of revelation. Exhausted, frightened, and possessed with the need to avenge their tortured and murdered buddies, a number of GIs in the platoon crack and turn into a murderous rabble who go on a rampage, murdering and raping Vietnamese peasants and finally torching the village suspected of harboring the enemy. Even the morally sensitive Taylor momentarily loses control and turns into a brute, repeatedly firing his rifle at a retarded villager to make him jump, although he ultimately recoils in guilty tears and regains his moral balance. The whole episode is handled by Stone without sensationalism as he gradually takes the audience through events that make comprehensible, even though not justifiable, the GIs blood thirsty state of mind. Stone is also a subtle enough director to convey by reaction shots that the platoon members do not respond as one: many of them are either frightened, stunned, or repelled by the actions of their fellow GIs.

The massacre scene also sets the stage for the conflict between two lifers, the headband-wearing doper-saint Sgt. Elias (Willem Defoe) and the war-loving, ruthless Sgt. Barnes (Tom Berenger), which dominates the film's second half. Both appear earlier at the base camp as charismatic leaders of two antipathetic groups within the platoon, Elias in the dope and rock music group and Barnes in the booze and card-playing one. But it's Elias's humane intervention during the massacre and his subsequent report of Barnes's barbaric murder of a Vietnamese woman to a higher-ranking officer that turns this conflict into a life-and-death struggle.

When their conflict is confined by Stone to battle action, the film may no longer be social realism but the screen is alive with the energy and tension generated by his fluid cross-cutting between Barnes, Elias, and the North Vietnamese and by tracking shots of the graceful Elias gliding through the brush. The sequence culminates in Elias's (who has volunteered to outflank the Vietnamese) being hunted, wounded, and left to die by the demonic Barnes.

Stone, however, is not content with the pure physicality of the conflict but conceives of the struggle in literary terms as well. Unfortunately, here the conception seems strained and clichéd. The seven-times wounded Barnes, his face crisscrossed with scars, is all too portentously referred to by Taylor as "our Captain Ahab" when the platoon enters the village bent on revenge. In a similar fashion, Barnes reveals himself to be a closet superman, whose assertion "I am reality" (when directly confronting Taylor and other potential fraggers out to avenge Elias) might well have been taken from the gnomic mutterings of *Apocalypse Now*'s Colonel Kurtz. Barnes is fearless and utterly without moral constraint. He is in Stone's terms a destructive force, ideally suited for the madness of Vietnam.

Elias is constructed along the same larger-than-life, mythical lines, except that he is the inversion of Barnes: a gentle and compassionate spirit. He talks about the stars, loves the United States, and is critical of a war he has become weary of. He is also tagged with the added burden of some oppressive Christian symbolism and dialogue. In one instance he greets Taylor, who has returned to the platoon after having his wounds attended, with the self-consciously significant "Here's our Chris, resurrected." But that bit of fancy dialogue is topped by his final gesture: arms raised crucifixion style (shot in slow motion), appealing

heavenward, as he is pursued to his death by swarms of North Vietnamese, while Taylor and the rest of the platoon watch helplessly from a
helicopter that has just rescued them.

Stone's camera focuses on both Elias and Barnes in ways that distinguish them from the rest of the GIs. Elias, as played by Defoe, has a
great deal of charm and an expressive face, and Stone heightens his
attractiveness by going for far too many significant close-ups, just as he
tends to use too many low-angle shots of Barnes to intensify his
frightening, forbidding power. To the extent that *Platoon* concentrates
on the Manichean and melodramatic struggle between Barnes and Elias,
the film begins to lose focus. The intrusion of these fabulistic figures on
the real landscape subverts the film's verisimilitude and at moments
reduces it to a pretentious version of traditional Hollywood action films.
Stone also means Barnes and Elias to serve as two symbolic fathers
warring for the soul of Taylor. But Taylor, who ultimately kills Barnes, is
too bland a character to convince us that this internal struggle has any
emotional reality for him and is anything more than a literary conceit of
Stone's.

On another level, the struggle between Barnes and Elias is supposed
to reflect the divisions in U.S. society about the war, but the film never
grants the split a political dimension. In fact, *Platoon* lacks a genuine
political perspective. It conveys varied expressions of pain and remorse
about the war ranging from Big Harold's (Forest Whitaker) despairing
lament that "I'm hurting real bad inside" to homicidal Bunny's casual
admission of a twinge of conscience for his barbarism. But save Elias,
not one of the GIs ventures a criticism, much less an act of defiance,
toward the war. They attribute their anguish to the death of buddies, the
atrocities they see or commit, and a general revulsion toward being
mired in a living purgatory.

Of course, it makes little sense for Stone to graft a developed political
consciousness onto men who are mainly interested in survival. These
are men who don't and wouldn't ask what political forces brought them
there, and once in Vietnam they discover that nothing else exists, the
outside world turning into a dream or being obliterated by what they
must confront daily.

Still, in the film's final moments, as he flies out of the war zone,
Stone's Taylor indulges in a florid, sermonizing voiceover about the
Vietnam experience. He exhorts us with the facile, ethnocentric idea that
the "enemy was in us," as if the war was fought mainly to purge the
demonic impulse from the interior of the nation and the self, and then
goes on to affirm that "those of us who did make it have the obligation
to build again, to teach others what we know, and try with what's left of
our lives to find a goodness and meaning to this life." This nebulous,
humane sentiment is harmless, but it hardly does justice to either what

Platoon itself depicts or the complex tangle of Vietnam. The war had its roots in the murderous cynicism of a foreign policy built on the U.S. need to demonstrate its national will and credibility and on a lengthy tradition of reflexive anticommunism. Despite our traumatic internal divisions and conflicts, an external enemy did exist: a nation and culture that was devastated by and suffered from the war in ways the United States never did.

The power of *Platoon* does not lie in Stone's vaporous attempt at political analysis or his penchant for literary turns or even his playing with the mythic. Although the film may not be the final word on Vietnam, it is nevertheless an antidote to dangerous patriotic cartoons like *Rambo* and metaphysically muddled works like *Apocalypse Now*. *Platoon* knows just how to place the war in its proper perspective of climate, terrain, fear, and death, and it is at its best when there is minimal or no dialogue, allowing the camera, through telling close-ups, to tell us all we want to know about the characters and their world.

The GIs in this film are neither given to self-indulgent heroics nor to patriotic rhetoric. In fact, most of them merely try to numb themselves to their surroundings and get out of the Vietnam charnel house in one piece, willing even to mutilate themselves to do it. It is in that striking image of self-mutilation and other concrete details that capture the day-to-day fear of an invisible and ubiquitous enemy that Stone succeeds in creating a richly textured portrait of the war. His talent for remembering how Vietnam looked and felt gave the film an affecting shock of recognition to vets and nonvets alike, making *Platoon*, despite its soporific narration and over-the-top mythologizing, the first real cinematic step taken by Hollywood in coming to terms with the truth about Vietnam.

There are, of course, inherent limitations to *Platoon*'s (and any film's) capacity for rendering the truth about Vietnam, for the daily ground and nature of the war shifted too often to be encapsulated in any one work of art. Indeed, the war was fought not only in canopied jungles against a stealthy, implacable guerrilla enemy but also from fixed positions against North Vietnamese regulars in the northern provinces, on search-and-destroy missions carried out against NLF units and main-force North Vietnamese regiments in the central highlands, and in skirmishes often fought from the gunnels of Naval patrol boats (LSTs) against NLF villagers amid the flooded rice paddies of the southern delta.

In a similar fashion, by setting the war around the time of the Tet offensive in late 1968, *Platoon* deals with the war at the moment when the notion of a winnable war had rapidly receded down a dark hole of despair and defeat. Saving one's ass, rather than the idealistic-sounding Johnsonian notion of winning the "hearts and minds" of the people, had become the articulated ethic of the day. It was an ethic ultimately rationalized and sustained by the cynical Nixon-Kissinger scenario of "peace with honor," which supplanted Johnson's rhetoric during the post-Tet years.

Stone himself never claims to provide the definitive version of the war. *Platoon* centers around his particular memories of Vietnam, and it is clear there are as many versions of the Vietnam experience as there are GIs who were over there. In fact, what's more interesting about the film is that despite its basically realist aesthetic, it constitutes a veritable catalogue of the symbolic figures developed by Hollywood in its attempt to sum up the Vietnam experience. Prominently appearing in *Platoon* are the superman, the hunter-hero, and the survivor. Even the wounded hero with his war-induced trauma is present, less in the shape of any one character than in the feeling that many of the film's GIs will return home to play out that melancholy, self-destructive role.

Nowhere is this tendency to recapitulate Hollywood's version of Vietnam more apparent than in Stone's depiction of Sgt. Barnes, another in a long line of Hollywood supermen. Barnes is an almost invincible killing machine who thrives on danger and death, and his pithy, metaphysical comments are a mere afterthought to his strong-willed quest for power and dominance. Barnes's drive is so potent that it even compels him to will his own death by commanding (challenging?) the revenge-bent Chris to kill him as he lies wounded.

The appearance of a romantic figure like the superman in *Platoon* demonstrates how successful Hollywood has been in creating recognizable and acceptable metaphors for the war. For audiences and film makers alike, the superman (in all his various guises) became the pre-eminent symbol of a war that had gone over the edge. Barnes, as Hicks of *Who'll Stop the Rain* and Kilgore of *Apocalypse Now*, is a character who maintains the notion that U.S. combat ability and courage remained still intact while at the same time personalizing the murderous lunacy of the war so that its larger historical, ideological, and social dimensions remain virtually unexamined.

In the person of Sgt. Elias a variation of the hunter-hero also makes his appearance. Although his character is touched with a bit too much Christian symbolism, he nonetheless acts in accord with the traditional outlines of the captivity myth. Elias has learned to survive in the jungle and has acquired the skills necessary to struggle against a fierce enemy but has not lost his sense of morality in spite of living in the savage wilderness.

In the context of *Platoon*, Stone uses the muscular saintliness of hunter-hero Elias to partially balance the superman's embrace of destruction. In addition to his presence providing some reassurance that the U.S. GI and the society itself has not been totally depleted of its decency and humanity, the hunter-hero supplies a vital link to an American myth deeply embedded in our national consciousness. Until

Platoon, this archetype's capacity for regenerative acts of violence had been primarily used by Hollywood as the basis for bloody fantasy images of victory over a variety of enemies. In this instance, there are no one-man victories over hordes of Communist Vietnamese, just a possible model for individual and perhaps even collective redemption.

In *Platoon*, the beneficiary of that idea of salvation is the Vietnam survivor, Chris Taylor, who is a classic example of that symbol. Taylor is transformed in the film from a callow recruit into a hardened veteran who has understood and survived both the horrors of the war and the portentous struggle for possession of his soul waged between the superman and the hunter-hero. Enveloped in the atmosphere of defeat, the only triumph is the survival of Taylor with his life and sense of moral values intact.

It is the particularity and ordinariness of the survivor's character that gives Stone the medium to convey the complex, everyday reality of combat in Vietnam. Even though his tepid portrait of Taylor is not especially rich in psychological nuance, Taylor's eyes give us a Vietnam both painfully commonplace and unique, one that the more grandiose, romantic heroes and cultural archetypes like Kurtz and Rambo never evoke. The survivor shares a realistic combat situation with other men who, in the main, come from specific social worlds and are not asocial, pop-metaphysical supermen (although *The Deer Hunter* still provides the most striking and illuminating images of the social world that a number of GIs came from) and whose responses to Vietnam are often shaped by their past histories. The survivor is a figure grounded in this world, a symbol of those who endured the Vietnam mad house and came out with some semblance of a moral victory. Given the nature of the Vietnam War, it is, oddly enough, the most genuinely hopeful version of the war that can possibly be imagined.

Ultimately, it was the moral victories (or more precisely the moral lessons) of Vietnam that were to serve as the theme of Oliver Stone's acceptance speech after receiving the Academy Award for best director (one of four that the film won). Stone said,

Through this award you really are acknowledging the Vietnam veteran and I think what you're saying is that for the first time you really understand what happened there, and I think what you're saying is that it should never happen again. And if it does, then these American boys died over there for nothing, because America learned nothing from the Vietnam war.[5]

Whether Hollywood did anything more than pay superficial lip service to the war's horror while simultaneously affirming the film's popular success is certainly open to question. What is certain is the impact the film had upon the GIs who served in Vietnam. Dedicated to "those who fought and died in Vietnam," *Platoon* was perceived by many of them as the first really authentic portrayal of the war. Among those who avowed the film's accuracy and power was Monte Newcombe, who served with Stone in Vietnam. Newcombe said that *Platoon* conveyed the "waste, corruption, filth, napalm, blood, and guts, the destruction and absolute craziness of that war."[6]

Significant for its moral and emotional resonance, *Platoon* marks (after much wavering) Hollywood's total acceptance of the Vietnam War as a fit subject for film. This is not meant to imply that film makers would not continue to exploit the war or would be able to get a handle on it, but a new yardstick existed now by which one could measure these films. Hopefully it would inspire more politically and intellectually sophisticated films illuminating other aspects and areas of the war.

It is within this new context that one can begin to analyze films like *Hanoi Hilton* (1987), *Gardens of Stone* (1987), and *Full Metal Jacket* (1987), all of which appeared soon after the release of *Platoon*. Unfortunately, Lionel Chetwynd's low-budget, polemical *Hanoi Hilton* adds nothing to our understanding of the war. This film, which deals with the ordeal of U.S. POWs in Hanoi's infamous Hao Lo prison looks like a tedious updating of Milestone's flag-waving, World War II film *The Purple Heart*. *Hanoi Hilton* features tired war-film chichés like sadistic prison guards and officers (the most brutal being a Cuban who is full of street talk and boasts of having lived in East Harlem) and long-suffering but heroic American captives. In addition, the film launches a diatribe against the antiwar movement with the camp's sophisticated "yellow menace" commandant informing the POWs that the war won't "be won in the delta," but in antiwar demonstrations in Berkeley and Washington. There is also a caricatured version of Jane Fonda (Gloria Carlin) who visits the camp to learn how the prisoners are treated and predictably is unable to see through the performance the North Vietnamese stage for her. As a result, instead of a serious treatment of the POWs' anguish (as in Stone's film, where the theme, common to both the grunts and the POWs, of survival as a form of heroism added stature), *Hanoi Hilton* only diminishes their experience.

This is not quite the case with Francis Coppola's *Gardens of Stone*. Despite being a dramatically lifeless work, it has the saving grace of some strikingly composed images in the carefully choreographed military burial rituals: honor guards, the riderless horse, a flag-draped coffin, and a bagpiper playing "Taps." These images set the scene for a film about tough, cynical Sgt. Clell Hazard (James Caan), a veteran of 27 years and three wars (World War II, Korea, and Vietnam), who is currently assigned to the army's elite unit the Old Guard, whose duties include presidential escorts and burials at "the garden" (Arlington National Cemetery). Clell is critical of the war but not for political reasons. He views it as a war where there is "nothing to win and no way to win it," but he loyally wants a transfer so he can help train draftees to fight and survive in the Vietnamese jungles.

Like Clell, *Gardens of Stone* clearly loves military life, paying homage to the vision of the army as a noisy, caring family. Clell has a brotherly relationship with warm, knowing Sgt. Major Goody Nelson (a role that demands little from James Earl Jones) and a surrogate son, Pvt. Jackie Willow (D.B. Sweeney), a gung-ho, colorless, army brat whose fondest dream is to go to Vietnam because he believes, in true Ollie North fashion, that "a soldier in the right place at the right time can change the world." The film also sentimentally exults in the barroom brawls and service banter that John Wayne and Victor McLaglen used to enjoy in John Ford's cavalry trilogy. In addition, Holmes has an unbelievable romantic relationship with an antiwar journalist, Samantha Davis (Anjelica Huston).

These conventional and undeveloped relationships take up so much footage that the issue of the war seems like an afterthought. In the midst of the opening burial scene Coppola imaginatively fills the soundtrack with the inchoate and ominous sounds of battle, but he never goes anywhere with it. This is especially troubling since the film is set during the time of the Tet offensive and the Old Guard spends much of its time burying Vietnam's victims. But the film does not bother to explore the effect of the war on the stateside army and says nothing about the war itself except for echoing current popular feeling that Vietnam was a suicidal, unwinnable conflict. Coppola saves most of his anger for the antiwar movement rather than for the government, constructing an embarrassing set piece where Clell is confronted at a garden party by a platitudinous, obnoxious antiwar activist and is forced to do the manly thing and break his jaw.

Obviously, Coppola now believes that the image of the GI must be rescued from all those Vietnam films, including his own *Apocalypse Now*, that treated them as anything less than earthy, compassionate souls. What is interesting about *Gardens of Stone* is not only that his vision of the army is a simplistic one but that the film's only real passion is reserved for the dead rather than the living. Indeed, the strongest images are found when the camera pans over the headstones in the gardens of stone and powerfully details the honor guard folding a ceremonial flag with military precision, handing it to a grieving widow or parent. For a few moments these images grant the film the haunted, mournful quality of an elegy (perhaps owing to the tragic accidental death of Coppola's son during the production), but it is not necessarily intended for those who died in Vietnam as much as for anyone who dies young needlessly.[7]

Among the immediate successor to *Platoon*, the only one to elicit a critical stir was Stanley Kubrick's *Full Metal Jacket* (1987), which has the misfortune to appear so soon after that generally acclaimed film that its own faults were magnified and its virtues were not given their due. Coming from Kubrick, the director of two notable war films (*Paths of Glory* [1975] and *Dr. Strangelove* [1964]), *Full Metal Jacket* aroused inflated expectations among those who were eager to see just how he would attack the Vietnam experience. Kubrick himself fueled these expectations by granting preproduction interviews during which he spoke of wanting to "explode the narrative structure of movies. I want to do something earth-shaking."[8]

As a result, it was no surprise that, among its mixed reviews, it often received a critical drubbing.[9] Some of the response had less to do with the film's flaws than the fact that the film may have been out of sync with the general public mood. Although not all critics were overwhelmed by *Platoon*, there was an appreciation of its realism. On the other hand, *Full Metal Jacket* had grander aspirations, dealing less with the concrete reality of Vietnam than with the military as an institution that breeds killers and projecting a vision of all men as potential destroyers and lovers of death.

This vision of the human condition, combined with the film's Olympian, detached tone, pervades almost all of Kubrick's work. It can be seen in the science fiction *2001: Space Odyssey* (1968), where HAL, the supercomputer that human beings have developed, is programmed to kill, as well as in *A Clockwork Orange* (1968), where a futuristic delinquent gang, living in an utterly sterile world, engage in orgies of violence. However, if Kubrick's remote style may suit the world evoked in these films, there is something essentially disturbing about its use in as passionate and immediate a universe as Vietnam.

Nonetheless, by the use of overbearing close-ups, drained colors, harsh white and cold blue lighting, minimal dialogue, and an unnaturally clean and severe barracks set in the film's stylized marine training-camp prologue, Kubrick succeeds in choreographing the transformation of unformed young men into trained killers. The opening shots of the recruits having their hair shorn and lining up like manikins around their bunks sets the tone. At the helm of this dehumanization process is an obscenity-spouting, bullying drill instructor, Sgt. Hartman (played by former marine drill instructor Lee Ermey). Hartman subjects his recruits to a relentless, sardonic, scatological barrage (breaking most sexual and racial taboos) that is so oppressively effective that he strips the men of their past identities and creates new ones for them, complete with names like Pvt. Joker (Matthew Modine), Pvt. Cowboy (Arliss Howard), and Pvt. Pyle (Vincent D'Onofrio).

Hartman's harangues often attain the pitch of a ribald opera or the imagistic richness of a poet of the profane. His corrosive humor can be also inspiring, leading the men in singing "Happy Birthday Dear Jesus" on Christmas Day and chanting "This is my rifle that is my gun, this is for fighting this is for fun," as they hold their crotches. He suggests, too, that God has a hard-on for marines because they kill everything they see and supply heaven with fresh souls. All his routines and invective are permeated with a sense of menace. And Kubrick has never been clearer about the connection between sex, aggression, and death—rifles and cocks (Hartman orders his men to give girls' names to their rifles)—a link that in *Full Metal Jacket* has grotesque results.

In this instance, it's Hartman's belief in aggression—the passion for the rifle and killing—that makes the men into "outstanding" marines. His greatest success is Pvt. Pyle, a slow-witted, awkward lump of a man whom he mercilessly victimizes and turns into the squad's scapegoat. Nevertheless, Hartman is able to transform him from a mild-mannered incompetent into a sharpshooting, demented killer. This brutalized monster never gets to display his skills in Vietnam, for the conditioning process backfires and he turns on his sadistic master in a visually striking, frightening murder-suicide scene, a close-up of a wild-eyed, slobbering Pyle enveloped in a ghostly white light first killing Hartman and then shooting himself in the head.

Unfortunately, the compressed power and brilliance of its 45-minute prologue makes the Vietnam portion of the film pale in comparison. Much of the problem lies in the fact that the film's central, choruslike figure Pvt. Joker (whose progress in the war the rest of the film follows) is a less-defined and striking character then the larger-than-life Hartman. Although played by Modine with a wry intelligence and a sense of irony, neither his cynicism about the war ("I wanted to meet people of an ancient and interesting culture and kill them") nor his schizoid relationship to it (wearing a peace symbol on his fatigues and inscribing "Born to Kill" on his helmet) make him a character one can connect with.

Joker's detachment is a projection of Kubrick's, and, rather than help reveal and synthesize (with a Brechtian form of irony) the nature of the war's madness, it merely acts as a medium for an impersonal and literal cataloguing of the war's absurdities. In his job as a correspondent for *Stars and Stripes*, Joker is witness to the kind of hype and packaging that went into our propaganda effort as his smooth, cynical editor announces at an editorial meeting, "We have two types of stories here: grunts who give half their salary to buy gooks toothbrushes and deodorant, winning hearts and minds, and combat action that results in a kill, winning the war." The goal is happy news, and even search-and-destroy missions are euphemistically turned into "sweep-and-clear" expeditions.

In a similar fashion, thrust into combat by the Tet offensive and soon engaged in house-to-house fighting in the rubble of Hue, Joker meets a pompous, ridiculous major, who tells him, "All I've ever asked of my men is to believe my orders as they would the words of God." Kubrick's heavy-handed use of irony here is matched by a scene where GIs are interviewed by a television camera crew. In this tedious and self-conscious sequence, each exhausted, wary grunt makes a comment that either exhibits his lack of comprehension of the nature of the war or his desire to put on the journalists: "You think we waste gooks for freedom. After we rotate back to the world we're gonna miss not having anybody around to shoot."

The ultimate irony inherent in Kubrick's send-up of this world of killers is that the film's most vital figures are the most murderous. Like Sgt. Hartman, the brutal, Ramboesque GI Animal Mother (Adam Baldwin) takes great pride in being crude and cruel. Still, it is he who rises to the situation and leads the squad in eliminating a young female sniper who has pinned them down and killed a number of his buddies. Of course, Kubrick does not endorse this world of war lovers, but, just like in *Clockwork Orange*, there exists here a powerful strain of sympathy for those figures whose openly barbaric behavior is at home in a nihilistic world. For Kubrick, it's the misanthropic and the near-psychopathic who dominate and often triumph in the midst of war's lunacy.

By the film's conclusion, the humane Joker (with the legacy of Sgt. Hartman goading him on) inevitably turns into a killer, finishing off the praying, wounded female sniper who is responsible for the squad's bloodbath. Shooting in close-up, Kubrick treats Joker's decision to execute the sniper as a great moral crisis. But the combination of Joker's pallid, undefined character and the young girl's plea to be shot subverts much of the moral resonance implicit in this choice.

Despite these weaknesses, Kubrick, as always, is a master of visual and aural images and effects. He has an unerring gift for using popular culture to memorably project his nightmare vision of reality. In *Full Metal Jacket* he juxtaposes violent, painful images with a soundtrack carrying banal party songs like "Wooly Bully" and "These Boots Are Made for Walking," and he concludes the film with the marines marching into a blazing sunset singing "The Mickey Mouse Club Song." It's a chilling moment that ironically fuses the murderousness of Vietnam with the synthetic innocence of the pop culture that helped shape the sensibilities of the young marines. In Kubrick's world of "shit," this is almost all that is left of their past lives. The scene evokes memories of the climax of *Dr. Strangelove*, in which Vera Lynn (singing a sentimental, World War II paean to British endurance, "We'll Meet Again") is heard against an image of an H-Bomb explosion. In a similar fashion, Kubrick demonstrates a talent for set design, and the desolate, lunar landscaped Hue he constructed from an abandoned gasworks outside of London is as inspired as the surrealistic war room and the superrealist interior of the bomber plane in *Dr. Strangelove.*

However, Kubrick's imaginative images do not lessen one's sense that the second half of the film is derivative. Thus, a spaced-out helicopter machine gunner who answers the question "How do you manage to shoot women and children?" with the terrifying reply, "Easy, you don't lead them too far," could have easily stepped out of Coppola's *Apocalypse Now.* And the sniper sequence, where one after another of the marines is picked off and dies in blood-cascading slow motion, is a more-eccentric variation on World War II films like *The Story of GI Joe* as well as reminiscent of Peckinpah's *The Wild Bunch.*

Despite the conventionality and ponderous ironies of much of the film's second half, Kubrick's dark view of human nature is probably the film's most problematic element. In *Dr. Strangelove*, Kubrick's savagely comic view of the cold war brilliantly demolishes the nuclear fantasies of both the Soviet Union and the United States. However, this is a more-abstract situation than Vietnam, played out in the main by top-level political and military strategists who hold the fate of the world in their hands. Given that apocalyptic fact, the film got to the heart of the matter without distinguishing or deciding between the defense policies of either country. For Kubrick, both sides are equally culpable and open to caricature and condemnation. And his vision of absurd, incompetent, and mad power wielders in this case is probably more dramatically and politically pointed than a subtle evocation of the causes and policies of the cold war.

To render the complexity of the Vietnam experience, a Hobbesian view of man is insufficient. Vietnam was a particular event where one side—the United States—bore more responsibility for what happened than the other by its pursuit of policies that were as immoral as they were militarily futile. Blaming it all on the innate brutality and corruption of man may aptly describe a great deal of the behavior of all sides in Vietnam, but it is an evasion of the political issues and culture surrounding the war and its specific historical context. Oddly enough, *Full Metal Jacket* seems more in need of another version of *Dr. Strangelove*'s war room than a reconstruction of the killing fields of Hue.

Still, there are moments where *Full Metal Jacket*'s pessimism-cum-nihilism has great emotional effect, as in Joker's statement, which can ultimately be viewed as the credo of the Vietnam survivor, "I am in a world of shit, but I am alive and I am not afraid." The pungency of that image, however, falls short of capturing the character of Joker or the war he fought in. There is just too much anguish and remorse pervading the memory of Vietnam for it to be totally conceived of in terms of pitiless irony and black humor. And if the full experience of the war is ever to be depicted in film, it will take both more compassion and more psychological and political ambiguity than Kubrick's virtuosity is able to achieve.

In the wake of *Full Metal Jacket* and *Platoon*, other films, like *Hamburger Hill* (1987), have begun to appear. Written by Vietnam veteran James Carabatsos (*Heroes*) and directed by British, former-Vietnam-documentarian John Irvin (*Dogs of War*, [1980] *Turtle Diary* [1985]), the film deals with the 101st Airborne's May 1969 attack on a hill in the Ashau valley. Captured by U.S. troops after ten days of 11 murderous assaults, eventually evacuated and then reoccupied by the North Vietnamese, the hill became a symbol of the impotence and futility of the whole war.

Hamburger Hill is a starkly realistic slice of life, centering on a squad of 14 young men who are flung into battle on a muddy hill enveloped in flames and death. The squad consists of white country boys, a couple of urban white ethnics, and four blacks. Much of their talk is barely intelligible and for the most part their anonymous faces and characters blur into each other, with the exception of a pained, exhausted Sgt. Frantz (Dylan McDermott) and an articulate, bitter, race-conscious black Corpsman (Courtney Vance).

There is nothing literary or formally adventurous about *Hamburger Hill*. Its strength lies in Irvin's gift for capturing the agonizing sights and sounds of combat: heads and arms are blown away; intestines spill out; U.S. helicopters mistakenly shoot down their own troops; and rockets, artillery, and machine guns go off without a pause. However, despite the power of these images, one becomes a bit numbed by it all—too many scenes of and too little feeling evoked for GIs taking their last breath. In these sequences, the film cries out for some of the dramatic vividness and individuation of *Platoon*.

But like *Platoon*, it falls short when it tries to provide even a semblance of a moral or political overview of the war. It does contain a couple of incisive scenes of black-white tension and black anger about their being "no niggers at Headquarters." But other scenes where GIs rage at the antiwar movement, repeating every slander ever invented (long-haired hippies sleeping with their wives and girl friends), although probably an accurate rendition of the view of many grunts, demonstrate just how limited the film's perspective on the war can be. The antiwar movement may have been insensitive and condescending to the GIs, but neither they nor the media (who are depicted here as callous voyeurs) were the people and institutions who made the decision to entrap the grunts in Vietnam. And Carabatsos and Irvin never suggest that the truth of the war went far beyond the rants and resentments of the men.

Hamburger Hill merely narrows its focus to a re-creation of the war's harrowing realities and the black grunts' nihilistic chant "It don't mean nothing, not a thing" in the face of them. One hopes for something more than a vision of a terrifying and meaningless conflict balanced off by an affirmation of the courage and loyalty of the men who suffered through it. Here are men who don't take drugs, shirk combat, or question that a hill must be taken. In the film's concluding scene, the camera zooms to the squad's three survivors, who sit on top of a hill stripped of vegetation, the wind howling. There are dead bodies strewn all about. It's an overwhelmingly bleak image, but one senses that Carabatsos and Irvin dimly believe that there is moral heroism involved in winning the hill just because it's there. *Hamburger Hill* provides a distinctive portrait of the war's appalling, violent surface and still leaves us in a moral and political morass.

Possibly the most powerful justification for a Vietnam film with a wider perspective comes from a note left at the foot of the Washington, D.C., Vietnam Veterans' Memorial, which states that "war destroys everything except memories." If these memories are ever to constitute anything more than a stirring catalogue of the war's horrors, then they must be tempered and shaped by some broader moral and political vision. That vision must do more than explain or conceive of the war in literary and philosophical terms that avoid the particularity of the conflict. Only when the political and social issues that were at the heart of the war are illuminated will the Vietnam war film become a true act of remembrance.

Whether or not films of this nature are ever produced (although we are in the long run optimistic) remains to be seen. What is certain is that the Vietnam War will continue to be a subject that Hollywood and the television industry will employ and exploit for a long time to come. It's a trend that is already evident in the long list of studios planning or already making films in a variety of genres (including a war comedy, *Good Morning, Vietnam*) with a Vietnam War background. And by late 1987, both cable and network television (HBO's *Vietnam War Story* and CBS-TV's *Tour of Duty*) had broadcast dramatic series about the war.

Of course, given the tendency of the entertainment industry to imitate past successes, it will probably take a bit longer for new ground to be broken. Nevertheless, recent films have begun to drop us into the depths of Vietnam without much of the fustian and escapist fantasy that mythic figures like the superman had once provided. Indeed, after watching these films, we may now echo those final words of the Vietnam War memoir *Dispatches:* "Vietnam, Vietnam, we've all been there."[10]

Notes

Introduction

1. Ronald J. Glasser, *365 Days* (New York: George Braziller, 1980), p. 5.

PART ONE: The War Film and Vietnam

1. Paul Fussell, *The Great War and Modern Memory* (New York: Oxford University Press, 1979), pp. 18-29.

2. James Agee, *Agee on Film: Reviews and Comments* (New York: Beacon Press, 1958), p. 45.

3. Tim O'Brien, *Going after Cacciato* (New York: Dell, 1978), p. 236.

4. Fred Silva, ed., *Focus on The Birth of a Nation* (Engelwood Cliffs, N.J.: Prentice Hall, 1971).

5. Richard Schickel, *D.W. Griffith: An American Life* (New York: Touchstone, 1985), pp. 212-302.

6. Michael T. Isenberg, *War on Film: The American Cinema and World War I, 1914-1941* (Teaneck, N.J.: Fairleigh Dickinson University Press, 1981).

7. Eric Rhode, *A History of the Cinema: From Its Origins to 1970* (New York: Hill and Wang, 1976), pp. 254-55.

8. Raoul Walsh, *Each Man in His Time: The Life Story of a Director* (New York: Farrar, Straus & Giroux Inc., 1974), pp. 185-95.

9. Rhode, *History*, pp. 255-56.

10. Norman Kagan, *The War Film* (New York: Pyramid, 1974), pp. 130-33.

11. John Clellon Holmes, ''15ᶜ before 6:30 P.M.: The Wonderful Movies of the Thirties,'' in *From the Crash to the Fair, 1929-1939*, program of the Public Theatre, October 29-November 11, 1979, p. 13.

12. Robert Sklar, *Movie Made America: A Cultural History of American Movies* (New York: Vintage, 1975), pp. 244-56.

13. *Ibid.*

14. Eric Sevareid, *Not So Wild a Dream: A Personal Story of Youth and War and the American Faith* (New York: Atheneum, 1978), p. 225.

15. *Ibid.*

16. *Ibid.*

17. Kagan, *The War Film,* pp. 66-70.

18. Agee, *Agee on Film,* pp. 171-75.

19. Kagan, *The War Film,* pp. 72-74.

20. Leonard Quart and Albert Auster, *American Film and Society Since 1945* (New York: Praeger, 1984), pp. 18-21.

21. *Ibid.,* pp. 34-35.

22. Eric F. Goldman, *The Crucial Decade And After: America, 1945-60.* (New York: Vintage, 1960).

23. Alfred Kazin, *Bright Book of Life* (Boston: Little, Brown, 1973), p. 81.

24. Victor S. Navasky, *Naming Names* (New York: Viking, 1980).

25. Nora Sayre, *Running Time: Films of the Cold War* (New York: Dial Press, 1982), pp. 79-99.

26. Goldman, *The Crucial Decade,* pp. 174-201.

27. Julian Smith, *Looking Away: Hollywood and Vietnam* (New York: Charles Scribner's Sons, 1975), pp. 39-40.

28. Sayre, *Running Time,* pp. 130, 185.

29. Joseph C. Goulden, *The Best Years: 1945-1960,* (New York: Atheneum, 1976), p. 433.

30. George C. Herring, *America's Longest War: The United States and Vietnam, 1950-1975* (New York: John Wiley & Sons, 1979).

31. Smith, *Looking Away,* pp. 105-7.

32. *Ibid.,* pp. 108-13.

33. Gilbert Adair, *Vietnam on Film: From the Green Berets to Apocalypse Now* (New York: Proteus, 1981), pp. 29-32.

34. Herring, *America's Longest War,* pp. 73-107.

35. William J. Lederer and Eugene Burdick, *The Ugly American* (New York: Crest, 1962).

36. Judith Crist, *The Private Eye, The Cowboy, and the Very Naked Girl* (New York: Paperback Library, 1970), pp. 160-61.

37. Smith, *Looking Away,* pp. 115-22.

PART TWO: The War That Dared Not Speak Its Name: Wounded Heroes and Supermen

1. Kenneth Keniston, *Young Radicals: Notes on Committed Youth* (New York: Harcourt, Brace Jovanovich Inc., 1968), pp. 229-56.

2. Paul Cowan, *The Making of an UnAmerican: A Dialogue with Experience* (New York: Viking, 1970), p. 11.

3. Richard J. Walton, *Cold War and Counter-Revolution: The Foreign Policy of John F. Kennedy* (Baltimore, Md.: Penguin, 1973), p. 142.

4. Peter Biskind, *Seeing Is Believing: How Hollywood Taught Us to Stop Worrying and Love the Fifties* (New York: Pantheon, 1983), pp. 51-98.

5. Susan Sontag, *Against Interpretation* (New York: Dell, 1969), pp. 212-28.

6. *Ibid.*, p. 215.

7. Quart and Auster, *American Film and Society*, pp. 78-82.

8. Norman Kagan, *The Cinema of Stanley Kubrick* (New York: Grove Press, 1972), p. 132.

9. Quart and Auster, *American Film and Society*, pp. 76-77.

10. Godfrey Hodgson, *America in Our Time: From World War II to Nixon, What Happened and Why* (New York: Vintage, 1978), pp. 274-352.

11. Norman Mailer, *Armies of the Night* (New York: Signet, 1968), p. 47.

12. John G. Cawelti, *Focus on Bonnie and Clyde* (Engelwood Cliffs, N.J.: Prentice-Hall, 1973), pp. 22-23.

13. Quart and Auster, *American Film and Society*, pp. 85-87.

14. Kagan, *The War Film*, pp. 119-121.

15. Adair, *Vietnam on Film*, pp. 33-52.

16. Renata Adler, *A Year in the Dark* (New York: Berkeley Books, 1969), pp. 199-200.

17. Gary Wills, *The Kennedy Imprisonment: A Meditation on Power* (New York: Pocket Books, 1983), p. 295.

18. Leonard Quart, "Altman's Films," *Marxist Perspectives* 1 (Spring 1978): 21-33.

19. Pauline Kael, *Deeper into Movies* (New York: Bantam, 1974), pp. 122-26.

20. William L. O'Neill, *Coming Apart: An Informal History of America in the 1960s* (New York: Quadrangle, 1971), p. 425.

21. Quart and Auster, *American Film and Society*, pp. 95-97.

22. *Ibid.*, pp. 94-95.

23. Adair, *Vietnam on Film*, pp. 76-82.

24. *Ibid.*, pp. 60-62.

25. *Ibid.*, p. 88.

26. Kael, *Deeper into Movies*, pp. 429-36.

27. Robert J. Lifton, *Home from the War: Vietnam Veterans neither Victims nor Executioners* (New York: Touchstone, 1973), pp. 35-71.

28. Stanley Karnow, *Vietnam: A History* (New York: Penguin, 1984), pp. 577-612.

29. *Ibid.*, p. 582.

30. Robert Hatch, "Films: Tracks,"*T he Nation*, March 17, 1979, p. 285.

31. Adair, *Vietnam on Film*, pp. 101-2.

32. Kael, *Deeper into Movies*, pp. 484-89.

33. Dixon Wecter, *When Johnny Comes Marching Home* (Boston: Houghton Miflin, 1944).

34. Albert Auster and Leonard Quart, "Hollywood and Vietnam: The Triumph of the Will," *Cineaste* 9 (1979): 4-9.

35. Vincent Canby, "Rolling Thunder! Film, Few Claps," *New York Times*, October 15, 1977, p. 20.

36. Rob Edelman, "A Second Look: 'Go Tell the Spartans'," *Cineaste* 13 (1983): 18-19, 54.

37. John Simon, *Reverse Angle: A Decade of American Films* (New York: Clarkson N. Potter, 1982), pp. 291-94.

38. Hodgson, *America in Our Time*, p. 354.

39. Jonathan Schell, *The Time of Illusion* (New York: Alfred A. Knopf, 1976), p. 91.

40. *Ibid.*, p. 382.

41. *New York Times*, November 28, 1984, p. 2e.

42. Karnow, *Vietnam*, p. 668.

43. *Ibid.*

44. *Newsweek*, December 14, 1981, p. 46.

45. Ed Roginski, *"'Who'll Stop the Rain,'"* *Film Quarterly*, Winter 1979, pp. 57-61.

46. D. H. Lawrence, *Studies in Classic American Literature* (Garden City, N.Y.: Doubleday, 1951), p. 73.

47. Auster and Quart, "Hollywood and Vietnam," pp. 4-9.

48. E. M. Forster, *Abinger Harvest* (New York: Harcourt, Brace, Jovanovich, 1964), pp. 136-41.

49. Joseph Conrad, *Heart of Darkness* (New York: Signet, 1959), pp. 57-142.

50. *Ibid.*

51. Virginia Woolf, *The Common Reader* (New York: Harcourt, Brace, Jovanovich, 1953), pp. 228-35.

52. Conrad, *Heart of Darkness*, pp. 57-142.

53. Friedrich Nietzsche, *Thus Spake Zarathrustra* (New York: Modern Library, undated), p. 126.

54. Eleanor Coppola, *Notes* (New York: Pocket Books, 1979), pp. 193-96.

55. Albert Auster and Leonard Quart, "Man and Superman: Vietnam and the New American Hero," *Social Policy* 11 (January-February 1981): 60-64.

PART THREE: Hunter-Heroes and Survivors

1. Richard H. Rovere, *Senator Joe McCarthy* (New York: World, 1966).

2. Laurence I. Barrett, *Gambling with History: Reagan in the White House* (New York: Penguin, 1984).

3. *New York Times*, November 28, 1984, p. 14.

4. *Ibid.*, February 2, 1985, p. 2e.

5. Robert Graves, *Goodbye to All That* (Garden City, N.Y.: Doubleday-Anchor, 1957), p. 287.

6. Mark Baker, *Nam: The Vietnam War in the Words of the Men and Women Who Fought There* (New York: Berkeley Books, 1983).

7. *Ibid.*, pp. 239-71.

8. *Ibid.*, p. 285.

9. Peter Goldman and Tony Fuller, *Charlie Company: What Vietnam Did to Us* (New York: Ballantine Books, 1983), p. 304.

10. Wallace Terry, *Bloods: An Oral History of the Vietnam War by Black Veterans* (New York: Random House, 1984), p. 15.

11. Joe Klein, *Payback: Five Marines and Vietnam* (New York: Ballantine Books, 1984).

12. Lou Cannon, *Reagan* (New York: Perigee Books, 1982), p. 271.

13. Goldman and Fuller, *Charlie Company*, p. xiii.

14. *The Wall Street Journal*, February-April, 1985.

15. John R. MacArthur, "A Plaintiff Ill-Used," *The New York Times*, February 25, 1985, p. E19.

16. William Shawcross, *Sideshow: Kissinger, Nixon, and the Destruction of Cambodia* (New York: Pocket Books, 1979).

17. Norman Podhoretz, *Why We Were in Vietnam* (New York: Simon and Schuster, 1982).

18. James Pinckney Harrison, *The Endless War: Vietnam's Struggle for Independence* (New York: McGraw-Hill, 1983).

19. Philip Caputo, *A Rumor of War* (New York: Ballantine Books, 1977), p. xiv.

20. Ron Kovic, *Born on the Fourth of July* (New York: Pocket Books, 1977), p. 108.

21. Norman Mailer, *Why Are We in Vietnam? A Novel* (New York: Berkeley Books, 1968), p. 224.

22. C. D. B. Bryan, "Barely Suppressed Screams: Getting a Bead on Vietnam Literature," *Harpers*, June 1984, pp. 67-72.

23. *Ibid.*, p. 67.

24. Ward Just, "Images of War: How America Recreates the 'Blood and Darkness'," *TV Guide*, January 29, 1983, pp. 2-4.

25. Leonard Quart and Albert Auster, "Cutter's Way," *Socialist Review* 12: 131-34.

26. Adair, *Vietnam and Film*, pp. 53-82.

27. David Sterritt, "A Small Circle of Friends," *Christian Science Monitor*, March 12, 1980, p. 18.

28. David Denby, "Making Love Not War," *New York Magazine*, March 24, 1980, pp. 76-77.

29. Terry, *Bloods*, p. 289.

30. *Ibid.*, p. 167.

31. Myra MacPherson, *Long Time Passing: Vietnam and the Haunted Generation* (New York: Signet, 1985), pp. 180-81.

32. *Ibid.*, p. 183.

33. *Ibid.*

34. *Ibid.*, p. 341.

35. Les Lescaze, "Vietnam Legacy: Inspired by Memorial, Veterans of the War Come into Their Own," *The Wall Street Journal*, April 4, 1985, p. 1.

36. Bill Paul, "Veterans Tale: Robert Garwood Says Vietnam Didn't Return Some American POWs," *The Wall Street Journal*, December 4, 1984, pp. 1, 11.

37. Stephen E. Ambrose, Rise to Globalism: American Foreign Policy, 1938-1970 (Baltimore, Md.: Penguin, 1971), p. 85.

38. William Shakespeare, *The Tragedy of Juilius Caesar* (New York: Washington Square Press, 1973), p. 85.

39. Stuart Byron, "The Searchers: Cut Movie of the New Hollywood," *New York*, March 5, 1979, pp. 45-48.

40. *Ibid.*, p. 46.

41. Richard Slotkin, *Regeneration through Violence: The Mythology of the American Frontier, 1660-1860* (Middletown, Conn.: Wesleyan University Press, 1973).

42. *Ibid.*, p. 562.

43. *Ibid.*, p. 563.

44. *Ibid.*

45. Judy Klemsrud, "Chuck Norris: Strong, Silent, Popular," *New York Times*, September 1, 1985, p. H14.

46. *New York Times*, July 1, 1985, pp. A1, 10.

47. *Ibid.*, September 2, 1985, pp. A1.

48. *Ibid.*, January 4, 1986, p. 3.

49. Angel Flores, ed. *An Anthology of French Poetry from Nerval to Valery in English Translation* (Garden City, N.Y.: Doubleday-Anchor, 1958), pp. 104-37.

50. Pauline Kael, "The Current Cinema: Unreal," *The New Yorker*, December 10, 1984, pp. 165-68.

51. Spalding Gray later created a one-man performance piece based upon his part in the making of *The Killing Fields* called, "Swimming to Cambodia." See Richard McKim, "Swimming to Cambodia," *Cineaste* 15, no. 4, (1987): 41-43.

52. Richard Grenier, "When It Comes to Movies, the World Looks to America," *New York Times*, September 25, 1985, p. H27.

53. Milan Kundera, *The Book of Laughter and Forgetting* (New York: Penguin, 1981), p. 3.

54. Seymour Hersh, *The Price of Power: Kissinger in the White House* (New York: Summit Books, 1983), pp. 174-83.

55. William Broyles, Jr., *Brother in Arms: A Journey from War to Peace* (New York: Alfred A. Knopf, 1986), p. 200.

56. *Ibid.*, p. 267.

57. *Ibid.*, p. 275.

58. Samuel G. Freedman, "The War and the Arts," *New York Times Magazine*, March 31, 1985, pp. 52-54.

59. Vincent Canby, "Screen: 'Alamo Bay'—Ethnic Strife in Texas," *New York Times*, April 3, 1985, p. 27.

60. John Culhane, "Louis Malle: An Outsider's Odyssey," *New York Times Magazine*, April 7, 1985, pp. 28, 68.

61. Steve Howard, "A Cinema of Transformation: The Films of Haile Gerima," *Cineaste* 14 (1985): 29.

62. Michael Herr, *Dispatches* (New York: Avon, 1978), p. 200.

63. Bryan, "Barely Suppressed Screams," p. 72.

PART FOUR: Confronting Vietnam

1. Karnow, *Vietnam*, p. 667.

2. Podhoretz, *Why We Were in Vietnam*, pp. 9-15.

3. Richard Corliss, et al., "Platoon: Vietnam, The Way it Really Was," *Time*, January 26, 1987, pp. 54-61.

4. John Del Vecchio, *The 13th Valley* (New York: Bantam, 1983), p. 132.

5. Bob Thomas, "Paul Hustles in 'Platoon' and Allen All Winners," *New York Daily News*, March 31, 1987, p. 5.

6. "Oliver Stone's Platoon Buddies Recall the War 20 Years Later," *People*, May 11, 1987, pp. 81-88.

7. Robert Lindsey, "Coppola Returns to the Vietnam Era, Minus Apocalypse," *New York Times*, May 3, 1987, pp. 19, 34.

8. Jack Kroll, "1968: Kubrick's Vietnam Odyssey," *Newsweek*, June 29, 1987, pp. 64-65.

9. Vincent Canby, "Film: Kubrick's 'Full Metal Jacket,' On Vietnam," *New York Times*, June 26, 1987, p. C3. See also Pauline Kael, "The Current Cinema: Ponderosa," *The New Yorker*, July 13, 1987, pp. 75-76; David Denby, "Death

Trap,'' *New York*, July 13, 1987, pp. 54-55; and Stanley Kaufmann, ''Blank Cartridge,'' *The New Republic*, July 27, 1987, pp. 28-29.

10. Herr, *Dispatches*, p. 278.

Bibliography

Books

Adair, Gilbert. *Vietnam on Film: From the Green Berets to Apocalypse Now*. New York: Proteus, 1981.

Adler, Renata. *A Year in the Dark*. New York: Berkeley Books, 1969.

Agee, James. *Agee on Film: Reviews and Comments*. New York: Beacon Press, 1958.

Baker, Mark. *Nam: The Vietnam War in the Words of the Men and Women Who Fought There*. New York: Berkeley Books, 1983.

Barrett, Laurence I. *Gambling with History: Reagan in the White House*. New York: Penguin, 1984.

Biskind, Peter. *Seeing Is Believing: How Hollywood Taught Us to Stop Worrying and Love the Fifties*. New York: Pantheon, 1983.

Broyles, William, Jr. *Brother in Arms: A Journey from War to Peace*. New York: Alfred A. Knopf, 1986.

Cannon, Lou. *Reagan*. New York: Perigee Books, 1982.

Caputo, Phillip. *A Rumor of War*. New York: Ballantine Books, 1977.

Cawelti, John G. *Focus on Bonnie and Clyde*. Engelwood Cliffs, N.J.: Prentice-Hall, 1973.

Conrad, Joseph. *Heart of Darkness*. New York: Sygnet, 1959.

Coppola, Eleanor. *Notes*. New York: Pocket Books, 1979.

Cowan, Paul. *The Making of an UnAmerican: A Dialogue with Experience*. New York: Viking, 1970.

Crist, Judith. *The Private Eye, the Cowboy, and the Very Naked Girl*. New York: Paperback Library, 1970.

Del Vecchio, John. *The 13th Valley*. New York: Bantam, 1983.

Flores, Angel, ed. *An Anthology of French Poetry from Nerval to Valery in English Translation*. Garden City, N.Y.: Doubleday-Anchor, 1958.

Forster, E. M. *Abinger Harvest*. New York: Harcourt, Brace, Jovanovich, 1964.

Fussell, Paul. *The Great War and Modern Memory*. New York: Oxford University Press, 1979.

Glasser, Ronald J. *365 Days.* New York: George Braziller, 1980.

Goldman, Eric F. *The Crucial Decade: and after America, 1945-1960.* New York: Vintage, 1960.

Goldman, Peter, and Tony Fuller. *Charlie Company: What Vietnam Did to Us.* New York: Ballantine Books, 1983.

Goulden, Joseph C. *The Best Years: 1945-1960.* New York: Atheneum, 1976.

Graves, Robert. *Goodbye to All That.* Garden City, N.Y.: Doubleday-Anchor, 1957.

Harrison, James Pinckey. *The Endless War: Vietnam's Struggle for Independence.* New York: McGraw-Hill, 1983.

Herr, Michael. *Dispatches.* New York: Avon, 1978.

Herring, George C. *America's Longest War: The United States and Vietnam, 1950-1975.* New York: John Wiley & Sons, 1979.

Hersh, Seymour. *The Price of Power: Kissinger in the White House.* New York: Summit Books, 1983.

Hodgson, Godfrey. *America in Our Time: From World War II to Nixon, What Happened and Why.* New York: Vintage, 1978.

Isenberg, Michael T. *War on Film: The American Cinema and World War I, 1914-1941.* Teaneck, N.J.: Fairleigh Dickinson University Press, 1981.

Kael, Pauline. *Deeper into Movies.* New York: Bantam, 1974.

Kagan, Norman. *The Cinema of Stanley Kubrick.* New York: Grove Press, 1972.

_____. *The War Film.* New York: Pyramid, 1974.

Karnow, Stanley. *Vietnam: A History.* New York: Penguin, 1984.

Kazin, Alfred. *Bright Book of Life.* Boston: Little, Brown, 1973.

Keniston, Kenneth. *Young Radicals: Notes on Committed Youth.* New York: Harcourt, Brace and World, 1968.

Klein, Joe. *Payback: Five Marines and Vietnam.* New York: Ballantine Books, 1984.

Kovic, Ron. *Born on the Fourth of July.* New York: Pocket Books, 1977.

Kundera, Milan. *The Book of Laughter and Forgetting.* New York: Penguin, 1981.

Lederer, William J., and Eugene Burdick. *The Ugly American.* New York: Crest, 1962.

Lifton, Robert J. *Home from the War: Vietnam Veterans neither Victims nor Executioners.* New York: Touchstone, 1973.

MacPherson, Myra. *Long Time Passing: Vietnam and the Haunted Generation.* New York: Signet, 1985.

Mailer, Norman. *Armies of the Night.* New York: Signet, 1968.

_____. *Why Are We in Vietnam? A Novel.* New York: Berkeley Books, 1968.

Navasky, Victor S. *Naming Names.* New York: Viking, 1980.

Nietzsche, Friedrich. *Thus Spake Zarathrusta.* New York: Modern Library, undated.

O'Brien, Tim. *Going after Cacciato.* New York: Dell, 1978.

O'Neill, William L. *Coming Apart: An Informal History of America in the 1960's.* New York: Quadrangle, 1971.

Podhoretz, Norman. *Why We Were in Vietnam.* New York: Simon and Shuster, 1982.

Quart, Leonard, and Albert Auster. *American Film and Society Since 1945.* New York: Praeger, 1984.

Rhode, Eric. *A History of the Cinema: From its Origins to 1970.* New York: Hill and Wang, 1976.

Rovere, Richard H. *Senator Joe McCarthy.* New York: World, 1976.

Sayre, Nora. *Running Times: Films of the Cold War.* New York: Dial Press, 1982.

Schell, Jonathan. *The Time of Illusion.* New York: Alfred A. Knopf, 1976.

Schickel, Richard. *D.W. Griffith: An American Life.* New York: Touchstone, 1985.

Sevareid, Eric. *Not So Wild a Dream: A Personal Story of Youth and War and the American Faith.* New York: Atheneum, 1978.

Shakespeare, William. *The Tragedy of Julius Caesar.* New York: Washington Square Press, 1973.

Shawcross, William. *Sideshow: Kissinger, Nixon, and the Destruction of Cambodia.* New York: Pocket Books, 1979.

Silva, Fred, ed. *Focus on the Birth of a Nation.* Engelwood Cliffs, N.J.: Prentice-Hall, 1971.

Simon, John. *Reverse Angle: A Decade of American Films.* New York: Clarkson-Potter, 1982.

Sklar, Robert. *Movie Made America: A Cultural History of American Movies.* New York: Vintage, 1975.

Slotkin, Richard. *Regeneration through Violence: The Mythology of the American Frontier, 1660-1860.* Middletown, Conn.: Wesleyan University Press, 1973.

Smith, Julian. *Looking Away: Hollywood and Vietnam.* New York: Charles Scribner's Sons, 1975.

Sontag, Susan. *Against Interpretation.* New York: Dell, 1969.

Terry, Wallace. *Bloods: An Oral History of the Vietnam War by Black Veterans.* New York: Random House, 1984.

Walsh, Raoul. *Each Man in His Time: The Life Story of a Director.* New York: Farrar, Straus and Giroux, 1974.

Walton, Richard, J. *Cold War and Counter-Revolution: The Foreign Policy of John F. Kennedy.* Baltimore, Md.: Penguin, 1973.

Wecter, Dixon. *When Johnny Comes Marching Home.* Boston: Houghton Miflin, 1944.

Willis, Gary. *The Kennedy Imprisonment: A Meditation on Power.* New York: Pocket Books, 1983.

Woolf, Virginia. *The Common Reader.* New York: Harcourt, Brace, Jovanovich, 1953.

Magazine and Newspaper Articles

Auster, Albert and Leonard Quart. "Hollywood and Vietnam: The Triumph of the Will." *Cineaste* 9 (Spring 1979): 4-9.

_____. "Man and Superman: Vietnam and the New American Hero." *Social Policy* 11 (January-February 1981): 60-64.

Bryan, C. D. B. "Barely Suppressed Screams: Getting a Bead on Vietnam Literature." *Harpers*, June, 1984, pp. 67-72.

Byron, Stuart. "The Searchers: Cult Movie of the New Hollywood." *New York*, March 5, 1979, pp. 45-48.

Canby, Vincent. "Rolling Thunder! Film, Few Claps." *New York Times*, October 15, 1977, p. 20.

_____. "Screen: 'Alamo Bay', Ethnic Strife in Texas." *New York Times*, April 3, 1985, p. 27.

_____. "Film: Kubrick's 'Full Metal Jacket,' On Vietnam." *New York Times,* June 26, 1987, p. C3.

Corliss, Richard, et al. "Platoon: Vietnam, The War It Really Was," *Time,* January 26, 1987, pp. 54-61.

Culhane, John. "Louis Malle: An Outsider's Odyssey." *New York Times Magazine,* April 7, 1985, pp. 28, 68.

Denby, David. "Making Love Not War." *New York Magazine,* March 24, 1980, pp. 76-77.

_____. "Death Trap." *New York Magazine* July 13, 1987, pp. 54-55.

Edelman, Rob. "A Second Look: 'Go Tell the Spartans'." *Cineaste* 13 (1983): 18-19.

Freedman, Samuel, G. "The War and the Arts." *New York Times Magazine,* March 31, 1985, pp. 52-54.

Grenier, Richard. "When it Comes to Movies, the World Looks to America," *New York Times,* September 25, 1985, p. H27.

Hatch, Robert. "Films: 'Tracks," *The Nation,* (March 17, 1979), p. 285.

Holmes, John Clellon. "15¢ before 6:30 P.M.: The Wonderful Movies of the Thirties." In *From the Crash to the Fair, 1929-1939, Program of The Public Theatre* (October 29-November 11, 1979), p. 13.

Howard, Steve. "A Cinema of Transformation: The Films of Haile Gerima." *Cineaste* 14 (1985): 29.

Just, Ward. "Images of War: How America Recreates the 'Blood and Darkness'." *TV Guide,* January 29, 1983, pp. 2-4.

Kael, Pauline. "The Current Cinema: Ponderosa." *The New Yorker,* July 13, 1978, pp. 75-76.

Kauffmann, Stanley. "Blank Cartridge." *The New Republic,* July 27, 1987, pp. 28-29.

Klemsrud, Judy. "Chuck Norris: Strong, Silent, Popular." *New York Times,* September 1, 1985, p. H14.

Kroll, Jack. "1968: Kubrick's Vietnam Odyssey." *Newsweek,* June 29, 1987, pp. 64-65.

Lescaze, Les. "Vietnam Legacy: Inspired by Memorial, Veterans of the War Come into Their Own." *The Wall Street Journal,* April 4, 1985, p. 1.

Lindsey, Robert. "Coppola Returns to the Vietnam Era, Minus Apocalypse." *New York Times,* May 3, 1987, pp. 19, 34.

MacArthur, John R. "A Plaintiff Ill-Used." *The New York Times,* February 25, 1985, p. E19.

McKim, Richard. "Swimming to Cambodia." *Cineaste* 15, no. 4 (1987): 41-43.

Paul, Bill. "Veterans Tale: Robert Darwood Says Vietnam Didn't Return Some American POWs." *The Wall Street Journal,* December 4, 1984, pp. 1, 11.

Quart, Leonard. "Altman's Films." *Marxist Perspectives* 1 (Spring 1978): 21-33.

_____. "A Step in the Right Direction." *Cineaste* 15 (1987): 6-7.

Quart, Leonard, and Albert Auster. "Cutters Way." *Socialist Review* 12: 131-34.

Roginski, Ed. "Who'll Stop the Rain," *Film Quarterly,* Winter 1979, pp. 57-61.

Sterritt, David. "A Small Circle of Friends." *Christian Science Monitor,* March 12, 1980, p. 18.

Thomas, Bob. "Paul Hustles in 'Platoon' and Allen All Winners," *New York Daily News,* March 31, 1987, p. 5.

New York Times, November 28, 1984, p. 14.

New York Times, February 2, 1985, p. 2E

New York Times, July 1, 1985, p. 1.10.

New York Times, September 2, 1985, p. A1.

New York Times, January 4, 1986, p. 3.

"Oliver Stone's Platoon Buddies Recall the War 20 Years Later." *People*, May 11, 1987, pp. 81-88.

Index

Above and Beyond, 24
Academy Awards, 78-79
Acheson, Dean, 9
Adler, Renata, 34
aerial footage, 4
Agee, James, 1, 7
Aiken, George, 79
Alamo Bay, 122, 126
Aldrich, Robert, 11, 55
Alice's Restaurant, 41-42, 88
Allen, Dede, 29
Allen, Karen, 89
All Quiet on the Western Front, 4-5
Altman, Robert, 35
Americana, 98
American Graffiti, 88
Americanization of Emily, The, 30
Anderson, John, 127
Anderson, Maxwell, 4
Andrews, Julie, 30
Apocalypse Now, 65-71, 79, 84, 88, 93,
    103, 114, 135, 138, 141, 145
Arlen, Richard, 4
Arnold, Edward, 86
Arrowsmith, 112
Ashby, Hal, 49, 85
Ashes and Embers, 126-29
Askew, Luke, 33
A Team, The, 112

Atlantic City, 121
Atlantic Monthly, 97
Attack!, 11
Ayres, Lew, 5

Bailey, F. Lee, 48
Baldwin, Adam, 144
Barry, Gene, 13
Bataan, 100
Battle of Algiers, The, 114
Battle Circus, 13
Battle Cry, 13
Beatles, 28
Berenger, Tom, 125
Berkeley Barb, 28
Berkoff, Steven, 108
Best Years of Our Lives, The, 7, 42, 96
Big Chill, The, 90
Big Parade, The, 3
Billy Jack, 42-44
Birdy, 124-26
Birth of A Nation, 2-3
Black Gunn, 49
black humor, 25-26, 29
Black Legion, 123
black market, 8
blacks, 96-97, 126-29
Black Sunday, 45
Blackwell, Evelyn, 127

Blalock, Norman, 128
bloodbath theory, 82
Bloods, 80
Blumenthal, Michael, 97
Bomber's B-52, 24
Bonnie and Clyde, 28-29
Boone, Daniel, 109
Boothe, Powers, 91
Bormann, Martin, 13
Born Losers, 42
Born to Win, 85
Boys in Company C, The, 55, 113
Brando, Marlon, 19, 42, 68, 85, 109
Bridge over the River Kwai, The, 11, 12, 100
Bridges, Jeff, 86, 87
Bridges at Toko Ri, The, 13
Broderick, James, 41
Broken Lullaby (Lubitsch), 5
Bronson, Charles, 48
Brooke, Rupert, 83
Brother in Arms: A Journey from War to Peace (Broyles), 120
Brown, Reb, 100
Broyles, William, Jr., 97, 120
Bryan, C.D.B., 84, 130
Buchanan, Pat, 118
Buddhists, 19
Bugsy Malone, 124
Bundy, McGeorge, 19, 56, 81
Burdick, Eugene, 19, 24
Bush Mama, 127
Bustin' Loose, 95

Caan, James, 140
Cage, Nicholas, 124, 126
Caine Mutiny, The, 11
Cambodia, 82, 116-17
Canby, Vincent, 52
captivity myth, 102, 103
Caputo, Philip, 83
Carabatsos, James, 146, 147
Carlin, Gloria, 140
Carradine, David, 98
Carradine, Keith, 91
Carradine, Robert, 50
Carter, Jimmy, 97
Casablanca, 13

catharsis, 2
Cazale, John, 62
CBS Reports, 80
Cease Fire, 129
Chaplin, Charlie, 3
Chariots of Fire, 113
Charlie Company: What Vietnam Did to Us, 80
Cherry, Col. Fred V., 95
Chetwynd, Lionel, 140
China, 9, 81-82
China Gate, 13-16, 22
Christie, Agatha, 91
Churchill, Winston, 13
Cimino, Michael, 58, 60, 61, 62, 63, 64, 72, 73, 79, 85, 129
Civil War, 2-3
Clockwork Orange, A, 142, 144
Cobb, Randall, 100
Cohen, Rob, 88
cold war, 8-9, 20-21
Cole, Nat King, 13, 15
Coming Home, 42, 49-52, 79, 84, 120
Commentary, 82
Communism, 9, 117-18
Communist China, 81-82
Conan the Barbarian, 99
Conrad, Joseph, 65, 68, 132
consciousness, 128
Cooder, Ry, 90
Cooper, Gary, 80
Cooper, James Fenimore, 59-60, 109
Coppola, Eleanor, 70
Coppola, Francis Ford, 65, 66, 67, 68, 69, 70, 71, 72, 79, 85, 129, 140, 141, 145
Cowan, Paul, 23
Cox, Ron, 96
Crane, Stephen, 134
credibility gap, 76
Crenna, Richard, 93, 94
Crist, Judith, 19
Crockett, Davy, 109
Crowther, Bosley, 28
Cuban missile crisis, 24
Culver, John, 57
Cummings, e. e., 83
Cutter's Way, 85-88

David, Keith, 134
Davis, Brad, 89
Davison, Bruce, 39
Death Wish, 48
decent interval, 52
Deer Hunter, The, 58-65, 72, 79, 84,
    85, 88, 93, 103, 120, 129, 139
Deerslayer, The, 60
Defoe, Willem, 135, 136
Deliverance, 91
Del Vecchio, John, 131
De Niro, Robert, 40, 47, 58, 85
Denton, Jeremiah, 76
De Palma, Brian, 40, 88
depression, 29
Dern, Bruce, 45, 46, 50
Devane, William, 46

Dickey, James, 91
Dickinson, Angie, 15
Diem, Ngo Dinh, 12-13, 17, 18, 19
Dietrich, Marlene, 8
Dillon, Kevin, 134
Dirty Harry, 48, 99
Dirty Dozen, The, 55
Dispatches (Herr), 84, 147
Dr. Strangelove, 24, 25-26, 142, 144, 145
Dog Soldiers (Stone), 57, 65
Dogs of War, 146
domino theory, 18, 82
D'Onofrio, Vincent, 142, 143
Dos Passos, John, 83
Douglas, Melvyn, 30
Dowd, Nancy, 49
draft, 40
drugs, 56
Dubois, W.E.B., 128
Durning, Charles, 55
Duvall, Robert, 36, 66
Dylan, Bob, 28
Dzunda, George, 62

East Village Other, 28
Eastwood, Clint, 48, 99
Easy Rider, 38-39
Eichorn, Lisa, 87
Eisenhower, Dwight D., 12, 18, 75

Eliot, T. S., 68
Elliot, Steven, 86
Emerson, Gloria, 84
*Endless War, The: Vietnam's Struggle
    for Independence* (Harrison), 82
Enforcer, The, 48
Englund, George, 19, 20
Ermey, Lee, 142
E. T., 94
Evans, Evans, 29
Evans, Gene, 10
Everything We Had, 80

Fail Safe, 24-25
Fallows, James, 97
female characters, 87-88
Field, Sally, 45
film noir, 48
Filson, John, 102
Fireman's Ball, 85
First Blood, 93-95, 98, 99, 107, 108,
    121
Five Gates to Hell, 18
Fix Bayonets, 11
Fonda, Henry, 24
Fonda, Jane, 50, 78, 85, 140
Fonda, Peter, 39
Force of Evil, 72
Force of One, 104
Ford, Gerald, 131
Ford, John, 31, 36, 63, 91, 101, 141
Foreign Affair, A, 8
Forester, E. M., 65
Forman, Milos, 85
Forster, Robert, 39
Foster, Jodie, 48
Four Friends, 90
Franciscus, James, 104
Frankenheimer, John, 26, 45
Friedman, Bruce Jay, 26
Friedrich, John, 89
Friendly Fire (Bryan), 84
From Hell to Eternity, 13
From Here to Eternity, 11
Fuller, Samuel, 9, 10, 13, 15
Full Metal Jacket, 140, 142-46
Furie, Sidney, 55, 113
Fussell, Paul, 1

Gabriel, Peter, 126
Gardens of Stone, 140-41
Garfield, John, 42
Garner, John, 30
Gayton, Joe, 99
General William Westmoreland v. *CBS,*
     80-81
Gerima, Hale, 126, 127, 128, 129
Germany, 3
Getting Straight, 39, 40, 88
Gilbert, John, 3
Glasser, Ronald J., 84
Going after Cacciato, 1, 78, 83
Golden Bough (Frazer), 68
Goldwater, Barry, 31
Good Guys Wear Black, 104, 105
Goodman, Paul, 28
Good Morning, Vietnam, 147
Go Tell the Spartans, 52-55
Gould, Elliot, 36, 40
Graham, Gerritt, 40
Graves, Robert, 77, 83
Great War and Modern Memory, The
     (Fussell), 1
Green Berets, The, 31-34, 38, 79, 103
Greene, Graham, 16, 19
Greetings, 40-41, 88
Griffith, D. W., 2, 3, 123
Gritz, James B., 99
guilt, 97
Gung Ho, 7
Guns of Navarrone, The, 19
Guthrie, Arlo, 41
Guthrie, Woody, 41

Hackman, Gene, 100, 101, 103, 108
Haggard, H. Rider, 1
Hamburger Hill, 146-47
Hanoi Hilton, 140
Harper's, 81
Harris, Ed, 121, 122
Harrison, James Pinckney, 82
Heard, John, 85, 86
Heart of Darkness, The (Conrad), 65
Hearts of the World, 3
Heaven's Gate, 85
Heller, Joseph, 26
Hemingway, Ernest, 83

Herodotus, 52
Heroes, 42, 45
Hershey, Barbara, 98
Hill, Walter, 90, 91, 92
Hi! Mom, 88
Histories, The (Herodotus), 52
Ho Chi Minh, 12, 13
Hollow Men, The (Eliot), 68
Holmes, John Clennon, 5
homecoming, 78, 81
Hopper, Dennis, 39, 46, 70
hostages, 80
Howard, Arliss, 142
humor, 25-26, 29
hunter-hero, 103, 104, 109, 138
Huston, Anjelica, 141
Hutton, Jim, 10

image, 57
imagination, 34
In the City of Fear (Just), 84
innocence, 16
Intimate Lighting, 85
Iran, 80
Iron Curtain, 9
Irvin, John, 146, 147
Isadora, 57
I Was a Communist for the F.B.I., 9

Jaglom, Henry, 46
Janssen, David, 31
Japanese, 7
Joan of Arc, 13
Joe, 48
Joffe, Roland, 113
Johnson, Don, 129
Johnson, Lyndon B., 27, 28, 35, 81,
     102, 137, 138
Johnson, Reggie, 134
Jones, James, 11
Jones, James Earl, 141
Jules and Jim, 89
Julius Caesar (Shakespare), 101
Jump into Hell, 18
Just, Ward, 84

Kaiser, Beast of Berlin, The, 3
Kasdan, Lawrence, 90

Kazan, Elia, 72
Kazin, Alfred, 8
Kelley, Walt, 92
Kennedy, John F., 12-13, 18, 27, 29, 31
Kennedy, Robert, 39
Kenniston, Kenneth, 23
Kerry, Bob, 76
Kerry, John, 76, 130
Khmer Rouge, 116-17
Kidder, Margot, 95
Killing Fields, The, 113-20, 126, 129, 130
King, Martin Luther, Jr., 39, 97, 123
King and I, The, 19
Kipling, Rudyard, 1
Kirkwood, James, 95
Kissinger, Henry, 45, 52
KKK (*see* Ku Klux Klan)
Korean War, 9-12
Kotcheff, Ted, 99
Kovic, Ron, 83
Kramer, Stanley, 24
Kubrick, Stanley, 142, 143, 144, 145, 146
Ku Klux Klan (KKK), 2, 3, 122-23
Kundera, Milan, 118
Kunen, James Simon, 39

Lacomb, Lucien, 122
Ladd, Alan, 13
Ladd, Cheryl, 112
Lancaster, Burt, 54, 55
Lannem, Les, 91
Laszlo, Andrew, 90
Laughlin, Tom, 42, 43
Law and Disorder, 85
Lawrence, D. H., 60
Lederer, William J., 19
Lenin, V. I., 30
Lennon, John, 119
literature, 83
Lombardi, Vince, 37
Lone Wolf McQuade, 104
Long, Shelly, 89
Longest Day, The, 19
Long March, The, 90
Long Riders, The, 91
Loo, Richard, 10
Lord Jim, 132

Los Angeles Free Press, 28
Los Angeles Herald-Examiner, 79
Lost Patrol, The, 91
Love, 63
Lovers, The, 121
Loves of a Blond, 8
Lowe, Edmund, 4
Luc-Godard, Jean, 29
Lynn, Vera, 144

MacArthur, Gen. Douglas, 11
MacArthur, John R., 81
McCarthy, Joseph R., 9, 26, 75
McDermott, Dylan, 146
MacGinley, John, 134
McLaglen, Victor, 4, 141
McNamara, Robert, 19, 81
McQueen, Steve, 104
Madigan, Amy, 121
Madman theory, 45
Magic Garden of Stanley Sweetheart, The, 88
Magnum Force, 48, 49
Magnum P.I., 112
Mailer, Norman, 28, 83, 91
Malden, Karl, 37
Malkovitch, John, 113
Malle, Louis, 121, 122, 123, 124
Manchurian Candidate, The, 26-27
Man I Killed, The, 4
Mankiewicz, Joseph, 16, 17, 18
Mansfield, Mike, 12
Manson, Charles, 48
March, Frederic, 8
martial spirit, 3
Marx, Karl, 8
Marxism, 128-29
Mary Poppins, 30
*M*A*S*H,* 35-36
Medium Cool, 88
Meet John Doe (Arnold), 86
memories, 147
Men, The, 42
Menges, Chris, 114
MIA (*see* missing in action)
Miami Vice, 112
Midnight Express, 132
Milestone, Lewis, 4, 5, 7, 140

Milius, John, 99, 101, 103
missing in action (MIA), 99-100, 102, 110-12
Missing in Action, 104-5, 106, 107, 110
Missing in Action 2: The Beginning, 104, 105-6
Modine, Matthew, 124, 126, 142, 143
Moll, Georgia, 17
morality, 56
Moreau, Jeanne, 89
Moriarity, Michael, 57
Mumford, Lewis, 25
Murmur of the Heart, 121
Murphy, Audie, 1, 16, 17
My Lai massacre, 44

Nam, 80
Napier, Charles, 108
National Liberation Front (NLF), 18
national will, 57, 60, 64
Nazis, 6
Newcombe, Monte, 140
New Left, 27-28
New Republic, 80
Newsweek, 57, 80, 97, 120
new wave techniques, 29
New York Times, 25, 28, 34, 52, 97, 113
New York Times Magazine, 114
Ngor, Haing, 113
Nhu, Ngo Ding, 18
Nietzche, Friedrich W., 57-58, 60
1960s, 29
Nixon, Richard M., 12, 38, 45, 57, 119
NLF (*see* National Liberation Front)
Nolte, Nick, 57
Norris, Chuck, 103-4, 108
North, Ollie, 141
nostalgia, 4
Notes (Coppola), 70
Not So Wild a Dream, 6
nuclear warfare, 23

Obenhein, William, 41
Objective Burma, 7
O'Brien, Tim, 1, 78, 83
Oh! What a Lovely War, 30
Okada, Eiji, 19
On the Beach, 24

Oswald, Lee Harvey, 48
Owen, Wilfred, 83

pacificism, 2-3, 4-5
parade, 81
Parker, Alan, 124, 125
Parker, Jameson, 89
Passer, Ivan, 85, 86
Paths of Glory, 11, 142
Patton, 37-38
Patton, Gen. George S., 66
PBS (*see* Public Broadcasting Station)
Pearl Harbor, 6
Peckinpah, Sam, 72, 145
Penn, Arthur, 28, 29, 41, 90
Platoon, 131-40, 141
Podhoretz, Norman, 82
Pogo, 92
Polansky, Roman, 72
Post, Ted, 52, 54
post-traumatic stress syndrome, 77
postwar period, 82
Powell, Dick, 13
Pramai, Kukrit, 20
Pressman, Michael, 95
Pretty Baby, 121
Pride of the Marines, 42
prophecy, 27
Prussian Cur, The, 3
Pryor, Richard, 95, 96, 97
PT-109, 19
Public Broadcasting Station (PBS), 80
Purple Heart, The, 7, 33, 140
Purple Hearts, 112-13
Puttnam, David, 113, 114
Pyle, Ernie, 7
Pynchon, Thomas, 26

Quiet American, The, 16-18, 21, 22
Quinn, Pat, 41

racism, 10-11, 15
Radford, Adm., 12
rage, 43-44, 78, 127
Rambo: First Blood Part II, 107-10, 129, 137
Ray, Aldo, 33

Reagan, Ronald, 31, 76, 80, 85, 107, 110
realism, 132
Reconstruction, 2
Red Badge of Courage, The, 134
Red Danube, 9
Redgrave, Michael, 17
regeneration through violence, 102, 105
Reisz, Karel, 57
Remarque, Erich Maria, 4
Retreat Hell!, 11
Return of the Secaucus Seven, The, 90
revisionism, 99
Rimbaud, Arthur, 108
riots, 40
rituals, 1, 61-62
Road to Glory, The (Hawks), 5
Robeson, Paul, 128
Robinson, Andy, 48
Robinson, Bruce, 113-14
Rocky, 94
Rocky IV, 107
Rogers, Charles, 4
Rogue's Regiment, 13
Rolling Thunder, 46-47
Rostow, Walt, 81
Roya, David, 43
R.P.M., 88

Sacks, Ezra, 88
Saigon, 13
Saigon, 64
St. Jacques, Raymond, 31
Salvador, 132
Sanders, Dennis, 19
Sanders, Terry, 19
Sands of Iwo Jima, The, 31
Sassoon, Siegfried, 83
Savage, John, 58
Sayles, John, 90
Sayonara, 15
Scarface, 132
Schaffner, Franklin, 37
Schlesinger, James, 57, 76
Schrader, Paul, 46, 47, 48
Scorcese, Martin, 47, 48
Scott, George C., 37

Scott, Sir Walter, 1
SDS (*see* Students for a Democratic Society)
Searchers, The, 101
Seeger, Alan, 83
Sellers, Peter, 25
Seresin, Michael, 125
Sevareid, Eric, 6
Shakespeare, William, 101
Sharkey, Ray, 96
Shatner, William, 99
Shaw, Stan, 55
Shawcross, William, 118
Sheen, Charles, 132
Sheen, Martin, 66
Shoulder Arms, 3
Shute, Nevil, 24
Sideshow: Kissinger-Nixon and the Destruction of Cambodia (Shawcross), 118
Siegel, Don, 48
Sihanouk, Prince, 119
Simon and Simon, 112
Slotkin, Richard, 102
Small Circle of Friends, A, 88-90
social realism, 132
Some Kind of Hero, 95-96, 98, 126
South, 2
Souther, Terry, 26
Southern Comfort, 90-92
Soviet Union, 8
Spellman, Francis Cardinal, 12
stab in the back thesis, 92
Stack, Robert, 100
Stallings, Lawrence, 4
Stallone, Sylvester, 93, 94, 95, 107, 108, 109, 110, 121
Stars and Stripes, 143
Star Trek, 99
Steel Bayonet, The, 11
Steel Helmet, The, 9-11, 13, 33
Stir Cracy, 95
Stone, Oliver, 131, 132, 134, 135, 136, 137, 138, 139
Stone, Robert, 57, 65
Stonekiller, The, 49
Story of GI Joe, The, 7, 132, 145
Strategic Air Command, 24

Strawberry Statement, The, 39-40, 88
Streep, Meryl, 62
stress, 77
Students for a Democratic Society
  (SDS), 27
Styron, William, 90
superman, 57, 71-73, 129; in *Apoca-
  lypse Now,* 65, 68, 70; in *The Deer
  Hunter,* 60, 63, 65; in *Platoon,* 138;
  Rambo as, 93; in *Who'll Stop the
  Rain,* 58
survivor, 10, 120-21, 126, 139
Sutherland, Donald, 36
Sweeney, D. B., 141
Sylvester, Harold, 100

Taxi Driver, 46, 47-48
Taylor, Delores, 43
teamwork, 7
television, 112
Ten Little Indians, 91
Tennyson, Alfred, 1
Test Pilot, 11
Tet offensive, 34-35
They Were Expendable, 31
Thieu, 82
Third World, 20
13th Valley, The (Del Vecchio), 132
Thirty Seconds over Tokyo, 7
Thomerson, Tim, 100
365 Days (Glasser), 84
Time, 12
To Hell and Back, 11
Tour of Duty, 147
Tracks, 46
Truffaut, Francois, 29
Truman, Harry, 9
Turgidson, Buck, 37
Turtle Diary, 146
Twilight's Last Gleaming, 55
2001: Space Odyssey, 142

Ugly American, The, 19-22
Uncommon Valor, 99-103, 105, 106,
  107, 110
*Uncounted Enemy, The: A Vietnam
  Deception,* 80-81
Unger, Joe, 54
United States, 57

Vance, Courtney, 146
veteran, 42-44, 78, 126-29
Victors, The, 19
Vidor, King, 3
Vietnamese, 63-64
Vietnam guilt chic, 97
Vietnam Veterans' Memorial, 80, 147
Vietnam War Story, 147
violence, 102, 105
Voigt, Jon, 50, 78
Von Cleef, Lee, 15
Vonnegut, Kurt, 26

Wahl, Ken, 112
Walk East on Beacon, 9
Walken, Christopher, 58
Walking Tall, 48
Walk in the Sun, A, 7, 132
Wall Street Journal, The, 80
Walsh, M. Emmet, 105
Walsh, Raoul, 4
Ward, Fred, 100
Warden, Jonathan, 40
War Hunt, 19
War Powers Act, 75
Warren Commission, 40, 41
Warriors, The, 90, 91
War's Peace, 2
Wasson, Craig, 54, 55
Waterston, Sam, 113, 114
Wayne, John, 1, 31, 34, 79, 93, 101,
  104, 122, 125, 141
Weinberger, Casper, 76
Wellman, William A., 4, 7
Westmoreland, Gen. William, 80-81
Wexler, Haskell, 39
Wharton, William, 124
What Price Glory?, 4
Wheeler, Harvey, 24
Wheeler, John, 131
When Willie Comes Marching Home, 36
Who'll Stop the Rain?, 57, 58, 138
Why Are We in Vietnam? (Mailer), 83,
  91
Wild Bunch, The, 29, 145
Wilder, Billy, 8, 29
Wild River, 72
will, 57, 60, 64, 70
Wings, 4

Winkler, Henry, 45
Winners and Losers (Emerson), 84
Woolf, Virginia, 65
women, 87-88
World War I, 3-5
World War II, 5-8

Xenephon, 90

Year of the Dragon, 132
Young Radicals (Kenniston), 23

Zapruder, 29

About the Authors

ALBERT AUSTER has taught at the College of Staten Island and Brooklyn College. He is currently an associate of *Cineaste* magazine and has contributed to many other magazines. He is also the author of *Actresses and Suffragists: Women in the American Theater: 1890-1920* and coauthor with Leonard Quart of *American Film and Society Since 1945.*

LEONARD QUART is Associate Professor of Cinema Studies at the College of Staten Island CUNY, and coauthor with Albert Auster of *American Film and Society Since 1945.* He is an Associate Editor of *Cineaste* magazine and a contributor to a wide variety of film and general magazines.

About the Authors